Paul Nash

Masterpieces of Art

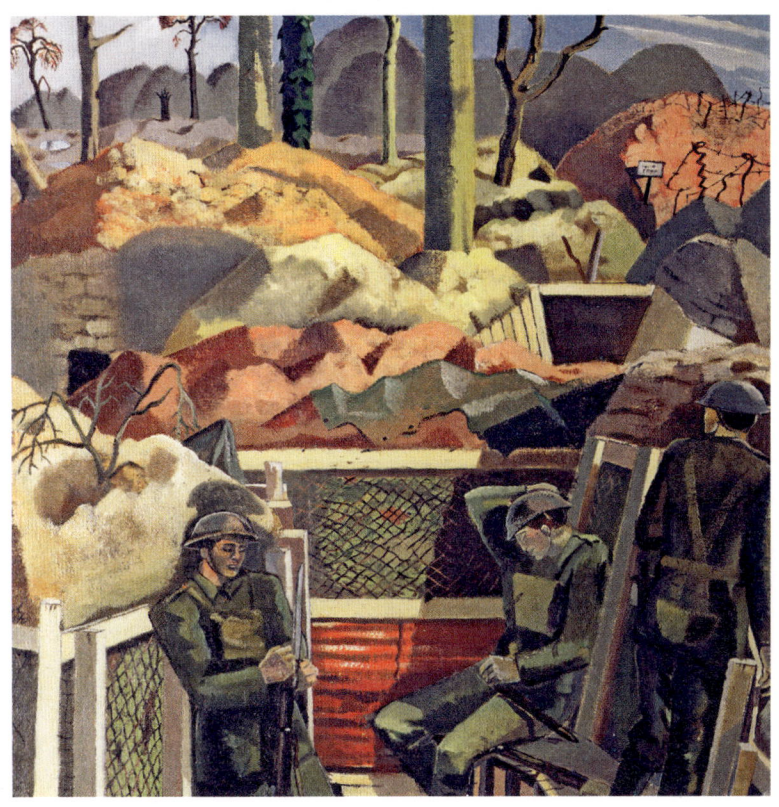

Publisher and Creative Director: Nick Wells
Commissioning Editor: Polly Prior
Art Director and Layout Design: Mike Spender
Digital Design and Production: Chris Herbert
Copy Editor: Ramona Lamport
Proofreader: Amanda Crook
Indexer: Helen Snaith

Special thanks to: Bethany Gooding, Laura Bulbeck

FLAME TREE PUBLISHING

6 Melbray Mews
Fulham, London SW6 3NS
United Kingdom

www.flametreepublishing.com

First published 2018

25
3 5 7 9 10 8 6 4

Front cover: *The Ridge, Wytschaete*, 1917 (detail)
Courtesy Private Collection/Photo © Christie's Images/Bridgeman Images

Back cover: *The Mule Track*, 1918 (detail)
Courtesy Imperial War Museum, London/Bridgeman Images

Image Credits: Courtesy **akg-images** and the following: Erich Lessing 47, IAM 108, De Agostini Picture Lib. 120; Courtesy **Bridgeman Images** and the following: Private Collection 1 & 32, 107; Private Collection/Photo © Christie's Images 3 & 62, 34, 84, 106, 124; Ferens Art Gallery, Hull Museums, UK 4 & 74; Private Collection/Photo © The Fine Art Society, London, UK 6 & 31, 10 & 95, 11 & 59, 38, 54; Imperial War Museum, London, UK 7 & 44, 25 & 50, 28 & 37, 42; Sheffield Galleries and Museums Trust, UK/Photo © Museums Sheffield 8 & 71; Manchester Art Gallery, UK 9 & 56, 15 & 33, 41, 57, 122; Art Gallery of New South Wales, Sydney, Australia/Watson Bequest Fund 1946 12 & 69; Art Gallery of New South Wales, Sydney, Australia/Gift of the Contemporary Art Society, London 1944 13 & 85; Ashmolean Museum, University of Oxford, UK 14 & 55; Wolverhampton Art Gallery, West Midlands, UK 16 & 68; Royal Albert Memorial Museum, Exeter, Devon, UK 17 & 94; Southampton City Art Gallery, Hampshire, UK 18 & 112, 89; Bradford Art Galleries and Museums, West Yorkshire, UK 19 & 77; Private Collection/Photo © Peter Nahum at The Leicester Galleries, London 20 & 114, 30, 81, 92 & 123, 98, 99, 113; Yale Center for British Art, Paul Mellon Fund, USA 21 & 118, 111; Pallant House Gallery, Chichester, UK/Hussey Bequest, Chichester District Council (1985) 22 & 80; Leeds Museums and Galleries (Leeds Art Gallery) U.K. 23 & 82, 46, 64, 103; Art Gallery and Museum, Kelvingrove, Glasgow, Scotland/© CSG CIC Glasgow Museums Collection 24 & 48; National Galleries of Scotland, Edinburgh 27 & 90, 61; Private Collection/Photo © Bonhams, London, UK 35, 36, 97, 119; Whitworth Art Gallery, The University of Manchester, UK 52 & 73; Tullie House Museum & Art Gallery, Carlisle, Cumbria, UK 58; Private Collection/Photo © The Maas Gallery, London 60; Harris Museum and Art Gallery, Preston, Lancashire, UK 65; Private Collection/Photo © Offer Waterman & Co. 66; Herbert Art Gallery & Museum, Coventry, UK 67; Birmingham Museums and Art Gallery 70; Private Collection/Photo © Lefevre Fine Art Ltd., London 72; Pallant House Gallery, Chichester, UK/On loan from a private collection 78, 117; Fitzwilliam Museum, University of Cambridge, UK 86, 110; National Gallery of Victoria, Melbourne, Australia 88; Private Collection/Photo © Crane Kalman, London 91; New Walk Museum & Art Gallery, Leicester, UK/Photo © Leicester Arts & Museums 96; The Cheltenham Trust and Cheltenham Borough Council 100 &128; Private Collection/The Stapleton Collection 102; National Museum Wales 104; Pallant House Gallery, Chichester, UK/Kearley Bequest through The Art Fund 109; Government Art Collection, UK 116; Courtesy **British Council Collection**: 79, 83, 105, 115, 125; Courtesy IWM/**Getty Images**: 39, 40, 43, 51; Courtesy Guy Bell/**REX/Shutterstock**: 26 & 49; Courtesy **TopFoto** and the following: Granger, NYC 76, World History Archive 87.

ISBN: 978-1-83562-281-0

Printed in China | Created, Developed & Produced in the United Kingdom

Paul Nash

Masterpieces of Art

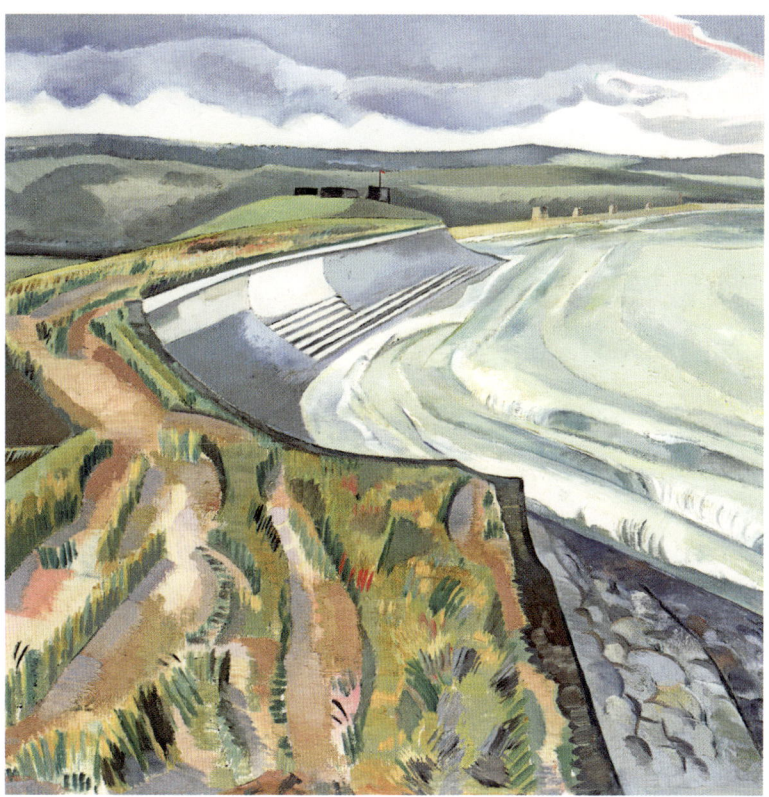

Michael Kerrigan

FLAME TREE
PUBLISHING

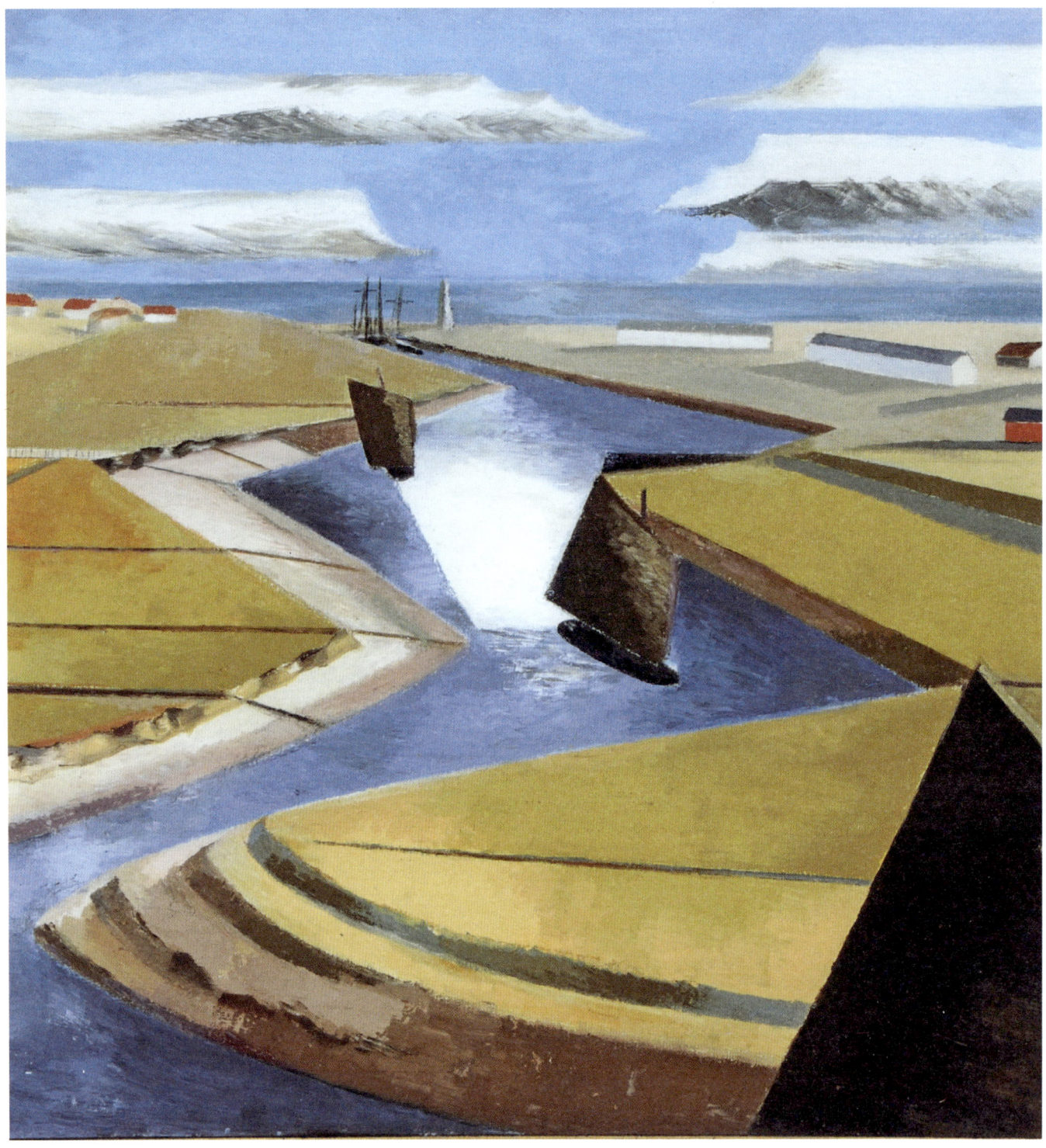

Contents

Paul Nash: Strange Beauty

6

The World Wars

28

Landscapes

52

Abstracts & Still Lifes

92

Index of Works

126

General Index

127

Paul Nash: Strange Beauty

Soldiers,' said Siegfried Sassoon (1886–1967) 'are citizens of death's grey land.' The image is evocative, if less than inspiring visually. Who would expect to find a life-affirming beauty on the battlefield? Why would anyone seek any sort of uplift here? Sassoon, of course, was one of the great War Poets of 1914–18; he spoke as a 'citizen' of the Western Front. A grey land indeed: we are familiar with its monochrome contours from a thousand black-and-white photos, but might not an artist find more colour here?

Not necessarily. Painter Paul Nash (1889–1946) first saw action as a soldier and then subsequently as a war artist – tasked specifically with finding a form of visual representation that could communicate life at the Front to a civilian audience back home. The conditions were certainly not too promising.

'Naked and Scarred'

One day, he wrote a letter to his wife Margaret at home in England. It was Good Friday, and the scene he described was a Golgotha:

Imagine a wide landscape flat and scantily wooded and what trees remain blasted and torn, naked and scarred and riddled. The ground for miles around furrowed into trenches, pitted with yawning holes in which the water lies still and cold or heaped with mounds of earth, tangles of rusty wire, tin plates, stakes, sandbags and all the refuse of war…. In the midst of this strange country … men are living in their narrow ditches.

Nash depicts the Western Front as a hell-on-earth: muddy, cratered, criss-crossed with barbed wire, cold and rat-ridden … and the men did not live

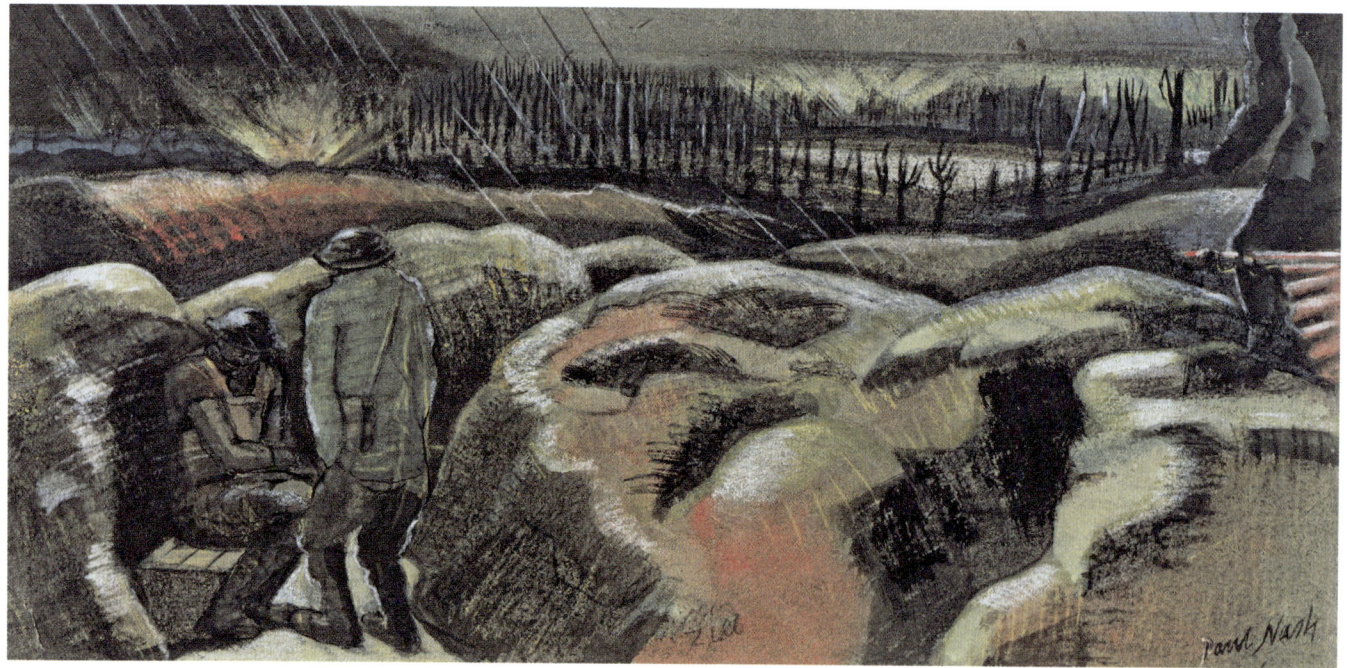

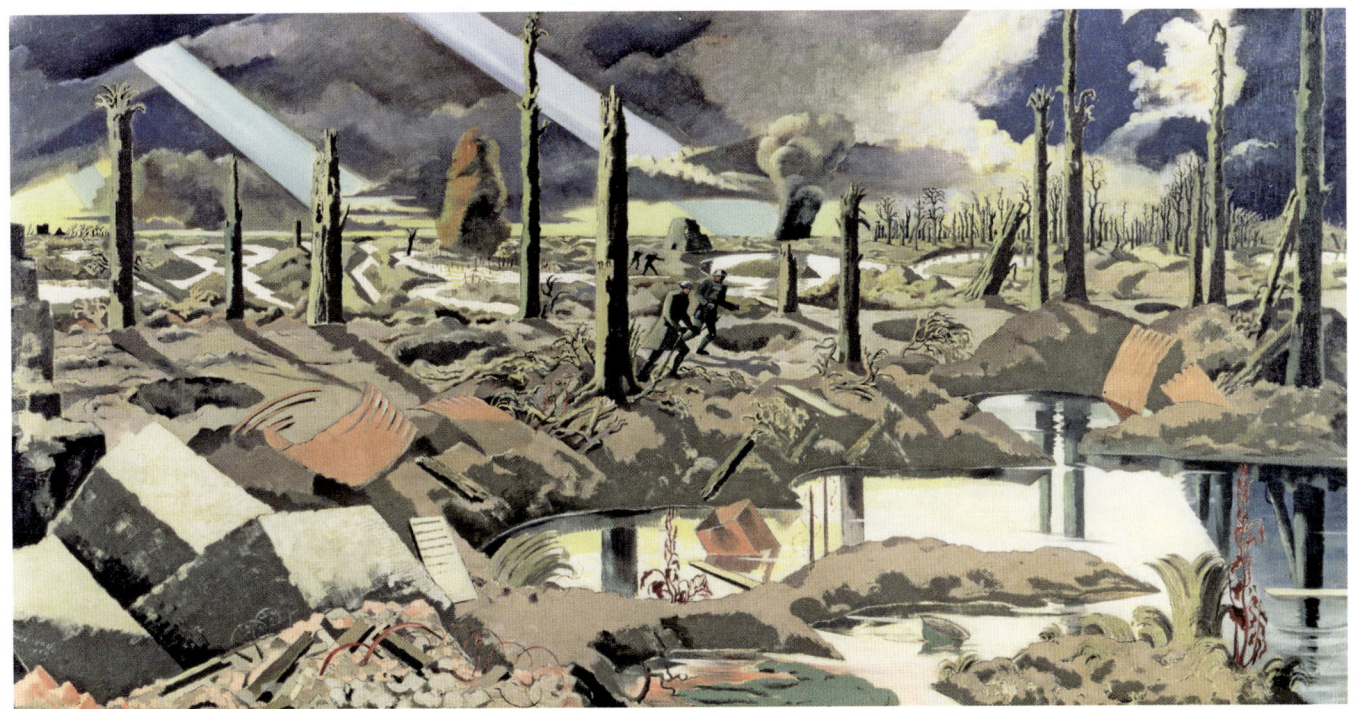

much better 'in their narrow ditches'. We see such rat-men cowering in Nash's picture *Shellburst, Zillebeke* (1917, *see* left and page 31), a drab, dun inferno of dreariness in coloured chalk. It is still recognizably a 'landscape', though, as we still see ragged-looking trees in the middle distance. It is a sort of poisoned pastoral, a scene of natural beauty turned grotesquely wrong.

Within the Wound

'The torn fields of France,' another War Poet, Isaac Rosenberg (1890–1918), was to call them. The phrase courts cliché until the anticipated 'green' is torn away. In a painting like *The Menin Road* (1919, *see* above and pages 44–45) – some 60 sq ft (almost 6 sq m) in size – the rural landscape is no more than a memory informing a nightmare scene of chaos and destruction. It is as if the tearing-open of the familiar fabric of a view we have seen and admired a million times has laid bare something new – something sinister, unsettling, but beautiful as well.

'My subject is war, and the pity of war,' wrote Wilfred Owen, the most famous of the War Poets. 'The poetry is in the pity,' he maintained.

Whether pity can really carry poetry – whether any emotion can in itself contain any art – is of course highly questionable. Nash undoubtedly felt that pity, although ultimately it was to harden into anger. However, he could not help seeing beauty at the Front as well. The moral outrage might remain a constant, but – and this could not but be troubling to anybody with a conscience – there was abundant artistic stimulation to be found.

The wickedness of war may have been everywhere before him, but so too was a visual scene that changed, not just with the circling seasons but with every shifting breeze, every passing cloud, every shower and every sunbeam (*see* page 32). He told Margaret as much in another letter home:

> *Everywhere are old farms, rambling and untidy, some of*
> *course ruined and deserted, all have red or yellow or green*
> *roofs and on a sunny day they look fine. The willows are orange,*
> *the poplars carmine with buds, the streams gleam brightest*
> *blue and flights of pigeons go wheeling about the field.*

Yet, he continued – and this was clearly a difficult thing for a thinking, feeling artist like Nash to come to terms with – it was not just Nature, obstinately asserting her beauty in the very face of war and destruction – war and destruction had their beauty too:

Mixed up with all this normal beauty of nature you see the strange beauty of war…. You look up and after a second's search you can see a gleaming shaft in the blue like a burnished silver dart, another and then another….

A painting like *Wire* (1919, *see* page 43) captures this 'strange beauty' to paradoxical perfection, as exquisite and, yes, as lovely as it is grim.

Waste Lands

The devastation to be seen on the ground in France was an all too real emblem of the destruction that the First World War had imposed on the wider Western order. It was not what had been expected. Even as hostilities broke out in the summer of 1914, the mood had been generally upbeat. This was, it was said, the war that would end all wars.

Predictions of it all being 'over by Christmas' proved groundless; a more pessimistic view took hold not just in the field, but on the Home Fronts too. The Russian Revolution of 1917 was the most obvious sign of a social collapse that threatened the existing political order Europe-wide. Whilst only in the Soviet Union was the workers' state (for better or worse) to be realized, there were major upheavals in Germany and France, and waves of strikes and demonstrations across Britain.

The War would leave behind it a 'Waste Land', as it was called in T.S. Eliot's famous poem of 1922, a key document of the Modernist movement in literature and art. Despite its name, Modernism did not cheerlead for change: in important ways, it was conservative in outlook. The use of disjointed text, allusion and literary montage that made 'The Waste Land' so innovative was Eliot's way of representing the social fragmentation and moral disintegration he saw reflected in modern life. These ideas had yet to be formulated when Nash was working on the Western Front. Even so, seeing action day after traumatic day, he was bound to be at the forefront in sensing that realities were changing, old assumptions exploding around him at every turn (*see* page 35).

An Idyll Unhinged

In fact, many years before the First World War, his childhood had given him a head start. Nash was born in London, spending his infancy in Earl's Court, but his father William, a barrister, had hailed from Langley, and his son's happiest childhood memories were to be of visits to his grandparents in their home in the Chiltern Hills. Formerly part of south Buckinghamshire Langley is now a suburb of Berkshire, lying just outside London's orbital motorway, the M25. In the early years of the twentieth century, however, this was a lovely, quintessentially English and rural setting.

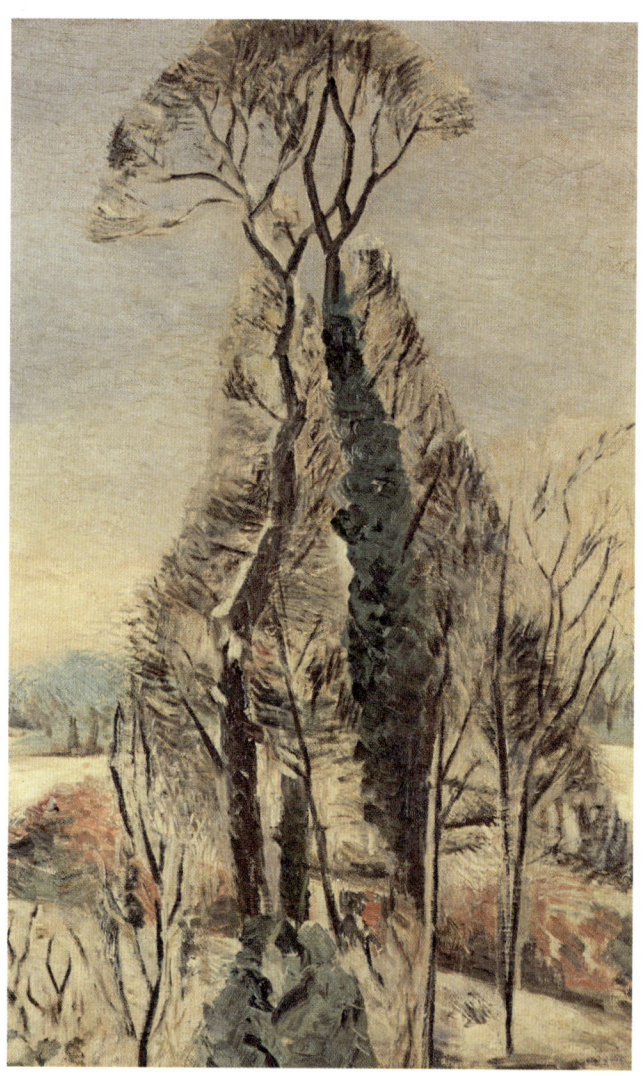

Even then, it was eminently commutable: indeed, when Nash was 13, his parents had a house built in Wood Lane, Iver Heath, from where William took a daily train into the city. By this time, however, Nash was boarding at Colet Court, the junior department of St Paul's School, beside the river at Barnes, west London. His schooldays, he remembered later, were 'a long and complicated purgatory', a time of 'misery, humiliation and fear'. For the moment, though, it was only Nash's unhappiness that marked him out. His academic results were ordinary at best. As for any artistic abilities, the record – from Nash himself, from his parents and from St Paul's – offers only silence on this subject.

Why, then, this 'misery'? The shock of separation from his parents must have underlined his sense of alienation, his growing nostalgia for a rural 'home' that had never actually been his. Nor could it realistically be now, however, for these fields too were 'torn', the peace of the countryside violently broken by the travails of his mother, Caroline. It had been her alarming slide into mental illness that precipitated William's decision to take his family from the city. As well as Paul, William and Caroline had two other children: John (1893–1977), who was also to become a well-regarded painter; and Barbara, who would become a gardener of note.

Roots of Inspiration

Exactly what Wood Lane House meant to Nash as a young boy cannot possibly be known to us now, of course. He did not have the experience nor was he articulate enough to record it as he may have done in adulthood. When he did recall its impact on him, it was to be many years later, in his memoir *Outline* (published posthumously, in 1949), and very much from the working artist's point of view:

Its magic lay within itself, implicated in its own design and its relationship to its surroundings. In addition, it seemed to respond in a dramatic way to the influence of light. There were moments when, through this agency, the place took on a startling beauty, a beauty to my eyes wholly unreal. It was this 'unreality', or rather this reality of another aspect of the accepted world, this mystery of clarity which was at once so elusive and so positive, that I now began to pursue and which from that moment drew me into itself and absorbed my life.

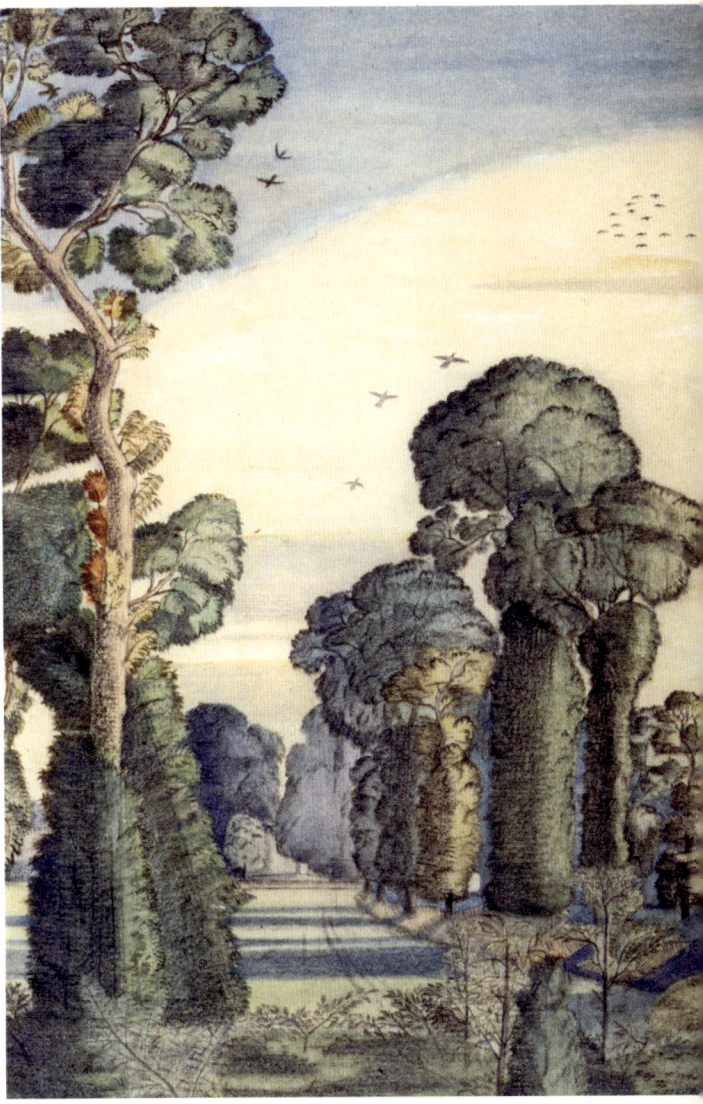

This idea that the beauty of a location might lie 'within itself' is surely significant, even if it is immediately qualified by the suggestion that it is also shaped in part by 'its relationship to its surroundings'. It implies a power or quality that is intrinsic to the place. The view that 'another aspect' underlines the immediately apparent, a 'mystery' which is at the same time a 'clarity' (and, perhaps, vice-versa) helps account for the unique poetic resonance of Nash's scenes. In *A Landscape at Wood Lane* (1913, *see* page 56), for instance, what seems a straightforward vista of parkland shimmers with mystic possibility – or is it menace?

Romantic Readings

Again, it is hard to know how conscious Nash was of these things in his boyhood. 'The child is father to the man,' wrote William Wordsworth (1770–1850), a major influence on Romantic English poetry and on landscape art. Nash's own recollections hardly bear this out: if he is to be believed, his artistic vocation came upon him when – apparently out of nowhere, at the age of 17 – he decided upon becoming a commercial artist.

At Chelsea Polytechnic and then from 1908 at the London County Council School of Photo-Engraving and Lithography, Nash made himself a master of the essential graphic arts. In addition to making himself 'a slick and steady machine for producing posters, show cards, layouts', however, he found himself taking an interest in art more generally, especially in the paintings of the Pre-Raphaelite founder Dante Gabriel Rossetti (1828–82). 'I have only to look at his designs to feel a burning desire to create something beautiful,' Nash said.

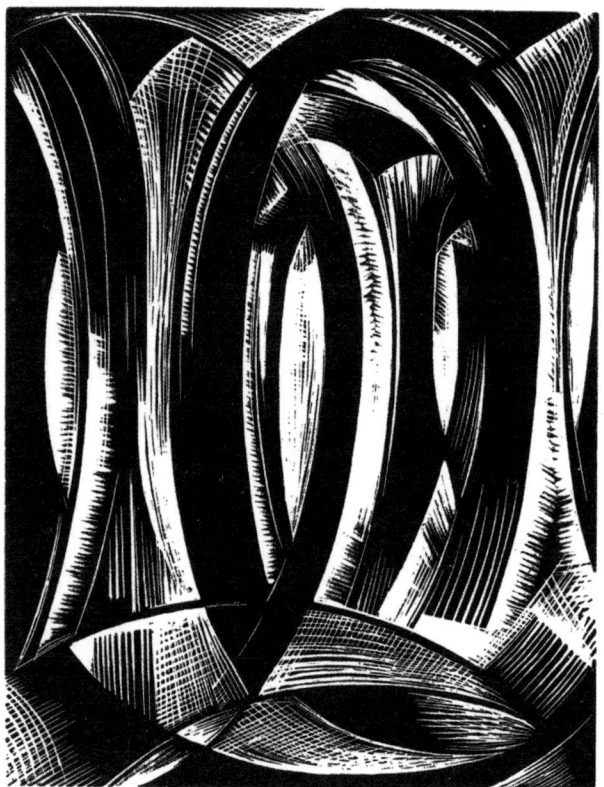

That desire was a distinctly adolescent one, it might be said. With their stylized female forms, their melancholy mood and their barely-there-but-inescapable suggestion of eroticism, Rossetti's pictures were perfectly adapted to the tastes of the self-consciously sad (and sexually repressed) Edwardian young man. However, his ravishing, romantic pictures apart, Rossetti inevitably led his admirers in a literary direction: not only were his subjects often literary but he was an accomplished poet as well.

From Guineas to God

Increasingly, however, Rossetti's influence was to be eclipsed by that of another, earlier painter-poet: William Blake (1757–1827). His verses, Nash said, 'taught me to open my eyes and look about me, above all, to search the skies'. There, memorably, Blake had claimed to see in the sun not 'a round disc of fire somewhat like a guinea' but 'an innumerable company of the heavenly host singing "Holy, holy, holy is the Lord God Almighty!"' It was not that what he saw with his 'corporeal eye' was not true, Blake insisted, but that it was not the whole truth: 'I look through it, and not with it,' he concluded.

Blake's brand of mystic poetry and philosophy was all his own, but it was profoundly to influence the younger poets of the Romantic movement, who in their turn were to influence English art and poetry for the remainder of the nineteenth century – and into the twentieth, as Nash's example shows. He himself was to express impatience with the 'Romantic' label. The grounds he gave for this, however, were that those qualities so characterized should only be seen as being in the best and fullest sense 'poetic' and, consequently, in the best and fullest sense painterly. He did not want Romanticism mentioned, in other words, only because its values were the alpha and omega of his art.

Crisis, What Crisis?

Nash's enrolment in 1910 at the Slade – the art school attached to University College London – did not just represent a minor coup for the young artist, it was a move upscale from commercial to 'fine' art. Furthermore, it was at the Slade at this time that, under the tutelage of Roger Fry (1866–1934), a dazzling new generation of English artists was just coming of age, creating what their drawing professor

Henry Tonks (1862–1937) called a 'crisis of brilliance' in the school. These fine talents included Christopher R.W. Nevinson (1889–1946), Edward Wadsworth (1889–1949), Mark Gertler (1891–1939), Stanley Spencer (1891–1959), Dora Carrington (1893–1932), Ben Nicholson (1894–1982) and William Roberts (1895–1980).

Nash may technically have been at school at the same time as these English 'Modernists' but he was not at school *with* them in a deeper sense. In such ebullient company, his nervousness and inexperience were always going to show; he did not shine alongside these adventurous spirits. Nor – if his own testimony is to be believed – did Professor Tonks leave him in much doubt of his shortcomings. He did not have the facility or obvious flair of his more famous contemporaries, and temperamentally Nash's artistic inclinations were more cautious – more consciously conservative, indeed. He did not so much miss the Modernist bus, as let it leave without him.

Little England ...

A risky decision, perhaps, but Nash had his integrity and a realistic sense of his own skills and limitations. Fortunately, it was to pay off handsomely. Around the end of 1911, he met Sir William Blake Richmond (1842–1921), whose work he had admired at that year's Royal Academy Exhibition. Richmond was an old and distinguished painter, for years the Slade Professor of Art at Oxford, but he was hardly forward-looking in his views. A classically English curmudgeon, he had slated Paul Cézanne (1839–1906) and the other French Post-Impressionists in their day, and now he knocked their champion on English soil, Roger Fry. He did, however, have real talents of his own and an insight into those of other, younger painters, and it was he who, having invited the young man to show him some of his early work, first saw all of Nash's limitations and potential strengths.

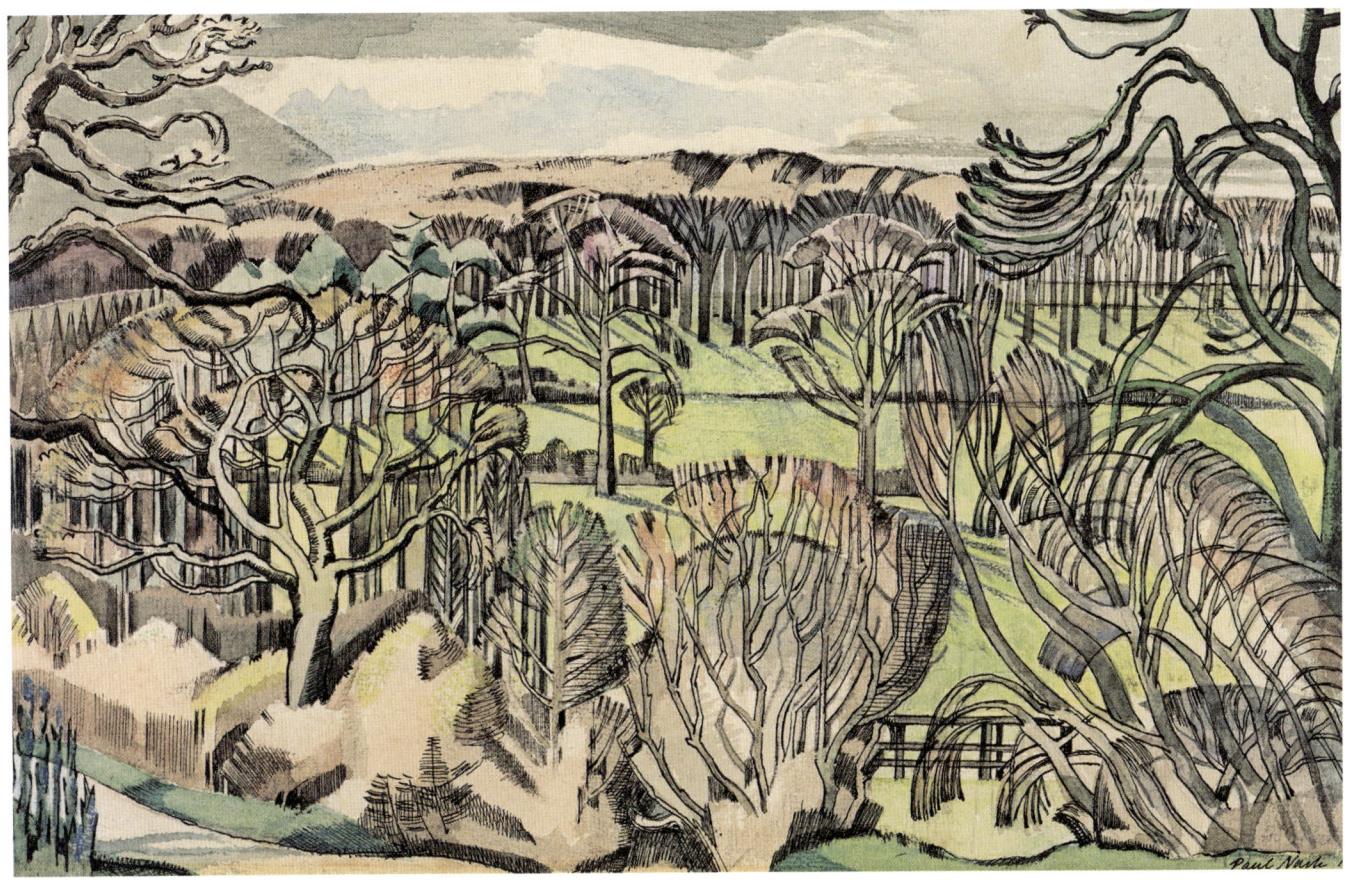

'My boy, you should go in for Nature,' he said. Given Richmond's age and authority, the remark had the air of an imperial decree. Nash certainly saw it that way. Within weeks he had moved back to his parents' home at Wood Lane House in Buckinghamshire and was consciously striving to make himself a landscape artist.

There was surely an element of self-mythologizing about this move and this 'conversion'. The real reasons for it were almost certainly more complex. Cynics have pointed out that Nash was uncomfortable trying to capture human figures (a weakness which would not have escaped the portraitist Richmond any more than it had his drawing tutor Tonks). More seriously, Caroline Nash had died the previous year and while her son was not explicitly to say so, it seems likely that her death would have brought his own relationship with his family, his father and his wider background, as well as his roots in the English countryside, into focus.

Small World …

Then, of course, there was what might be seen as his artistic antecedents. Nash's new mentor, William Blake Richmond, had himself been named after the famous poet and artist. His father, George, had been at 'the' Blake's deathbed. An important painter in his own right, George Richmond (1809–96) had with fellow-artists, Edward Calvert (1799–1883) and Samuel Palmer (1805–81), formed a little group of disciples to the (by this time ageing) visionary. They called themselves 'The Ancients' and once their prophet and inspiration had passed on, gathered regularly to commemorate him at Samuel Palmer's home in Shoreham, Kent. Nash, inspired in his turn, was to make a pilgrimage to Shoreham.

He had already read and come to love Blake's prophetic poems (surprisingly, Blake's painting seems to have influenced him less profoundly). There is no doubt that Nash saw his 'connection' with William Blake and with this visionary company as auspicious, and it inspired him as he set about his self-invention as an artist.

Back to Front

That self-invention had to be a conscious one, though, and despite Wordsworth's claim that poetic art was a 'spontaneous overflow of emotion', it was not to be that straightforward for Nash. The new Nash vision was explicitly mystic, and obviously Blakeian, as he explained in a letter to a friend: 'I turned to the landscape not for the landscape's sake but for "the things behind", the dwellers in the innermost: whose light shines thro' sometimes.'

However, Blake's ability to see 'the universe in a grain of sand' – to see past the sun-as-guinea to the sun-as-angelic-host – did not come as easily to Nash. A painting, to his way of thinking, had to have some subject, distinct and distinctly delineated; Nature was still very much a 'background'. 'At first,' he recalled:

I was unable to understand a devotional approach to a haystack and listened doubtfully to a rhapsody on the beauty of its form. Such objects, and indeed, the whole organic life of the countryside, were still, for me, only the properties and scenes of my 'visions'. Slowly, however, the individual beauty of certain things, trees particularly, began to dawn on me.

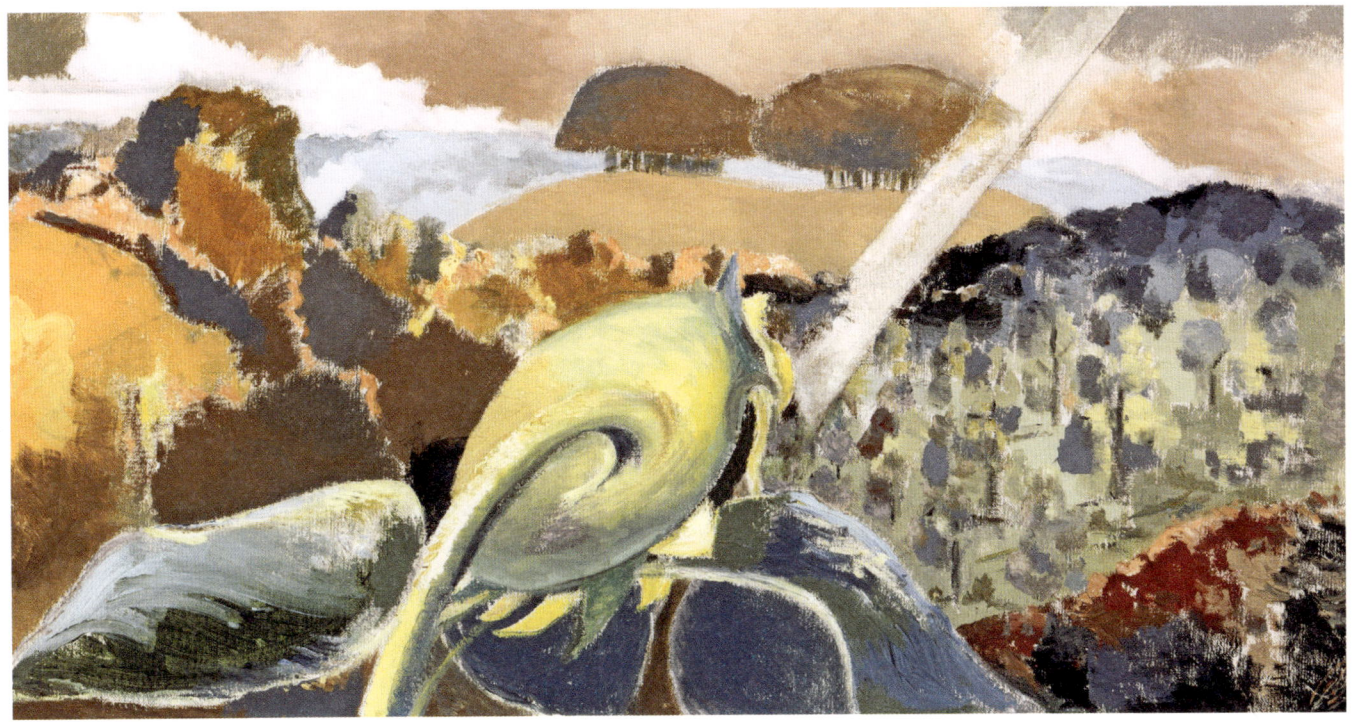

'What Images?'

Trees and woods were to populate Nash's paintings from now on (*see* pages 57 and 59). Nash maintained that trees were people – and 'wonderfully beautiful people' at that – possessing an immeasurable charisma in his work. Part of their appeal, of course, was that they were old, their lifespan putting human lifespan into a lengthy historical perspective, as some verses he wrote around this time makes clear:

> *O dreaming trees, sunk in a swoon of sleep*
> *What have ye seen in these mysterious places?*
> *What images? What faces?*
> *What unknown pageant thro' these hollows moves*
> *At night? What blood-fights have ye seen?*
> *What scenes of life & death? What haunted loves?*

Who was really dreaming, though? The trees or he who gazed at them and saw in their 'sleep' the human dramas they must have dumbly witnessed? Paradoxically, Nash appears to have found an excitement in their impassivity; their quietness testifies to generations of human 'noise' (*see* page 54).

One particular cluster near Wood Lane House, 'The Three', crop up again and again in his work, as though Nash wanted to record them in every season, in every sort of weather and in every mood. So closely, so intimately, indeed, does he capture their character that sometimes, as in *Iver Heath, Buckinghamshire – Snow* (1927–28, *see* page 71), we can hardly see the trees for the collective copse they form and for the mysterious emotion they embody.

'Strange Enchantment'

Another couple of copses atop adjacent hills at Wittenham Clumps, not far from Wallingford, Berkshire (now in Oxfordshire), caught Nash's attention when he visited his uncle at nearby Sinodun House. The letters he wrote to another friend, Mercia Oakley, show the hold the sight established over him and the ways in which his appreciation of it evolved. He mentions it first in 1911, at which point, whilst he clearly does feel there is something 'more than' a few trees on hills, he invests the scene with (a conventionally classical) pagan promise:

The country around and about is marvellous – grey hollowed hills crowned by old old trees, Pan-ish places down by the river wonderful to think on, full of strange enchantment ... a beautiful legendary country haunted by old gods long forgotten.

By September 1912, however, Nash was well into his artistic voyage of self-discovery and perceiving new dimensions to what he saw at Wittenham. 'I had come out to get a drawing of the Clumps,' he told Mercia in another letter:

I wanted an image of them which would express what they meant to me. I realised that I might well make a dozen drawings and still find new aspects to portray.... As I began to draw, I warmed to my task. For the first time, perhaps, I was tasting fully the savour of my own pursuit. The life of a landscape painter.

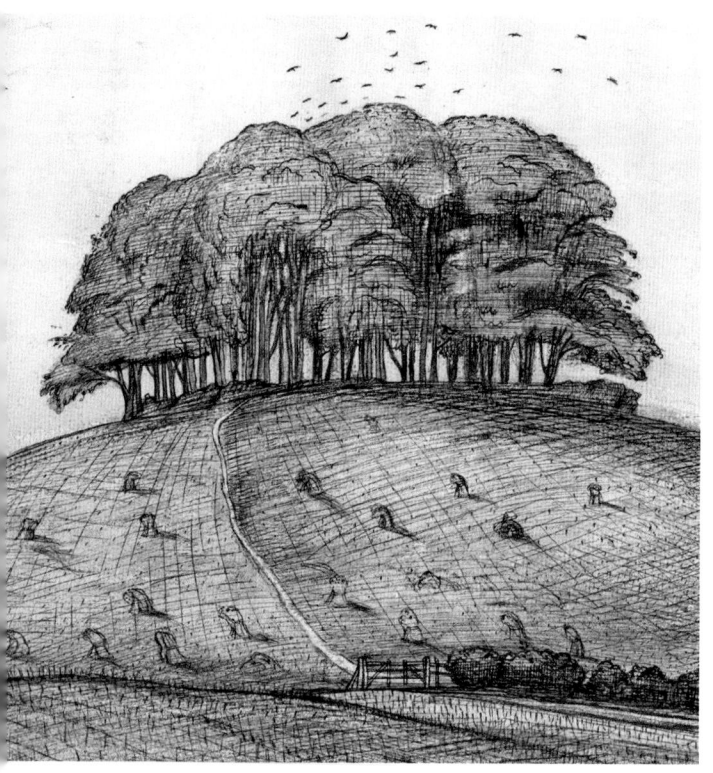

The sense of an immanent life is every bit as present, but the note of learned whimsy has been dropped to give place to a more personal – if less exhibitionist and high-flown – appreciation. And, as important, to a more matter-of-fact and technical tone, that of the committed painter for whom every 'new aspect' is a new artistic possibility (*see* pages 55 and 81).

'A New Kind of Boadicea'

In the meantime, Nash had met his future wife. Brought up in Cairo, Margaret Odeh (1887–1960) was the daughter of a Coptic priest. A history graduate of St Hilda's College, Oxford, she was also a leading suffragist. In 1909, she had helped to found the Women's Tax Resistance League. The WTRL shared the same principle as that in the American Revolution that there should be no taxation without representation. Conversely, it also believed in 'No Vote? No Tax!'

Margaret's courage and resolve alike appear to have impressed Nash. He was later to recall a demonstration in which she had been carried in the back of a milk-cart, facing down the threats of a hostile mob. Margaret 'charged through the crowd in a storm of missiles and floating leaflets ...', he said, 'standing erect in the milk chariot like a new kind of Boadicea'. A committed social reformer, Margaret had done important work with central London's prostitutes as well. Women from this cruelly marginalized group were to turn out in considerable numbers to see her marry Nash at the church of St-Martin-in-the-Fields in December 1914.

Off to War

By this time Margaret's new husband was himself a warrior of sorts. The First World War was already five months old and Nash had enlisted in the Artists' Rifles early on. Like many of his contemporaries, he had signed up with some reluctance but he did not feel especially strongly against the War. In fact, as he and his comrades cooled their heels in England, he grew increasingly impatient to be closer to the real action. Not until the middle of 1916 was he selected for officer training and not until February 1917 was he sent to the Front.

It was a comparatively quiet time to be arriving at the Ypres Salient – though terrible scenes of fighting had taken place there previously during the First and Second Battles of Ypres, and were to again a few months later, in the Third Battle (or Passchendaele) in July to November 1917. There was certainly devastation here, but with spring approaching fast, Nash could enjoy the sights and sounds of Nature's reawakening in a rural scene that was not so different from Buckinghamshire or Berkshire. War, for now, was far from being 'hell'.

Indeed, Nash told Margaret in a letter home, the sense that after so long he was actually there and doing his duty was uplifting:

It seems absurd, but life has a greater meaning here and a new zest, and beauty is more poignant.

That 'beauty' was not just to be found in an undulating countryside that was strikingly close to that of southern England but even in the infrastructure of war itself:

Oh, these wonderful trenches at night, at dawn, at sundown! Shall I ever lose the picture they have made in my mind?

War Artist

Well, yes, he did in fact – or, rather, he reinterpreted what he saw in the light of longer experience. First, though, three months after his arrival, Nash was invalided home. His war wound was sustained, bathetically, by a fall into a trench which left him with a broken rib. A couple of weeks later, the situation worsened again in France: his comrades went over the top into the attack – and in many cases to their deaths. Nash recognized how fortunate he had been, but that was not the same as appreciating the whole horror of what had happened. His rosy view of the War remained intact.

The ink and watercolour work he did at this time reflected this naivety, which may in turn have endeared them to those in authority at home. Living up to its all but oxymoronic title, *Chaos Decoratif* (1917, *see* right and page 33) sums up the capacity of Nash to find the bright side in a scene of what was essentially destruction. Suffice it to say that

when Nash went back to the Front in Flanders in October 1917, it was with the status and the privileges (the access and transport facilities) of an official war artist.

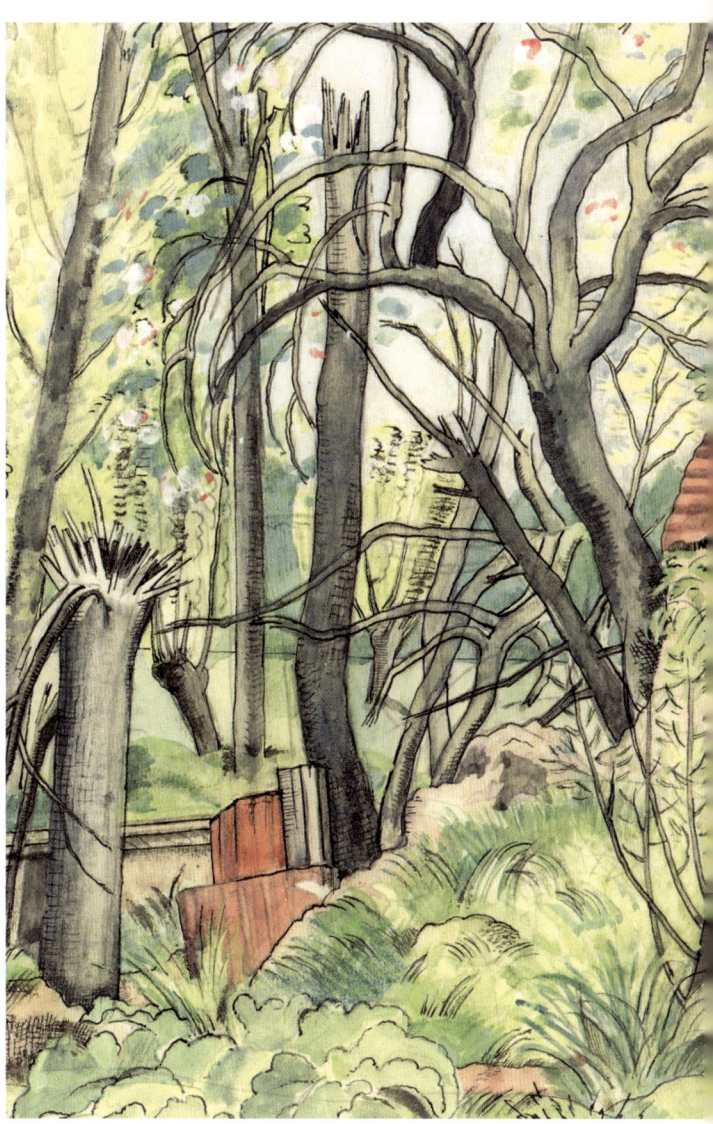

However, he was returning to a very different war. Through the months of his recovery, the Third Battle of Ypres had been building in a grim crescendo, which was just coming to its climax when Nash arrived. Mud, mist, barbed wire, the howl of sirens, the scream of shells, the *whump!* of mortars, the crack of rifles, the stammer of machine-gun fire and, maybe worse, the eerie silence of encroaching gas – the whole now-stereotypical Western Front experience in its quintessence, in other words. Nothing had prepared Nash for its hideousness, but in his resolve to bear some sort of witness he scribbled frantically away in pen and ink, painting over this in watercolour and often producing several finished works in a single day.

His letters home to Margaret now had a very changed tone, with Nash having a different view of himself and of his role:

> *I have seen the most frightful nightmare of a country…. Sunset and sunrise are blasphemous, they are mockeries to man…. The rain drives on, the stinking mud becomes more evilly yellow … the black dying trees ooze and sweat and the shells never cease…. I am no longer an artist interested and curious, I am a messenger…. Feeble, inarticulate, will be my message, but it will have a bitter truth, and may it burn their lousy souls.*

The sense that he was 'no longer an artist' – that what he was seeing was somehow more important than his painting – perhaps made Nash's decision to reconsider his earlier abandonment of human representation easier (though the War Office would, of course, have expected him to include more figures). Stark figures stalk several of his scenes of Passchendaele (*see* pages 39 and 41). As often, though, we see an unpeopled, black and grey Gehenna of devastation (*see* pages 36 and 38), a landscape drained of humanity and of life.

Home Again

Drained all but dry of humanity and life himself, Nash returned home to a nervous breakdown and sought to work his way back to equilibrium by applying himself to wood engraving. The immediate result was a series of seven evocative pictures: *Places*. As their title suggests, each attempted to capture the quintessence of some spot that was important to him and to reveal its *genius loci* – the spirit of the place.

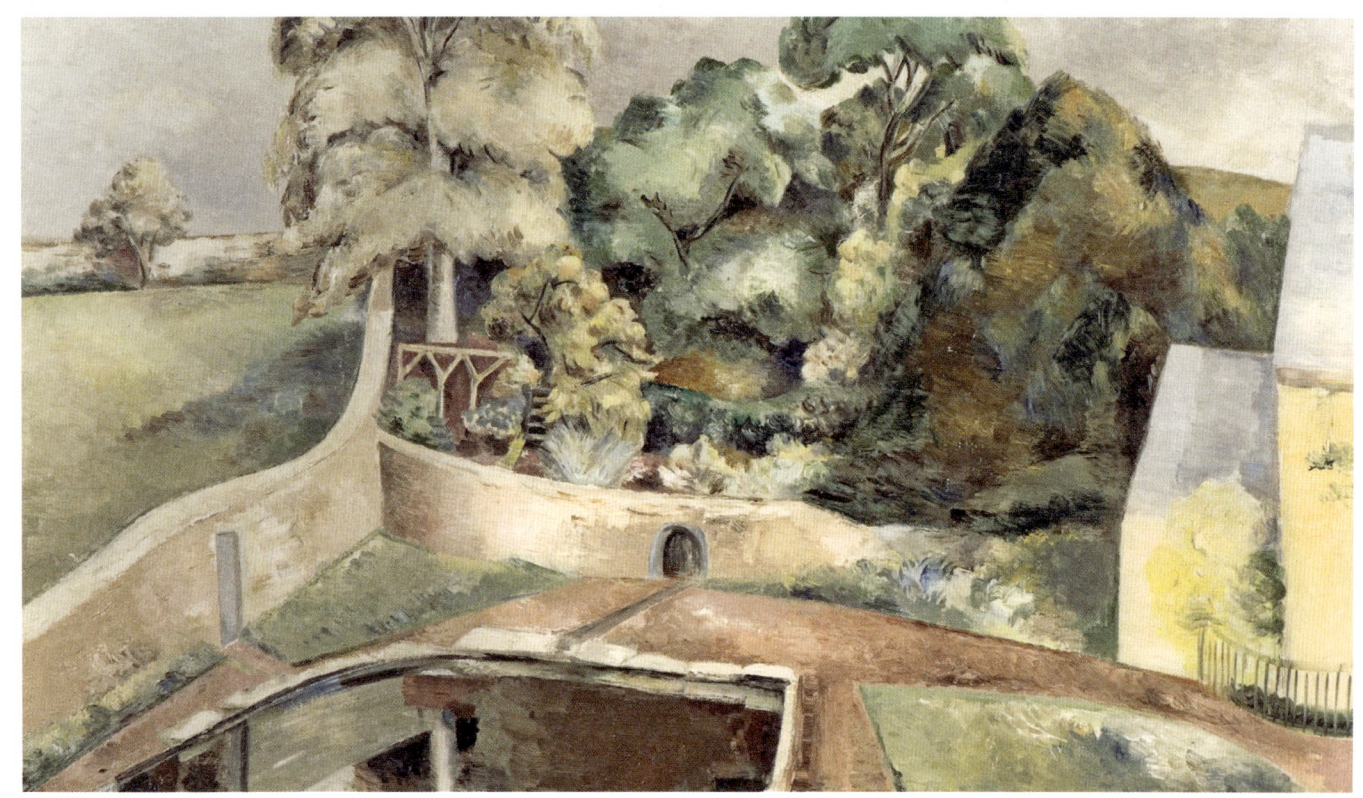

Soon he was painting again, but still for the most part in a minor mode. A cloudy sky casts a sinister shadow on the tussocky grass around *Sheepfold, Romney Marsh* (1920, *see* page 60), whilst foliage from a tree on the left seems to claw its way into the picture. As the months went by, however, there were signs of this gloom lifting; of a restoration of colour to what had been dismal scenes. *Cumberland Landscape* (1924, *see* page 66) seems flooded with warm sunshine. Gone, definitively, is the young man who was 'unable to understand a devotional approach to a haystack' (*see* page 12): that is proven explicitly in the glowing golds, the warming reds and tans of *The Stackyard* (1925, *see* page 67).

Into the Wood

The First World War had no more ended melancholy than it had ended war. Nash's spirit was always meditative, and sometimes moody. Despite the beauty of the engraving *Au Bords du Bois* ('At the Edge of the Wood', 1921, *see* right and page 94), the trees crowd in just oppressively enough for us to imagine ourselves getting lost there, like children in a fairy tale. *A Wood* (1926; an illustration for the tragedy *King Lear* by William Shakespeare) inspires the same sort of existential unease, but more explicitly.

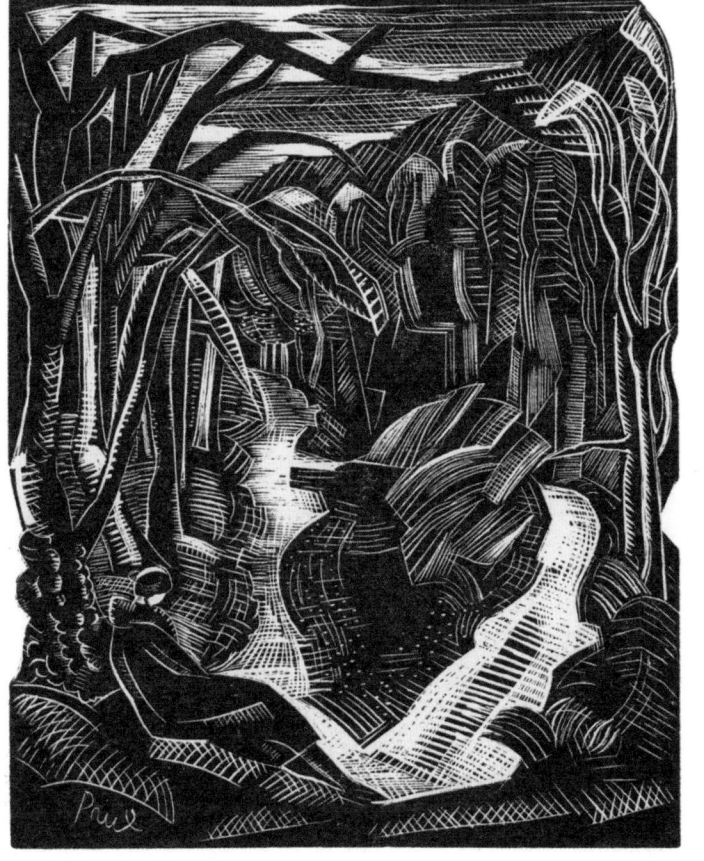

We feel something of the same claustrophobia looking at *Heaven* (1924, *see* page 95), a woodcut-illustration Nash prepared for the biblical Book of Genesis. It illustrates the Creation and the division God made on the second day between the waters and the sky. The emphasis, accordingly, is not on open, endless space, but on the cramped structure of curved columns Nash

imagined holding up the heavens and thereby separating them from the surface of the waters.

Moments of Reflection

More interestingly, Nash was exploring the assumption he had had since as long ago as his days of 'Dreaming Trees' (*see* page 13) that there were other realities implicit in the immediately 'real'. In *Mirror and Window* (1924, *see* page 97), we see a systematic breaking-down of boundaries – between the mirror and the room it reflects, and between the still-life flowers on the windowsill and the autumnal woods outside.

Its origins uncertain (all we know is that it was painted some time between 1923 and 1938), *Nostalgic Landscape* makes a similar sort of visual pun (*see* page 96): this time, it is a setting sun that we see reflected in the circular window of the antique tower around which this oddly dreamlike painting is composed. The painting, with its geometric play, suggests an appreciation of the *Pittura Metafisica* ('Metaphysical Painting') of Giorgio de Chirico (1888–1978) which was to inform a good deal of Nash's work between the wars.

The counterpointing of curling, looping natural forms and more rigidly architectural shapes can be seen in such comparatively conventional-looking works as *Dead Spring* (1929, *see* page 109). As time went on, in paintings such as *Coronilla Landscape* (1929, *see* page 110), Nash took this same opposition to stranger lengths.

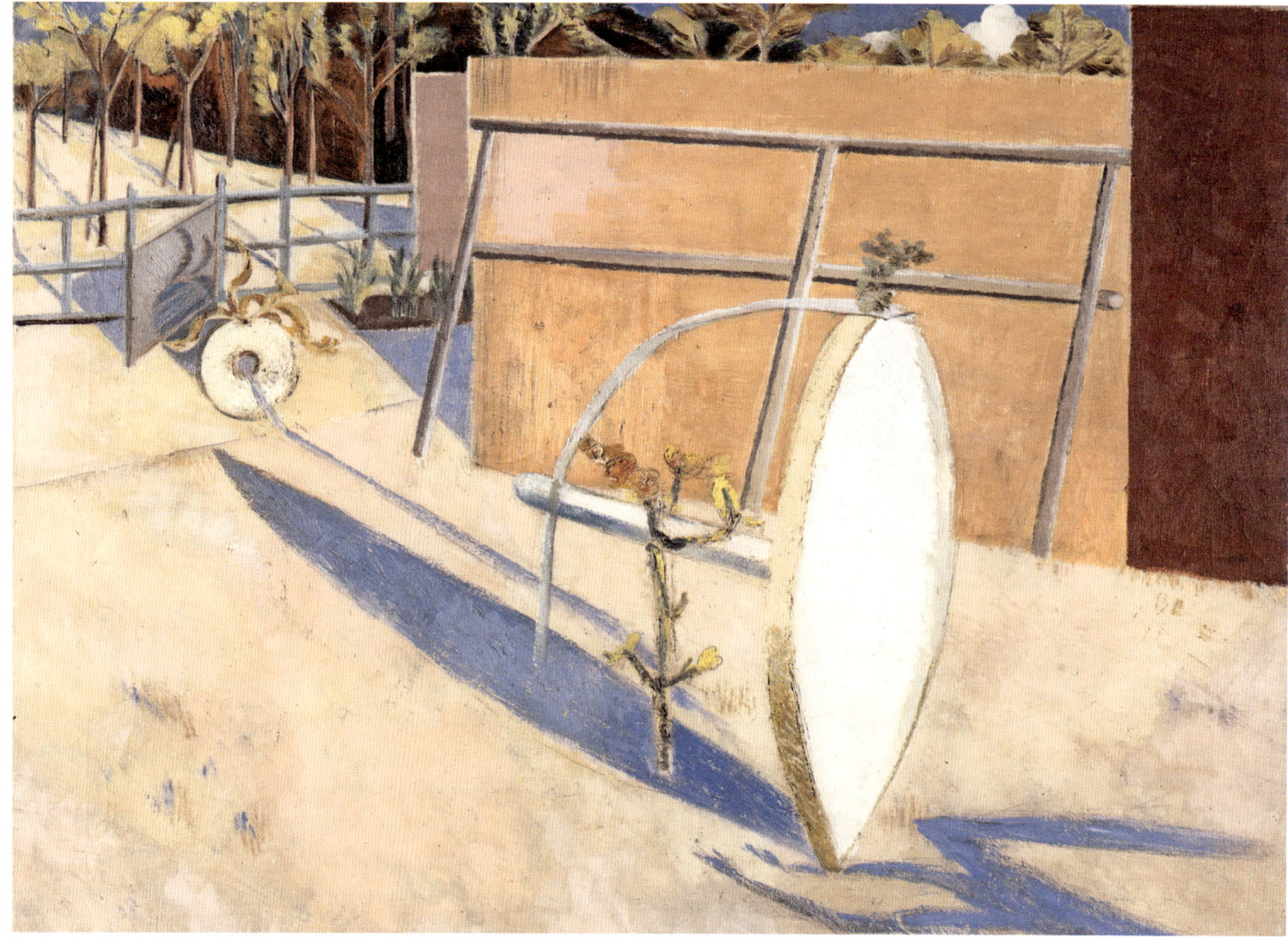

Dark Dreams

None, perhaps, so outré as those in *The Archer* (1930 – but apparently returned to and modified several times over the next 12 years – *see* above and page 112). Here, an upright ovoid, held up by a curved support (the 'bow' of this inanimate 'archer'?) seems to point with a (phallic?) projection past a growing plant towards a nearby disc- (or vagina-?) like 'target'. The shadows in the foreground and the squared-off planes of the walls behind seem straight out of De Chirico, although the vegetation behind it belongs to conventional landscape art. The overall effect is unfathomable – uncharacterizable, even – except in the absurd visual code of dream.

Surrealist Soldiers

While Nash had been experiencing the infernal horrors of the battlefront in Flanders, the French poet and critic André Breton (1896–1966) had found another hell behind the lines. His work with shell-shocked soldiers in a mental hospital in Nantes had brought him face-to-face with the kind of conflicts the War uncovered in the human mind. The ravings of his patients may not have been rational, but how could they have been 'wrong' when they so clearly vented thoughts and feelings from somewhere deep within their minds? In many cases, Breton realized, these 'madmen' spoke with a greater eloquence and a more profound poetic power than he himself could muster.

This had in its turn helped focus Breton's interest in finding a form of expression for what he saw as a new dimension: the 'surreal'. He called it this because it was literally a sort of super-reality (*sur* as a prefix means 'above' or 'beyond' in French). Surrealism, Breton suggested, would combine the ideas and imagery of the subconscious with those of the reality of which we were consciously aware. In his *Surrealist Manifesto* of 1924, Breton called for artists to practise what he called 'psychic automatism' – allowing imagery to stream straight from their subconscious, unmediated by the thinking or actively composing mind. This would produce an art that was in an important sense 'scientific', systematically unpacking the subconscious in all its violence, obsessiveness and turbulence.

Being British

Like many French artistic fashions, Surrealism met with considerable resistance in England and was slow to make its presence felt. Nash himself was in any case instinctively conservative, as we have seen. He had long since set himself against the artistic avant-garde he had seen advancing under his brilliant contemporaries at the Slade (*see* page 10). He still shared some of their impatience with the past, however, and experienced the tug of Modernism; the whole thing was a big dilemma, he acknowledged. As he wrote in 1932: 'Whether it is possible to "go modern" and still "be British" is a question vexing quite a few people today.'

But being British in some unquestioning way was not an option for one who had seen the sort of things he had on the Western Front. Nash's experiences of war had helped colour his experiences of the peace that followed. He had learned the hard way that human nature contained its hatreds; that, even in its times of apparent calm and contentment, society had its darker, more destructive side.

Abolishing the Artist

That dark unconscious was to be found delineated in French Surrealism in a way it simply could not be in English pastoral poetry or academic art. Whilst Nash may have felt nostalgic for the old aesthetics, the shock of war had shaken the assumptions they

depended on: hence his insistence, in Flanders, that he was 'no longer an artist' (*see* page 16). Far from feeling philistine, the 'scientific' claims of Surrealism would have struck a pleasing chord with a painter who yearned to find a way of getting past the accustomed conventions to a deeper truth.

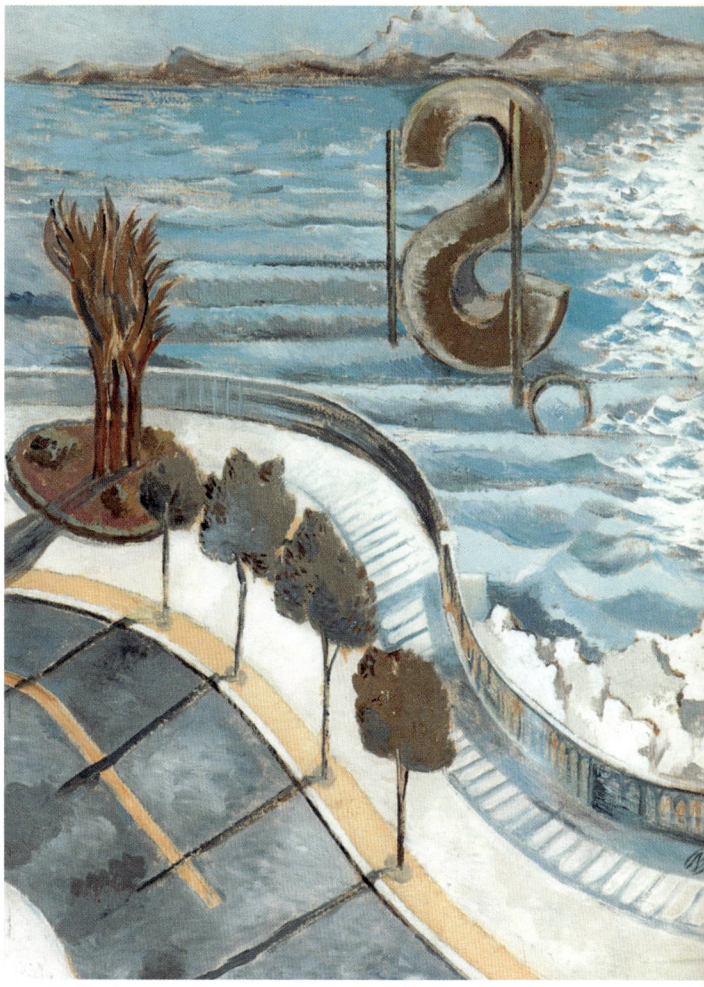

The radicalism of this shift should not be underestimated; it amounted to an acknowledgement that the artist was merely the instrument of his or her unconscious psyche. As the English Surrealist poet Hugh Sykes Davies (1909–84) explained in *New Verse* magazine (April/May 1936): 'This hypothesis rules out at once all ideas of "inspiration", "aesthetic intuition", since they imply the notion of free-will….'

The true Surrealist was, in other words, literally and completely self-effacing – although how many Surrealists there actually were by this definition must be doubtful. The impressive company in which Nash's works were shown at that summer's International Surrealist Exhibition at the New Burlington Galleries in Mayfair, London testifies to the existence of outstanding 'stars'. In addition to De Chirico, it included Pablo Picasso (1881–1973), Max Ernst (1891–1976), Joan Miró (1893–1983), René Magritte (1898–1967) and Salvador Dalí (1904–89). There were sculptures and other art-objects by Jean (Hans) Arp (1886–1966) and Alberto Giacometti (1901–66) – not to mention by André Breton himself.

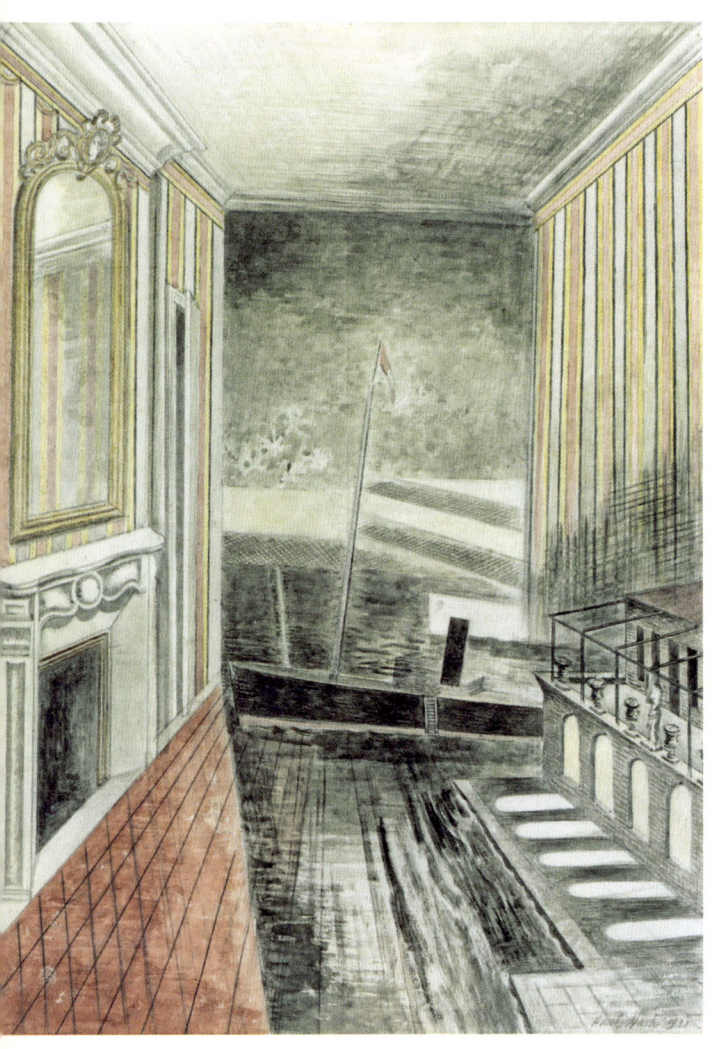

The 'Living Animate'

It was a high point for Nash, although it also marked the only period when he gave any indication of being fully signed-up to the Surrealist project. How far any given artist actually attained the sort of 'psychic automatism' Surrealism theoretically demanded is impossible to assess. The whole point of our 'subconscious' is that we do not know about it; still less can we hope to apprehend that of another person. While Nash quite clearly found things in the theory to appeal to his artistic instincts, he seems only to have followed it selectively. Arguably, indeed, it was no more than a way of recycling Romanticism for the modern era, but it gave him a new perspective on an age-old English scene.

What Breton's work, with its Freudian foundation, did seem to offer him was a theoretical underpinning for instincts of his own. Nash had long had a feeling that the reality we see was not the whole story; he sensed the presence of a life, invisible yet immanent, in the landscape. The idea of the countryside having an 'unconscious' – which his art might apprehend – made real sense in Surrealistic terms. By May 1937 Nash had formulated his thinking sufficiently to characterize it (in an article he contributed to *Country Life*) as 'the mystery and mysticism of the "living animate"'.

Tree-Trunks *Trouvés*

Like other Surrealist – or Surreal-ish – painters, Nash was intrigued by what French modern artists had characterized as *objets trouvés* or 'found objects'. These were random items with no inherent artistic properties, which could however be re-presented in the form of art. In psychoanalytic terms, they might be seen as the sort of random 'slips' Freud had identified as offering little glimpses of the otherwise suppressed subconscious mind.

Nash did not use urinals, as Marcel Duchamp (1887–1968) had done, or scrap-metal assemblages like José de Creeft (1884–1982), but items he had stumbled on outdoors in the countryside. A gatepost, a gnarled and rotten tree stump, a ragged sea stack, a fossil, a twisted stick … utterly strange when seen in isolation, such things could be interpreted as expressions of a natural unconscious. In the trouble he took to view these items in relation to their surrounding English landscape, as in *Event on the Downs* (1934, *see* page 116), Nash found his way of being 'modern' and 'British' at the same time.

A Surrealist in Swanage

The two principles came together nicely in one of the incidental treasures of Nash's career, his book on *Dorset* (1936) for the famous Shell Guide series. Nash and Margaret moved to Swanage in 1934 so that he could complete this work. He was delighted to find the little town a riotous collage of different architectural styles and decked out with 'found objects' in apparent readiness for his arrival. Local builder George Burt (1816–94) had bought up odd statuary, street furniture and a miscellany of other monuments from clearance sites in London and placed them haphazardly around the streets of his Swanage home.

The perfect setting, then, for Nash's own attempt at 'Seaside Surrealism'. *Dorset* was to be a great deal more than just a guide, as were all the Shell Guides. Poet John Betjeman (1906–84) was general editor for what in these more congested (and eco-conscious) times sounds like an improbable project, but which in those days of the 'open road' and auto-touring made perfect sense. The company might have been primarily interested in petrol sales, but it was happy for Betjeman to proceed with a series that in many ways rediscovered the British countryside.

Like later guidebooks, they offered information on everything from climate to wildlife and on attractions from geological features to stately homes. The difference was the easy-going organization, the idiosyncratic approach allowed, and the highly personal and even quirky tone. Betjeman's authors were writers and artists, and he wanted and expected them to express themselves. At first glance, Nash's *Dorset* strikes the modern reader as quite preposterously self-indulgent, but it is a work both of art and literature in its own right.

County-nance

Starting out from the clichéd phrase 'the face of the earth', Nash decides to imagine a more near literal Face of Dorset. 'As I see it,' he wrote:

there appears a gigantic face composed of massive and unusual features; at once harsh and tender, alarming yet kind, seeming susceptible to moods but, in secret, overcast by a noble melancholy – or, simply, the burden of its extraordinary inheritance.

A lot to read into a topography. But there was more: this 'face' did not just bear the imprint of the past, it animated and expressed it daily, registering changes of mood like any living man or woman: '… There are certain places, at certain times, where the record of some drama can start into life as a scar glows with sudden memory….'

If the county's towns and villages, its harbours, roads and railways could all be interpreted as delineating some centuries-long history, its landscape also registered the events of 'a more distant time':

'These, indeed, have left indelible marks in her countenance, which is scarred and furrowed from end to end.'

These scars and furrows might be the work of geological forces or of human ones – the effects of agriculture and urbanization in once-pristine countryside. What really fascinated Nash, though, was the inheritance of that prehistoric era in which, in the absence of written records – or the more advanced construction methods that would make the demarcation clearer – the works of nature and of humanity seem to meld. A modern building – or even a medieval or Roman ruin – stood in its surroundings, but was clearly separate from them. Maiden Castle was, at once and eternally, both 'hill fort' and 'hill'.

Cultural Contours

Not surprisingly, Nash's investment in Wittenham Clumps was meanwhile only growing. They were, he said, 'the Pyramids of my small world'. For at Wittenham, too, there would have been an Iron Age fort, the contours of the Clumps not just natural inclines

but works of defensive engineering, with a role in a community's life over generations.

And, it followed, a great deal of human drama. If the 'dreaming trees', in pushing their physical roots into the soil, extended metaphorical ones into the past through which they had grown – with all its 'blood-fights', its 'scenes of life & death' and 'haunted loves' (*see* page 13) – the archaeological site concealed the same sort of record in its strata.

This ambiguity; this difficulty in establishing where archaeology ends and topography begins gives these antique earthworks a special charisma in Nash's work. The great mound at Silbury, Wiltshire, for example, is a sort of stylized hill, raised up directly out of the earth, a tumulus or barrow – a more regular version of a common natural feature. For Nash it was a focus of fascination. Megaliths are slabs or spikes of (often unworked) rock, set upright, in some mysterious but unmissable relation to the terrain around them. Nash found creations of this kind the best sort of 'found objects' and painted them again and again during the 1930s.

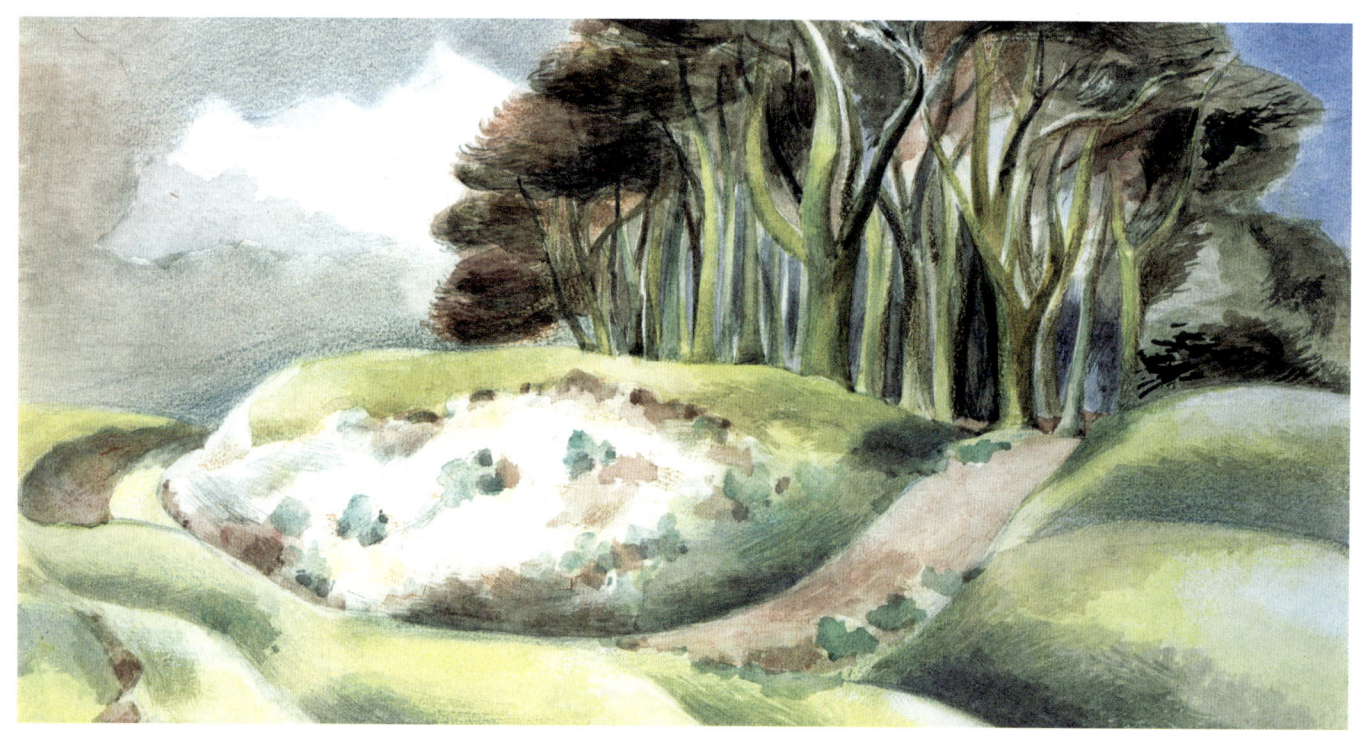

The Avebury Effect

Avebury, in Wiltshire, is Britain's biggest stone circle by some distance, but until recently it was by and large passed over in favour of Stonehenge. The latter is iconic, of course, its characteristic lintels giving it a special 'constructed' charisma, whereas Avebury is just an assemblage of simple standing stones. Stonehenge stood in isolation too, splendidly complemented by its downland surroundings, a gigantic jewel in a setting of emerald green. Avebury, almost 1 km (⅝ mile) in circumference, sprawled across a large area of woods, tussocky green grazing and working farmland – and, indeed, in one corner there was a medieval village.

Nash, who first visited Avebury in 1933, felt drawn to these Cinderella standing stones. The way the country had evolved around them was a major part of their attraction. 'Some were half covered by the grass,' he noted:

> Others stood up in cornfields, were entangled and overgrown in the copses, some were buried under the turf. But they were wonderful and disquieting, and, as I saw them then, I shall always remember them.

We see them that way now ourselves, in *Landscape of the Megaliths* (1934, *see* page 79). Here a continuous plane of white seems to soften still further the demarcation between the stones and the wider landscape in which they stand.

'Repair and Revenge'

For the modern poet Adam Thorpe (b. 1956), in 'Neolithic' (2003), Wiltshire's West Kennet Long Barrow documents generations of 'repair and revenge', the fundamental rhythm, it might be suggested, of human life. Thorpe was to use Nash's work to illustrate his book-length essay *On Silbury Hill* (2014), his meditation on a monument Nash had tried to tackle visually (*see* page 91). 'Flower petals have been found in a Neanderthal grave,' Thorpe points out, 'probably cast in as the simplest form of metaphorical or symbolical reflection.' But, he continues:

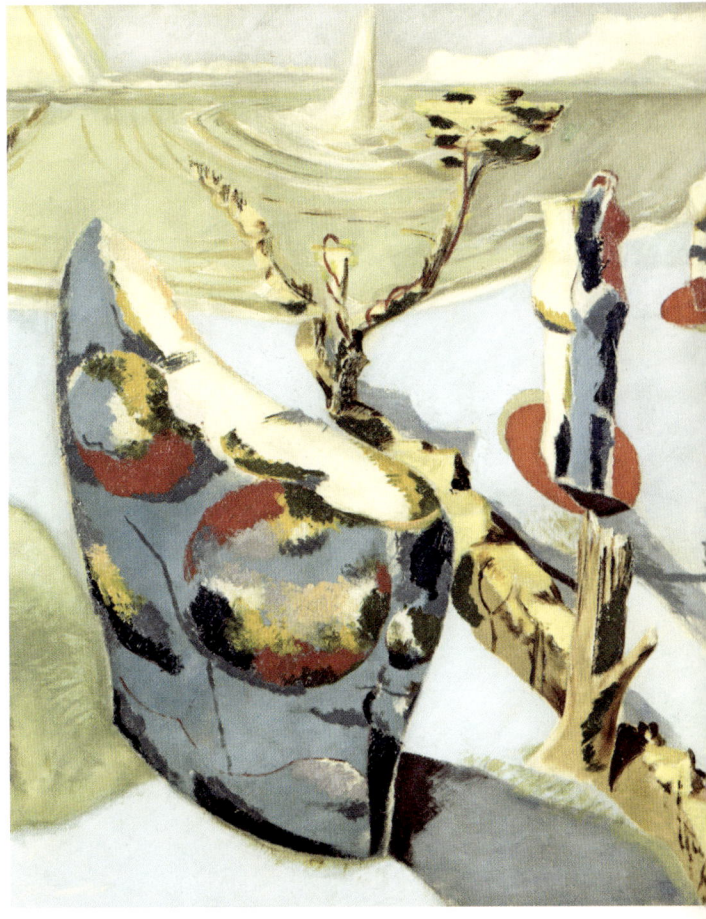

The human rituals and thoughtscapes of prehistory – a period which takes up all but the last few millennia's tiny fraction of our total time on Earth so far – remain closed to us, since history begins with writing and only writing records such things.

'Closed' it may be, but it is a vital book; the more so for the fact of its unwritten-ness, for what we *do* know of history tends to hide the things we do not, leaving deeper mysteries of life and time to go unremarked. Every age sets its stamp on the earth, but prehistory's stamp was paradigmatic in its uncommunicativeness, its secrets emblematic for those left behind by later generations. At the same time, their power seems ever-present. As the crowds that gather each year at Stonehenge and Avebury to celebrate the summer and winter solstice testify, certain rhythms of human existence have been constant.

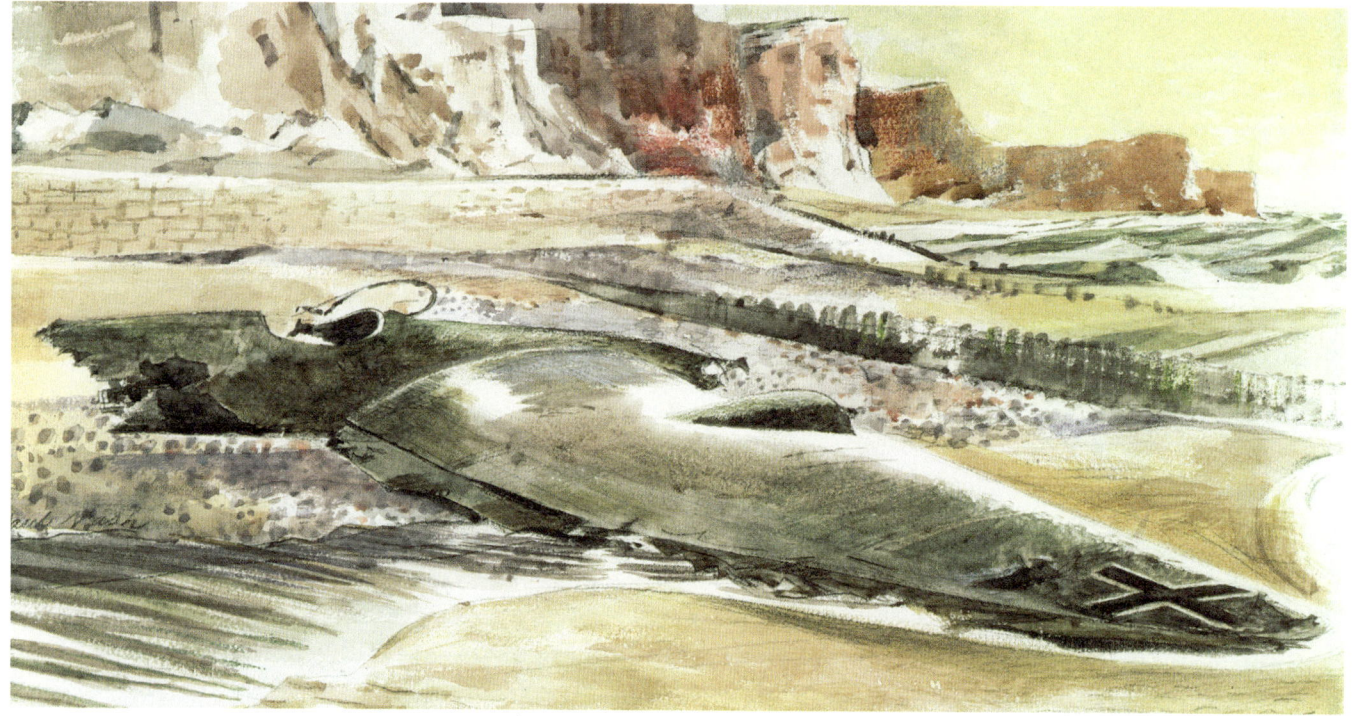

Unit One

Nash had found in the prehistoric past his route to contemporaneity, in Avebury his point of access to the present day. It was a natural next step for him now to establish his first and only avant-garde movement: in June 1933, he proclaimed the foundation of Unit One. This group, he said, 'may be said to stand for the expression of a truly contemporary spirit, for that thing which is recognized as peculiarly *of to-day* in painting, sculpture, and architecture.'

Among those who signed up for the group, committed not to attack English art but to expand its scope by incorporating the abstract and surrealist dimensions, were painters Edward Wadsworth, John Armstrong (1893–1973), Ben Nicholson and Edward Burra (1905–76), and the sculptors Henry Moore (1898–1986) and Barbara Hepworth (1903–75). As Nash's notes for the Unit One touring exhibition of 1934–35 made clear, he remained wedded to his view that lyricism and landscape were essential to Englishness in even the most modern and surreal art.

Real-World Problems

An interest in Surrealism did not of course preclude a concern with a more immediate reality, and in the 1930s there was plenty of reality to go around: the Great Depression, the rise of Fascism in Italy and of Nazism in Germany, and in 1936 General Franco's coup in Spain and the bloody Civil War that followed. Spanish artists such as Picasso, Dalí and Miró all obviously had a direct stake in the fortunes of their homeland but other artists and intellectuals were moved by what they saw as a life-and-death crisis for democracy. Even Nash – though, by the standards of his generation fairly disengaged politically – felt strongly that freedom was under threat and had to be defended from the forces of the Right. He wanted to do his bit as a democrat and as an Englishman, and – once the Second World War began – as a painter too.

Real World War

Neither his age (he was now in his fifties) nor his health (he had serious asthma) would permit the kind of frontline role Nash had had in the First World War. But he still very much wanted to play his part. As an official war artist attached to the Royal Air Force, he was to spend most of his time in southern England, over which – between July and October 1940 – the Battle of Britain was fought.

Nash was intrigued by the whole idea of flight – for its sheer excitement and for the new perspectives he saw it opening up over his beloved English landscape. He was bitterly disappointed when his health would not let him take to the air himself. Such enthusiasms notwithstanding, he was never going to forget the lessons he had learned at Passchendaele about the utter nightmare that a real war could be. By the early summer of 1940, however, western Poland had already been occupied; Norway, Denmark and the Low Countries had been seized soon after. France had been invaded and, with Germany's aerial offensive across the English Channel now well under way and a seaborne invasion seemingly on the cards, Britain evidently had no option but to fight.

Continuities

'War,' wrote Carl von Clausewitz (1780–1831), 'is the continuation of politics by other means.' War art was the continuation of art-as-usual for Nash. His paintings from this period are more of a piece than perhaps might be expected with the 'civilian' art he had created in the preceding months and years. In part by necessity, in part by choice, he kept to the artistic course he had long been following, rather than going out of his way to adapt to his new – and obviously more 'public' – role.

Earthbound as he was, Nash had to observe the air war from some distance, so even when he represented the sky, it was generally in the context of a landscape with strong thematic parallels to the sorts of work he had done before. But he also seems to have seen in the destruction of the War an accelerated version of that same old cycle of 'repair and revenge' he had seen in the story of civilization as a whole. Hence the series of downed planes he portrayed, incongruously positioned where they had crashed and come to rest, like steel-and-canvas, camouflage-painted standing stones.

'The Personality of Planes'

Although always, as we have seen, alert to the unlikely beauties to be found in the field of battle, Nash had never been an enthusiast for war. Not when he had first joined up and certainly not by the time the Armistice came, when after long and traumatic months in the thick of the fighting, he had marked his return to civilian life with a nervous breakdown (*see* page 16). A fish out of water in his English public school (in those days, arguably, a military academy under another name), he did not seem to have developed either the jingoistic patriotism or the boyish *machismo* that prevailed among what was then his country's 'officer class'.

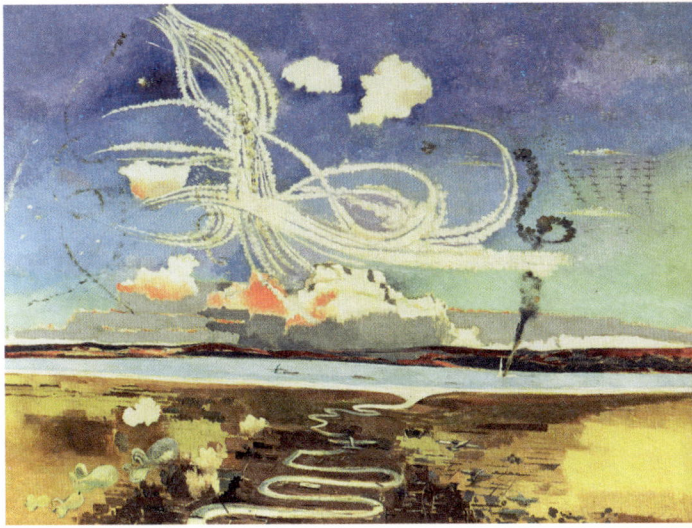

Nash did find an excitement in the idea of flight but as his ambitions to be airborne were thwarted by his failing health, his perspective on the planes that had become his subjects was in some ways not ideal. The German Messerschmitts and Heinkels he saw were either distant specks in the sky or crashed carcasses, unceremoniously brought down to earth. And if the fighters, bombers and transporters of the RAF were intact when he saw them, they were nevertheless grounded, out of their 'natural' element; he never really got to see them do their stuff. Hence, perhaps, his peculiar relationship with what he quickly came to see, semi-seriously, as living, half-human characters, quirky and vulnerable – rather than as roaring, flying, firing, fighting machines.

Nash was even to contribute an article to *Vogue* magazine's March 1942 issue on what he called 'The Personality of Planes', which opens up an interesting window on the way he thought. It is odd to think that this most serious of artists was a fervent admirer of the work of Walt Disney (1901–66), and surprised James Thurber (1894–1961), the American cartoonist, when he met him on a visit to the US with his knowledge and appreciation of American 'comic art'. In other ways, of course, Nash's anthropomorphizing of aircraft can be seen as simply an extension of his old idea of the 'living animate' (*see* page 20).

In any case, like his own art earlier – or, for that matter, perhaps that of any artist at any time – Nash's work during this period sought to do the best it could with the challenges it faced. *The Battle of Britain* (1941, *see* page 50), for example, makes a virtue of necessity in offering a stunning, civilian's eye view of the drama being acted out above everybody's heads across the southern English sky. It works at once as a tribute to 'the Few' in their fighters fending off the Luftwaffe's attack, and as a continuation of Nash's work with found objects (here the random patterns made by vapour-trails) and geometric forms.

Moonlit Mortality

However, the masterpiece from this period (some would argue, from his whole career) is the German-titled *Totes Meer* ('Dead Sea', 1940–41, *see* below and page 49). What initially appears to be a billowing sea is actually entirely static, a dump of aircraft wreckage outside Oxford where wings and fuselages arc up like breaking waves. This is archaeology-in-waiting, a new stratum of destruction which only the centuries will successfully settle and inter. Again, however, it depends for its emotional impact on the touch of anthropomorphism it suggests, the sense of

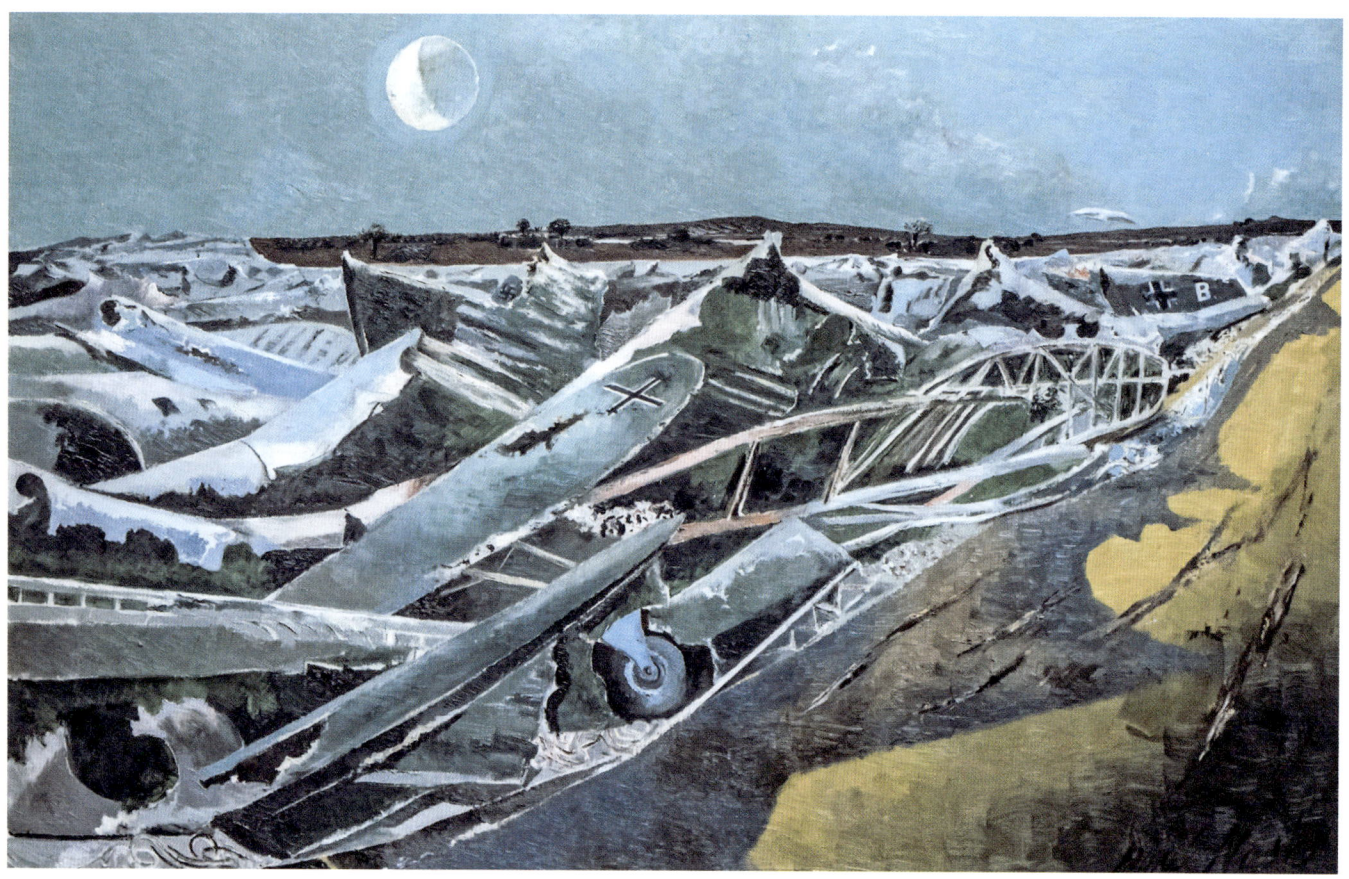

(spent) life in the randomly piled airframe 'bodies' we are looking at – for a sea to be 'dead', it has at some point had to be 'living'. 'You might feel', wrote Nash, that 'this is a vast tide moving across the fields', only then to realize that 'no: nothing moves'.

It is metal piled up, wreckage. It is hundreds and hundreds of flying creatures which invaded these shores….

And, potentially, with some mysterious capacity to live again:

By moonlight, the waning moon, one could swear they began to move and twist and turn as they did in the air.

In fact, the feeling that this scene is living and that it is utterly inert seems to alternate in the consciousness like the ebb and flow of the tide. One way or another, the scene is haunted – not with ghosts or spirits in the conventional sense, but with 'a pervasive force baffled yet malign' which 'hung in the air', as Nash said in his letters to Margaret from Ypres, Belgium in 1917.

Conclusions

Victory, welcome as it was, can hardly have been ecstatic for so sensitive an artist, especially one who had passed this way before – and intensely painfully – after the First World War. Nash had, in any case, learned long since to see the progress of the world and the ways of human history as something that 'scarred and furrowed' (*see* page 22) our collective face. What could be more welcome than release? His visionary fire renewed in his resignation, he worked out these feelings in such stunning paintings as *Landscape of the Vernal Equinox (III)* (1944, *see* right and page 90).

Since his student days an admirer of Blake, in recent years Nash had become especially enamoured with the painter-poet's little lyric, 'Ah! Sun-flower'.

Ah Sun-flower! weary of time,
Who countest the steps of the Sun
Seeking after that sweet golden clime
Where the traveller's journey is done.

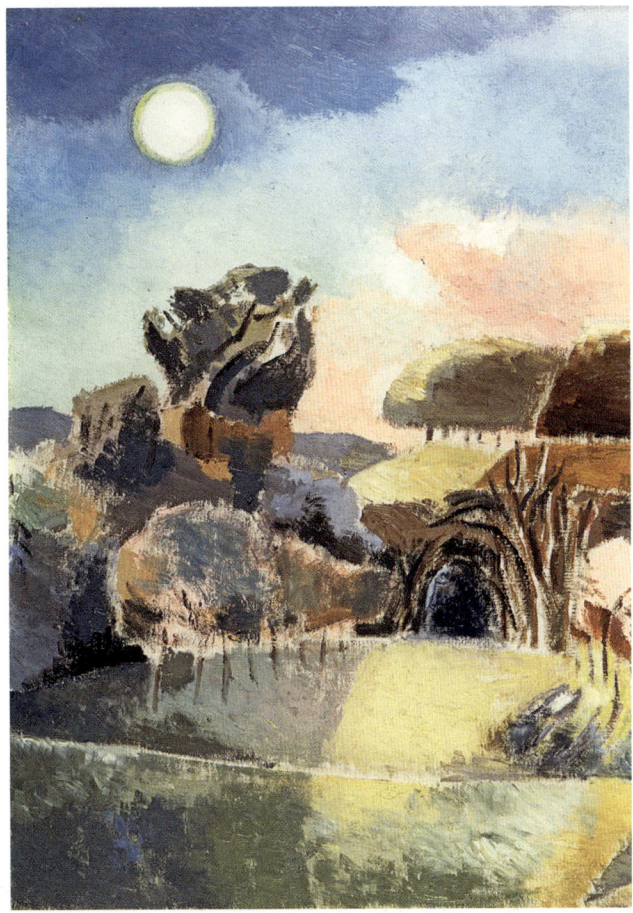

Turning, tracking the sun it so resembled as it pursued its daily circuit across the sky, the flower would never get to join it; and with every dawn it would have it all to do again. Human life was like that, Nash realized. His own life's journey all but done by now, he attained a sort of stoic triumph in late works like *Eclipse of the Sunflower* (1945, *see* page 125). Here, the moon, like the mundane 'guinea' of the philistine's view (*see* page 10), seeks to block out the poet's vision of the angel host. It fails, though, and in that failure creates a richer and more complex art.

This, surely, was Paul Nash's achievement: to find the beauty in brute destruction and, in all life's horrors, at least the possibility of redemption. That work done, in the summer of 1946 Nash caught pneumonia and on 11 July died in his sleep.

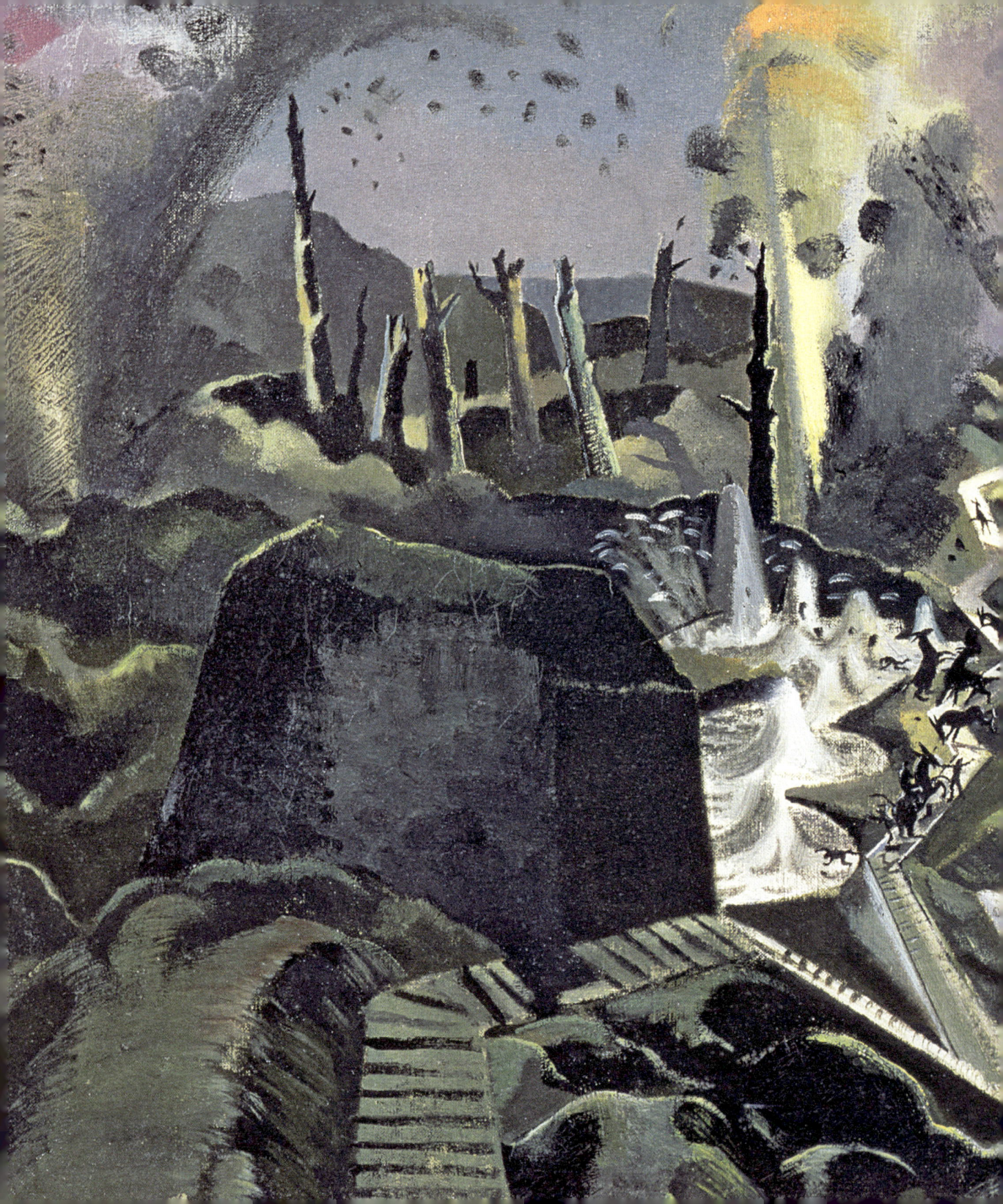

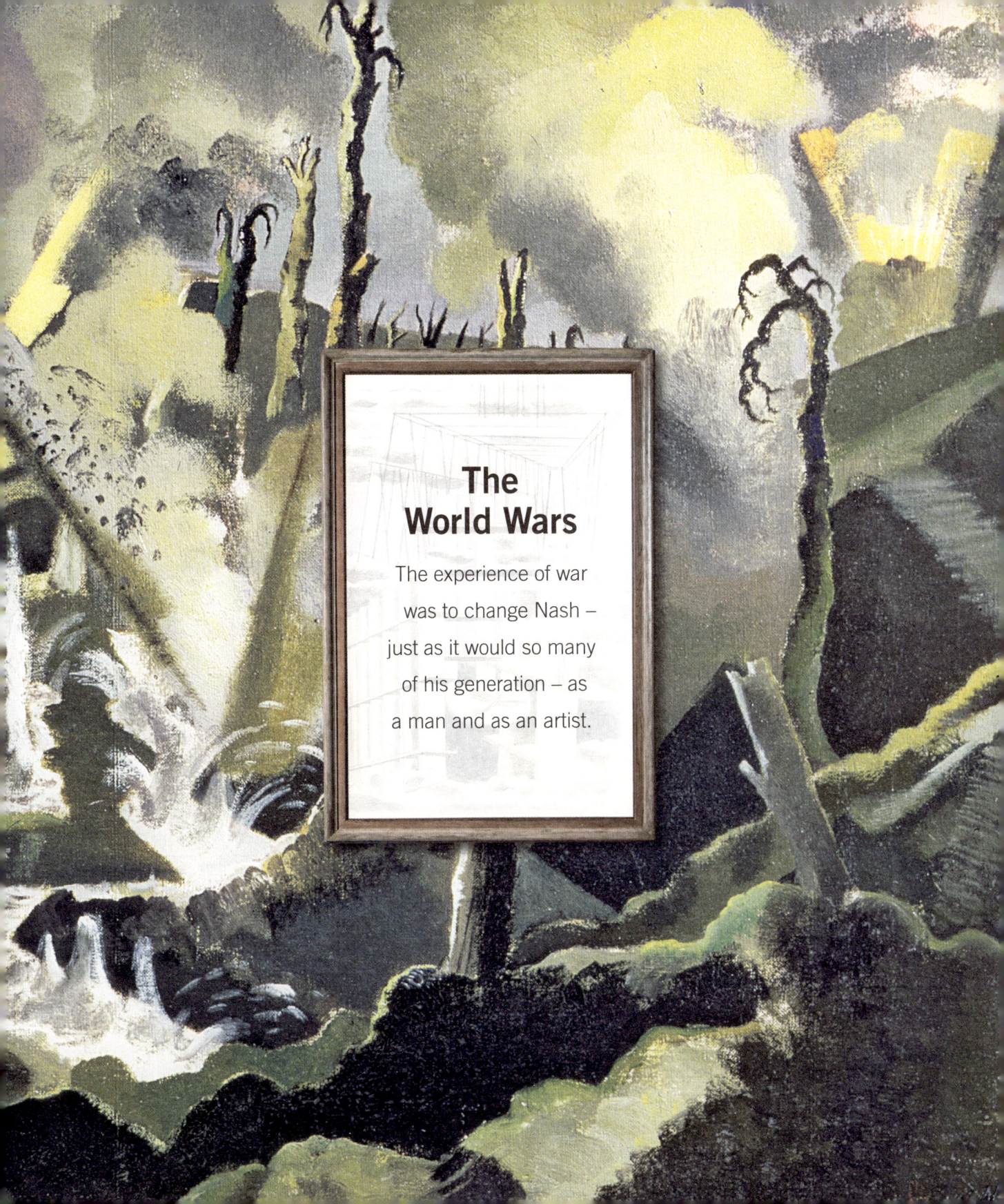

The World Wars

The experience of war
was to change Nash –
just as it would so many
of his generation – as
a man and as an artist.

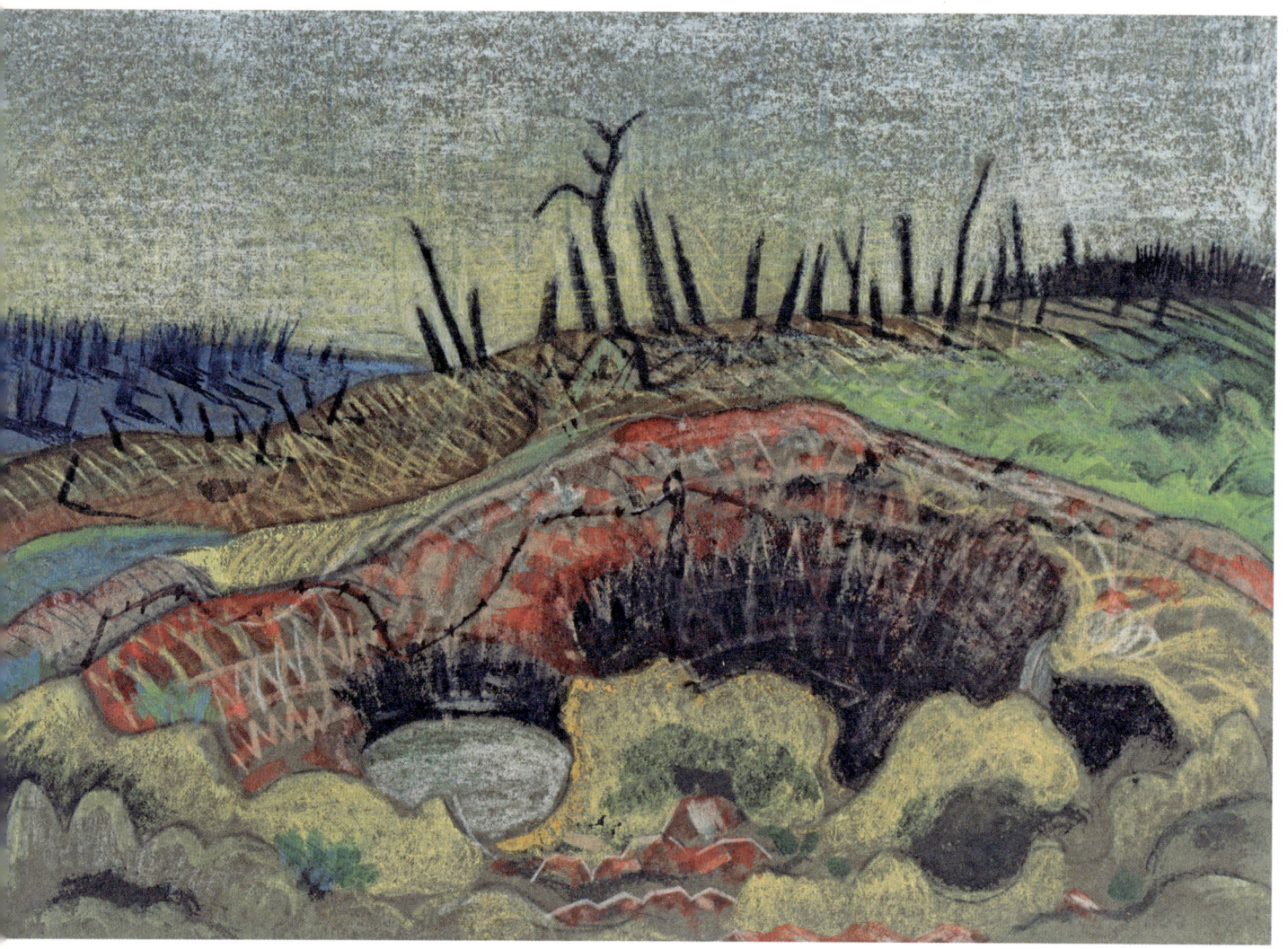

A Farm, Wytschaete, 1917
Ink, chalk and watercolour on brown paper, 25.7 x 35.9 cm (10 x 14 in)
• Stapleton Collection

'The ground ... pitted with yawning holes in which the water lies still and cold or heaped with mounds of earth....' The Western Front was its own world, with its own luridly exotic palette for the painter.

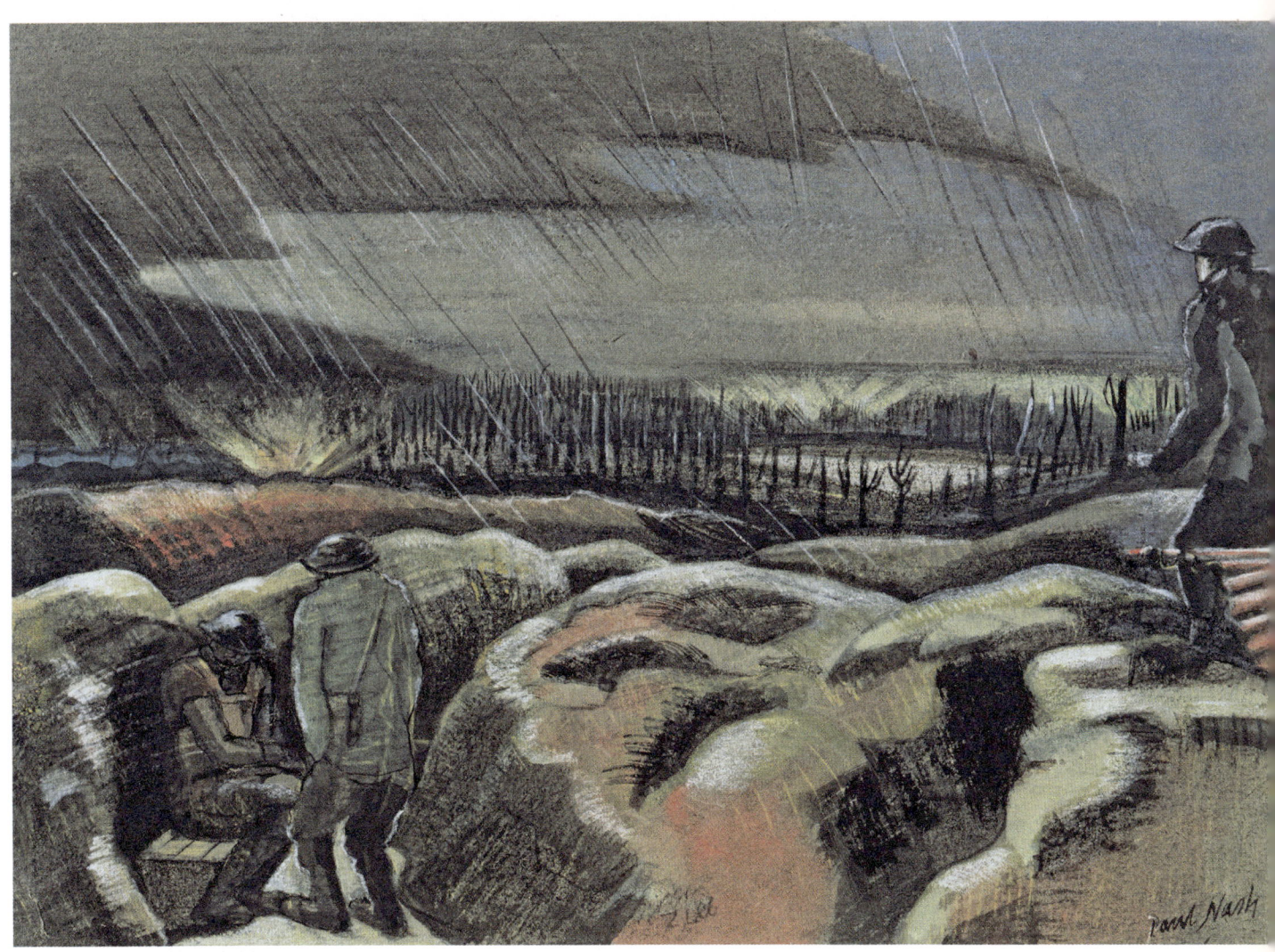

Shellburst, Zillebeke, 1917
Coloured chalks on brown paper, 22 x 28 cm (8¾ x 11 in)
• Private Collection

In this area south-east of Ypres, artillery fire was so frequent that shrapnel showers seemed part of the weather, much like the weeks of incessant rain. Lake Zillebeke, a triangular reservoir, is visible just below the horizon.

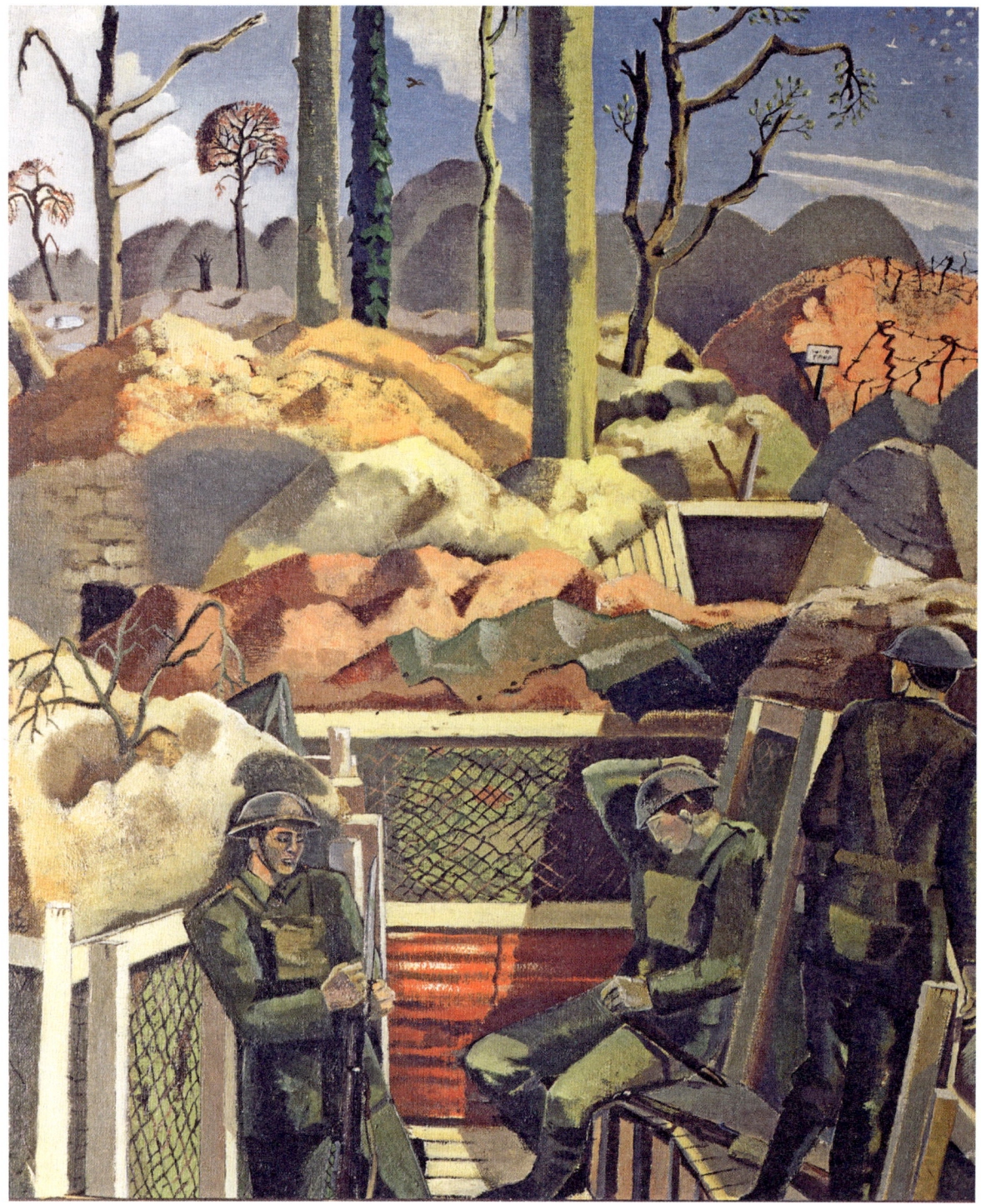

Spring in the Trenches, Ridge Wood, 1917
Oil on canvas, 60.9 x 50.8 cm (24 x 20 in)
• Peter Nahum at the Leicester Galleries

The Front seems almost inviting here. There is certainly something a little topsy-turvy (the reds, russets and tawny browns beneath the blue sky would seem to suggest an autumnal setting), but it is by no means an unappealing scene.

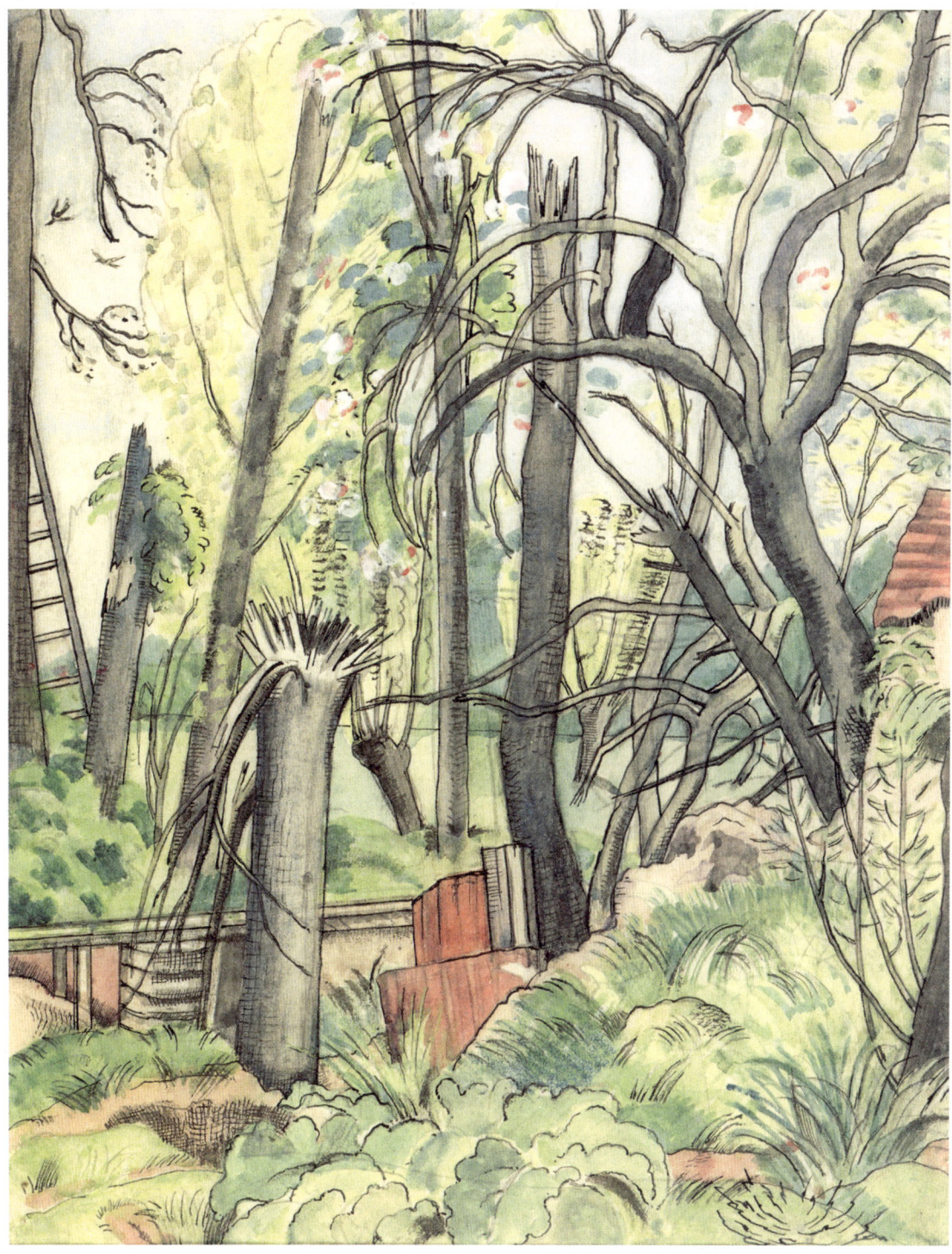

Chaos Decoratif, 1917
Ink and watercolour on paper, 25.3 x 20 cm (10 x 8 in)
• Manchester Art Gallery

Two worlds, two imaginative spheres collide in utter confusion here. Nash depicts a scene of sylvan peace and calm in which, however, the tops of the trees have been shot away, whilst at ground level defensive earthworks have encroached.

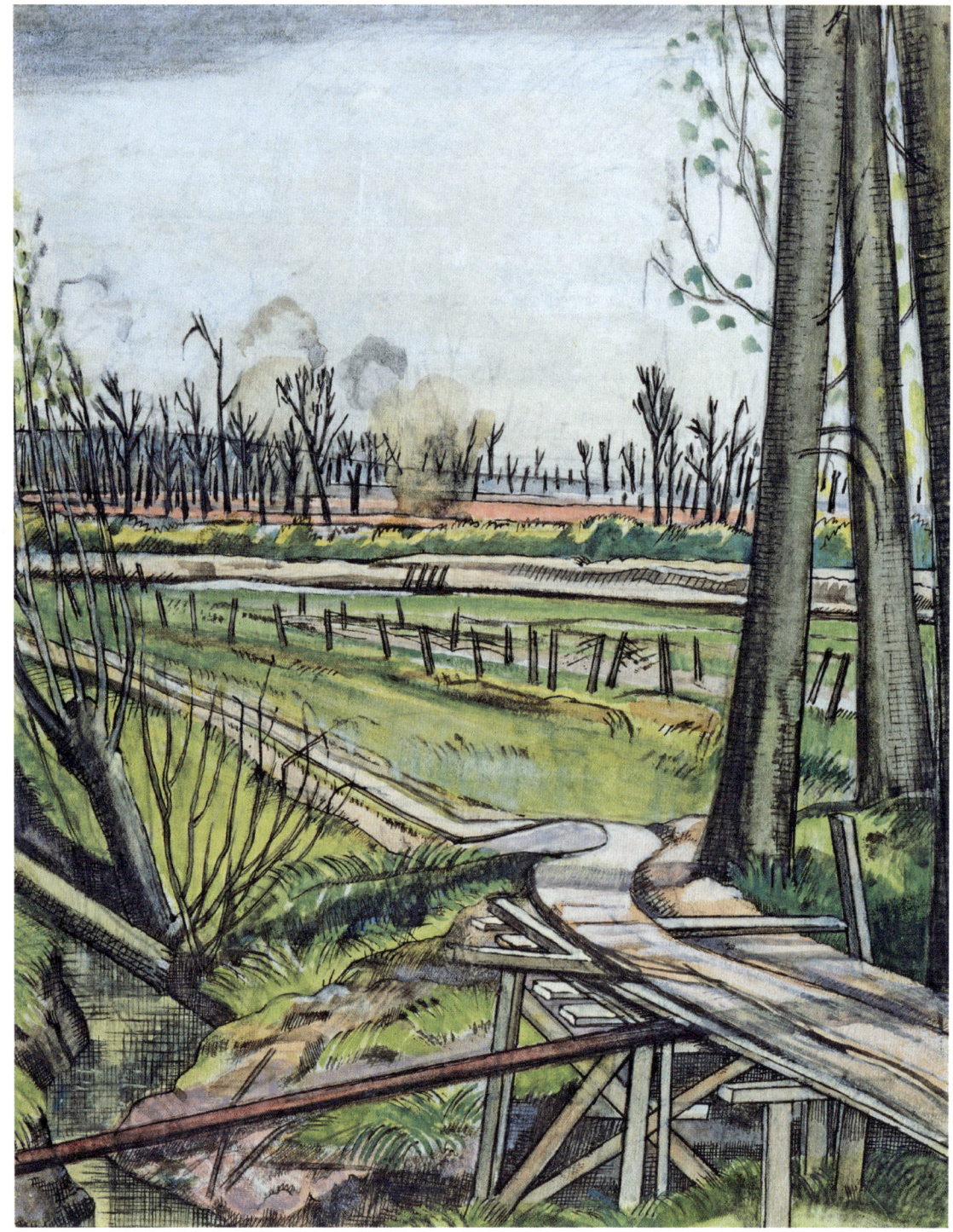

The Ridge, Wytschaete, 1917
Ink, chalk and watercolour on paper, 24.1 x 19.1 cm (9½ x 7½ in)
• Private Collection

Thousands were killed and wounded in the battle for Wytschaete Ridge, Belgium, on 7 June 1917. Here, however, it all seems peaceful if a little threadbare, the green grass growing in defiance of the destruction.

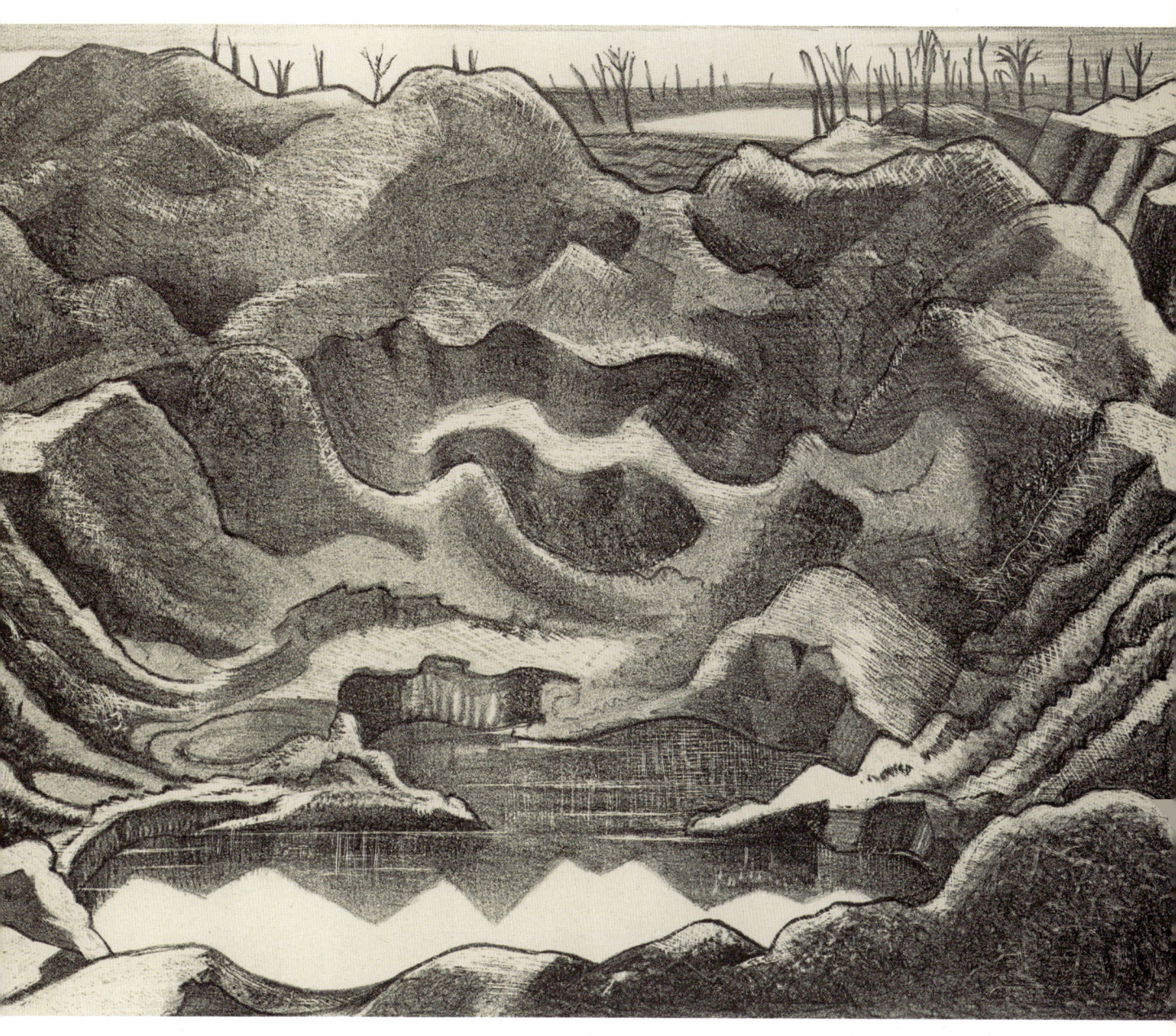

The Mine Crater, Hill 60, Ypres Salient, 1917
Black and white lithograph, 35.5 x 45.5 cm (14 x 18 in)
• Private Collection

Desperate to dislodge the Germans from Hill 60, the British sent sappers to tunnel below.
On 7 June 1917, as the Second Battle of Messines began, explosive charges sent the whole
position sky-high. What had been a hill was now a hole.

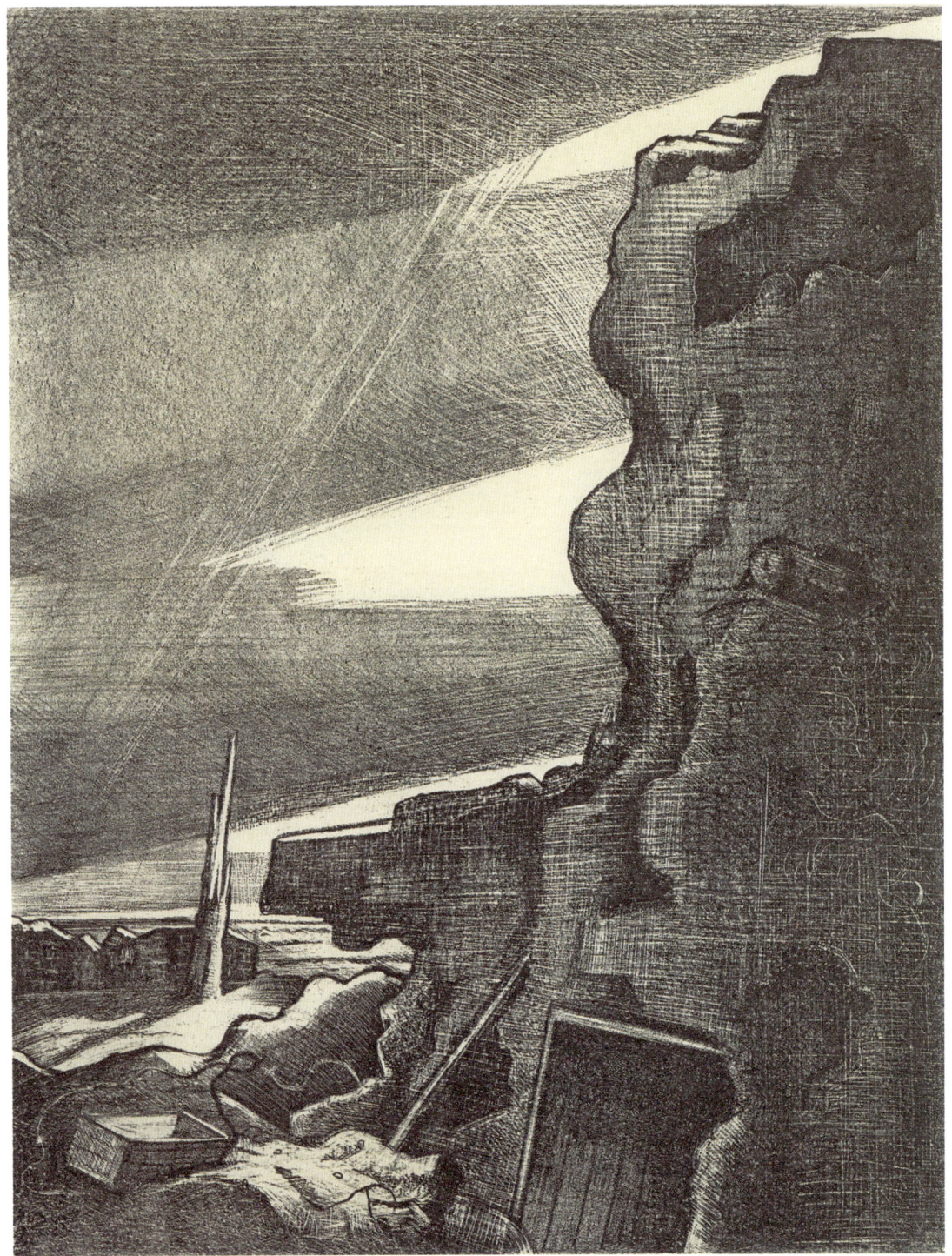

German Double Pill Box, Gheluvelt, 1918
Lithograph, 46 x 35.5 cm (14 x 18 in)
• Private Collection

If the building is a ruin, surrounded by abandoned equipment, the tree against the skyline is little more than a ragged spike. A scene from what Siegfried Sassoon called 'death's grey land'.

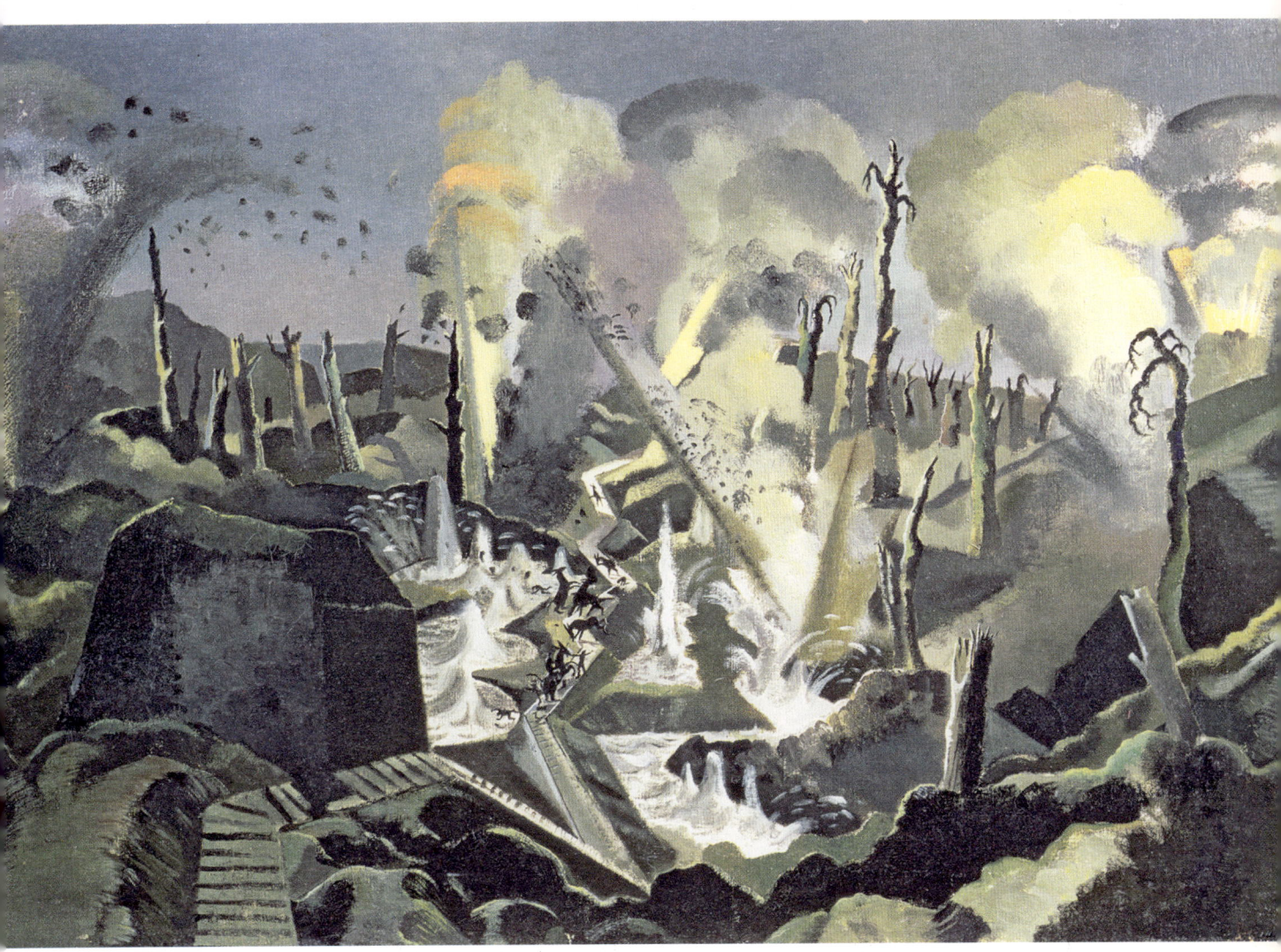

The Mule Track, 1918
Oil on canvas, 61 x 91 cm (24 x 36 in)
• Imperial War Museum, London

Just discernible in the zig-zag of the duckboard track, the silhouetted shapes of terror-stricken mules and men rear and contort as falling shells land all about them, sending up clouds of smoke and fountains of mud and water.

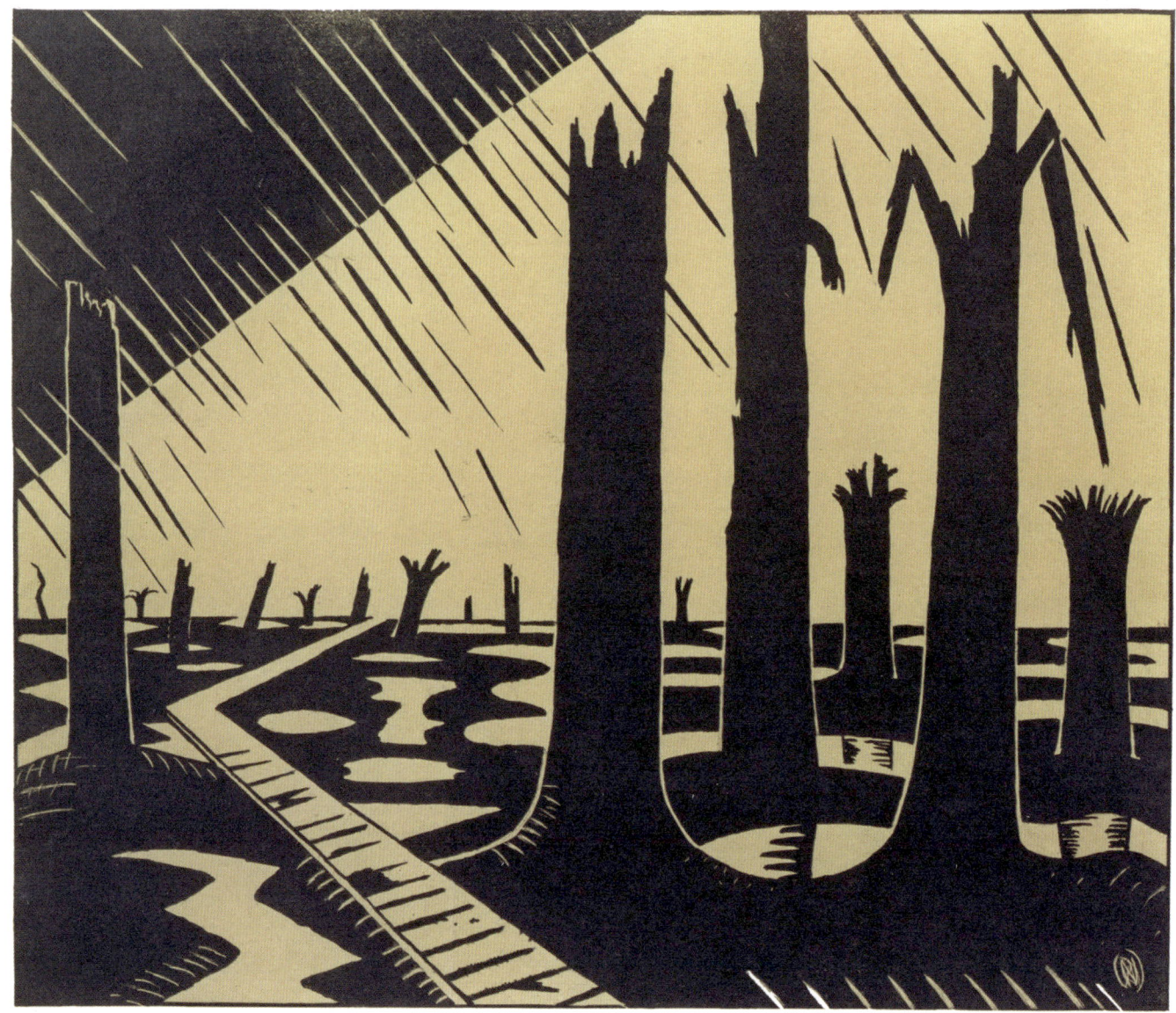

Void of War, 1918
Lithograph, 37.1 x 44.4 cm (14½ x 17½ in) • Private Collection

The poster image for a Paul Nash exhibition of this name, 'The Void of War' is starkly striking. It lives up to its title in showing us a scene of emptiness; a landscape drained of all animation and of all life.

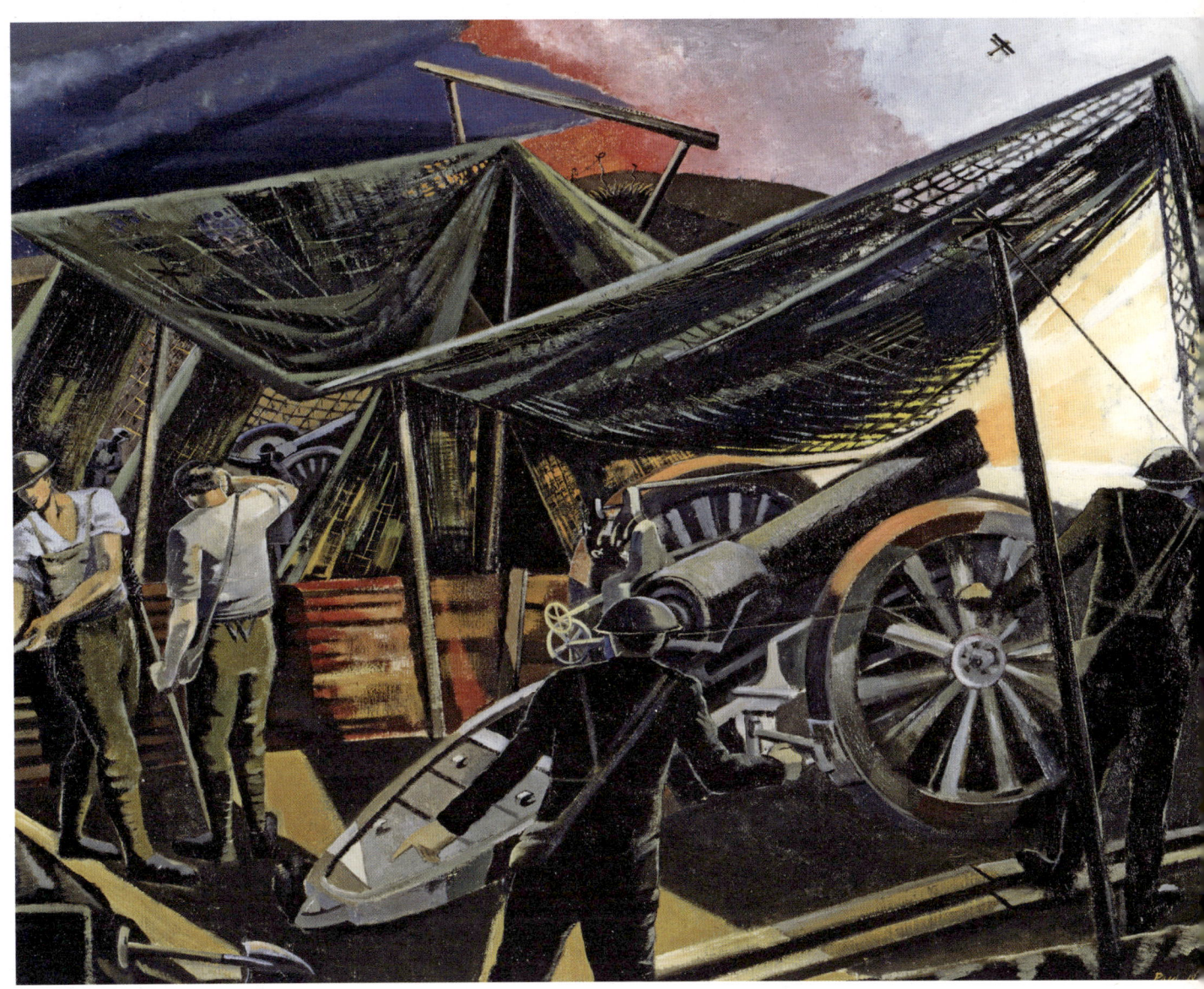

A Howitzer Firing, 1918
Oil on canvas, 71 x 91 cm (28 x 36 in)
• Imperial War Museum, London

One gunner shields his eyes while his comrades look on in wonder at the searing
sun-blast from the muzzle of their howitzer, as it makes a momentary noon amid
the darkness of a Flanders day.

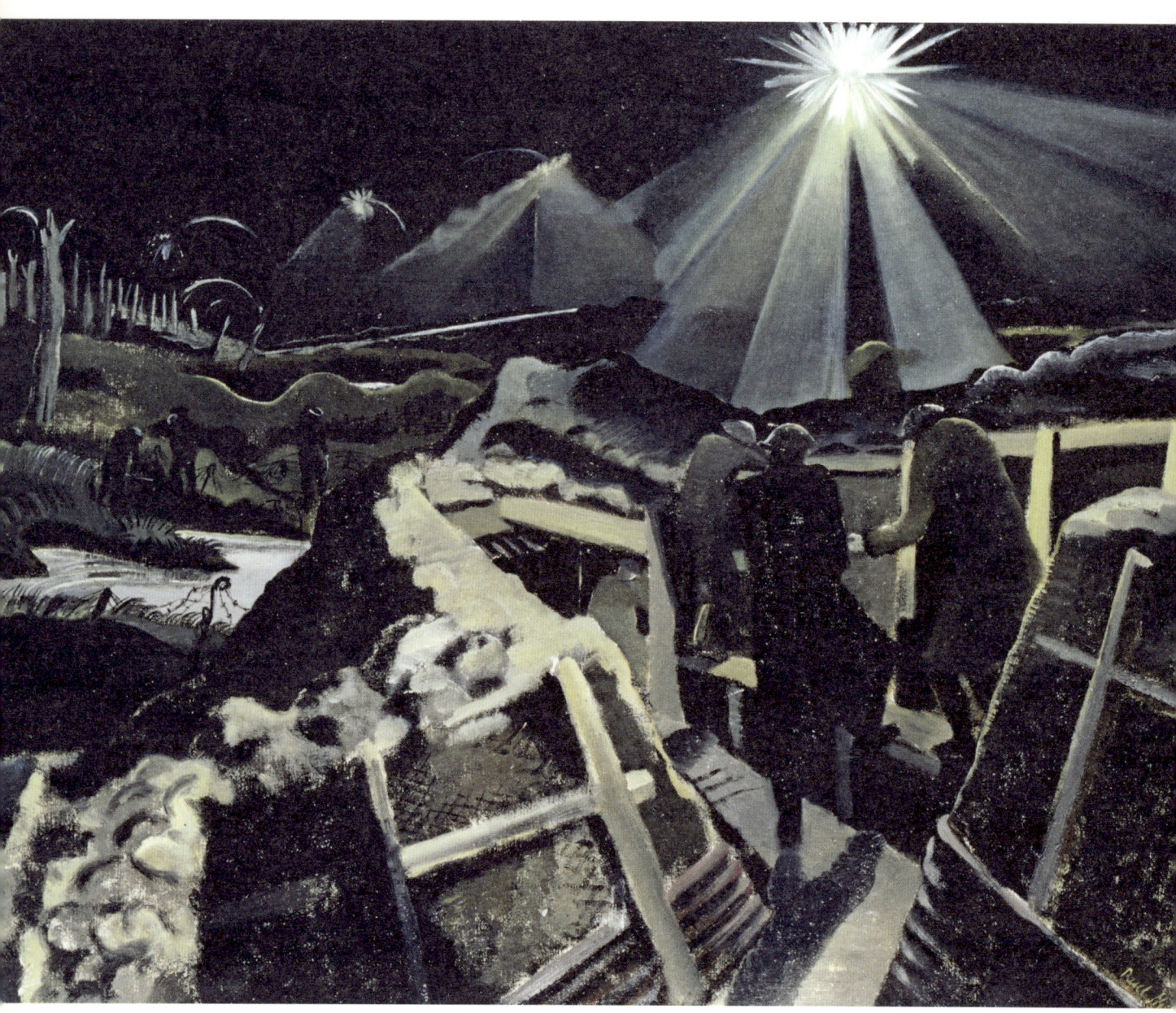

The Ypres Salient at Night, 1918
Oil on panel, 71 x 92 cm (28 x 36¼ in)
• Imperial War Museum, London

Star shells cast a baleful light upon the battlefield below, where three men in a trench avert their eyes. Further figures stand darkly silhouetted in the distance, across the eerily illuminated waters of a crater-lake.

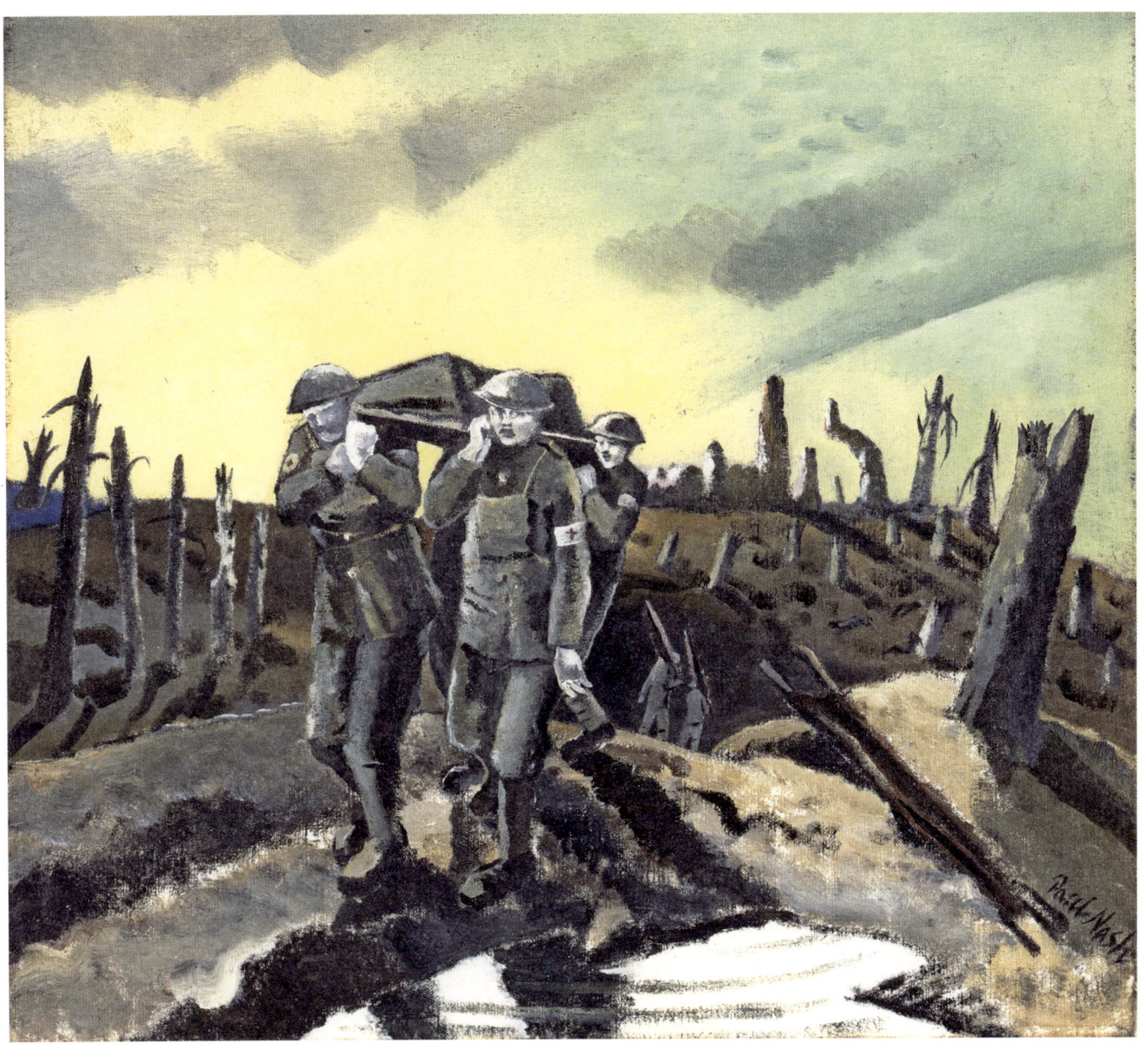

Wounded, Passchendaele, 1918
Oil on canvas, 46 x 51 cm (14 x 20 in)
• Manchester Art Gallery

Up to half a million men were killed or wounded at the Third Battle of Ypres. It was Nash's baptism of fire at the Front. He returned that October, nominally a veteran, but unprepared for the full ferocity of the fighting.

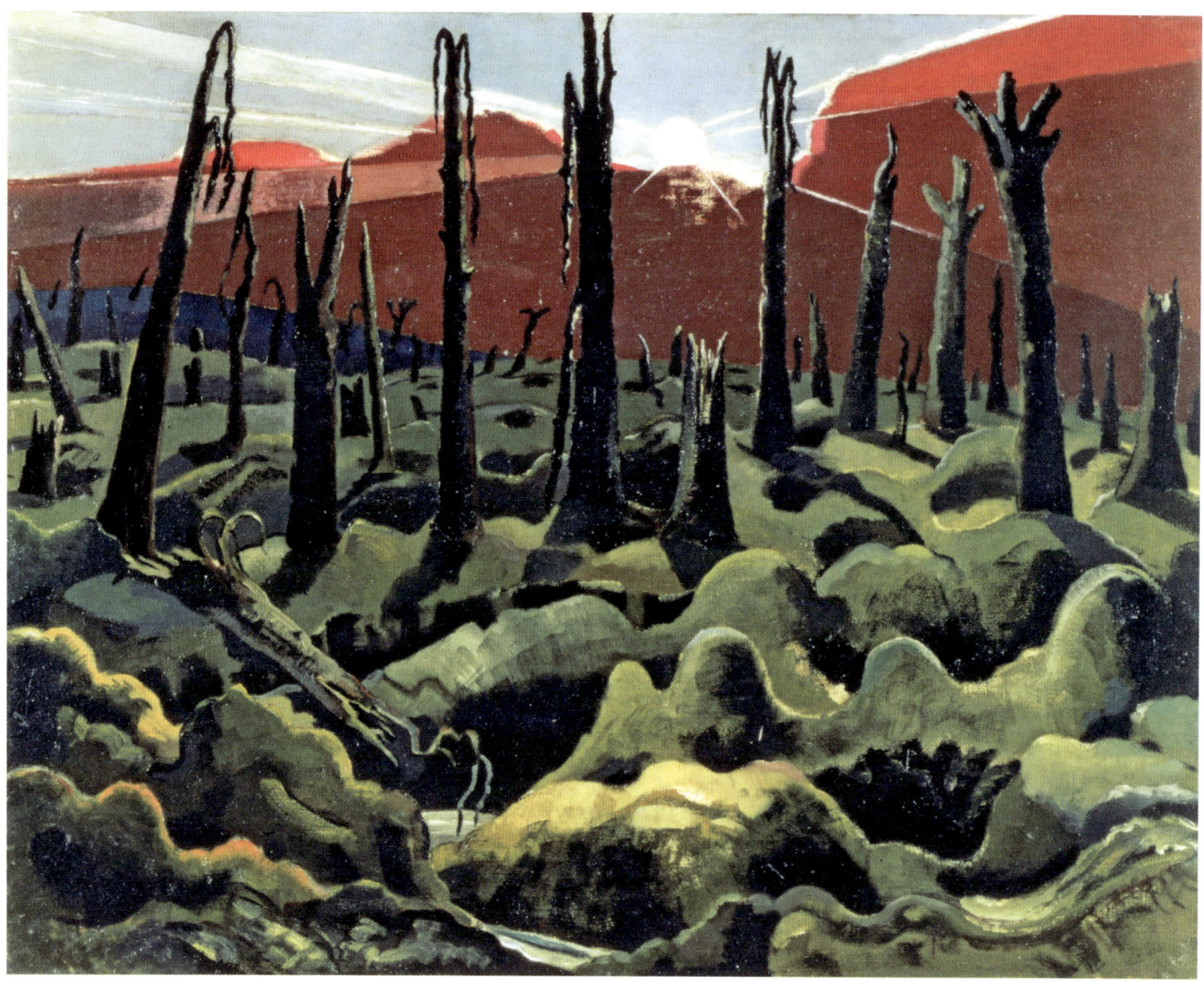

We Are Making a New World, 1918
Oil on canvas, 71.1 x 91.4 cm (28 x 36 in)
• Imperial War Museum, London

The morning sun rises above a skyline of red hills, lighting a landscape stubbled with snapped-off trees and pitted and pocked by falling shells. Is this a scene of hope or of irredeemable despair?

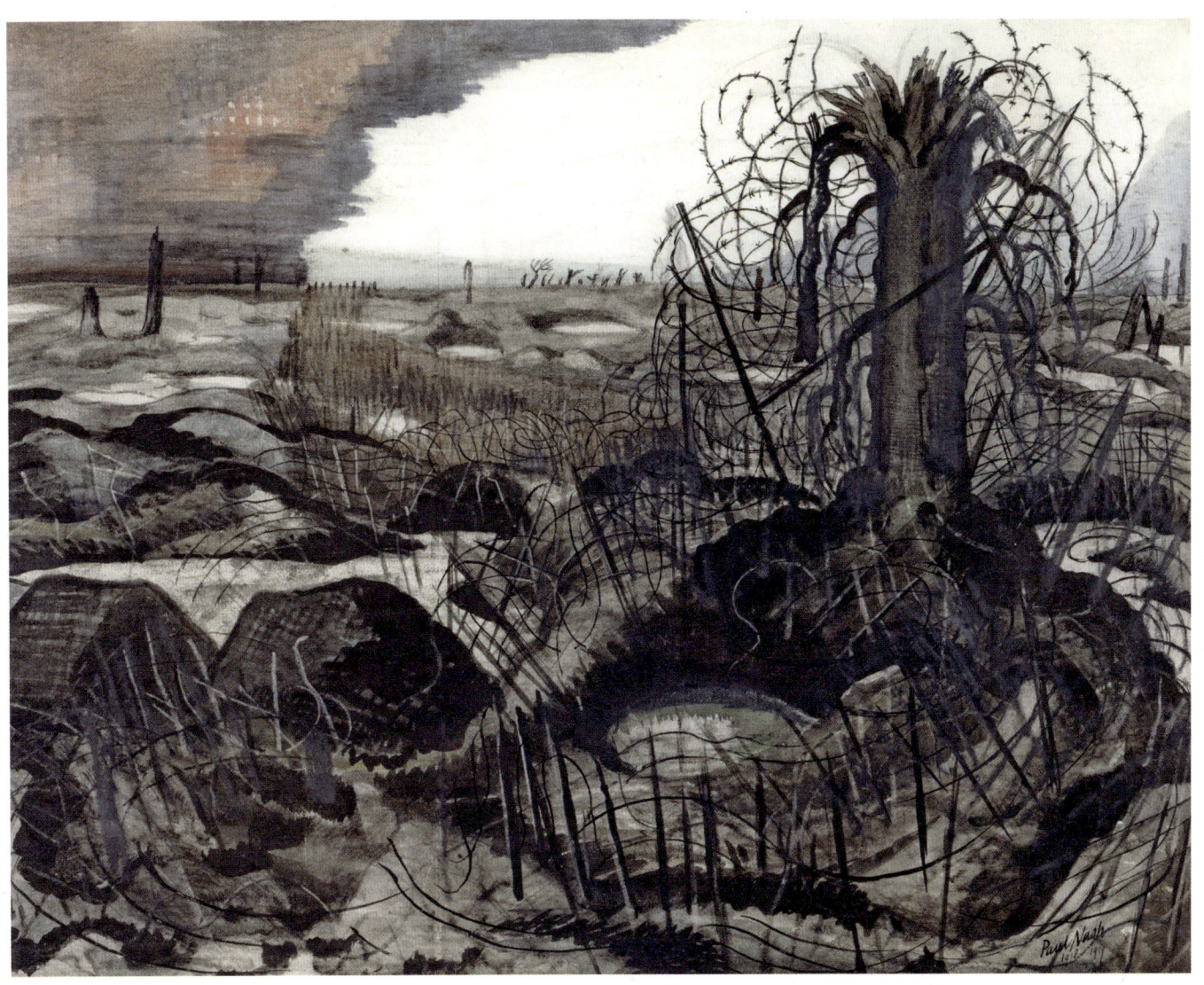

Wire, 1919
Ink, chalk and watercolour on paper, 48.9 x 63.5 cm (19½ x 25 in)
• Imperial War Museum, London

The grass has gone and the trees have been blasted away, but no matter, warring men have replaced them with an *ersatz* vegetation of their own: a veritable thicket of black barbed wire.

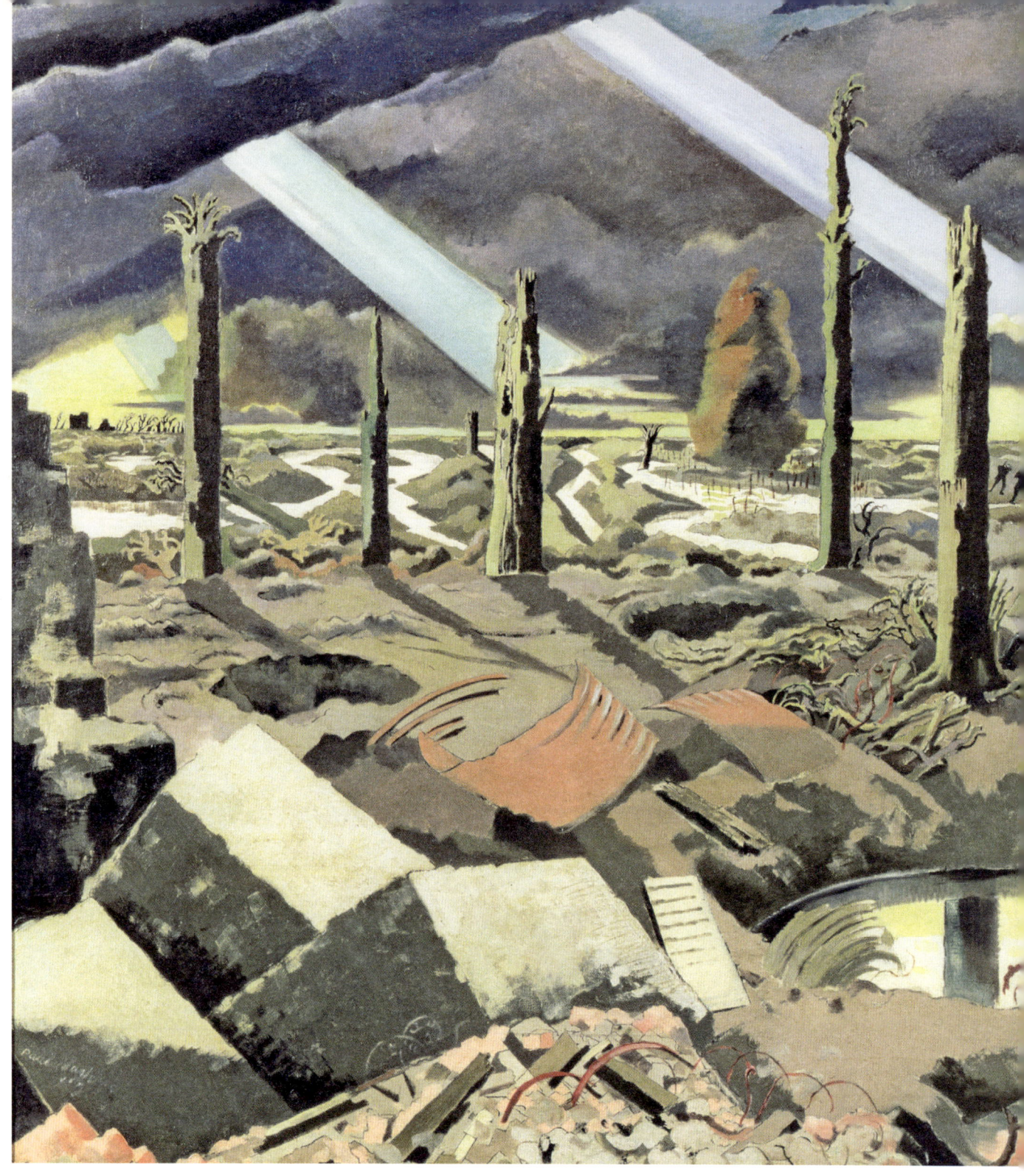

The Menin Road, 1919
Oil on canvas, 71.1 x 91.4 cm (28 x 36 in)
• Imperial War Museum, London

'The picture,' Nash himself explained, 'shows a tract of country near Gheluvelt village in the sinister district of "Tower Hamlets", perhaps the most dreaded and disastrous locality of any area in any of the theatres of War.'

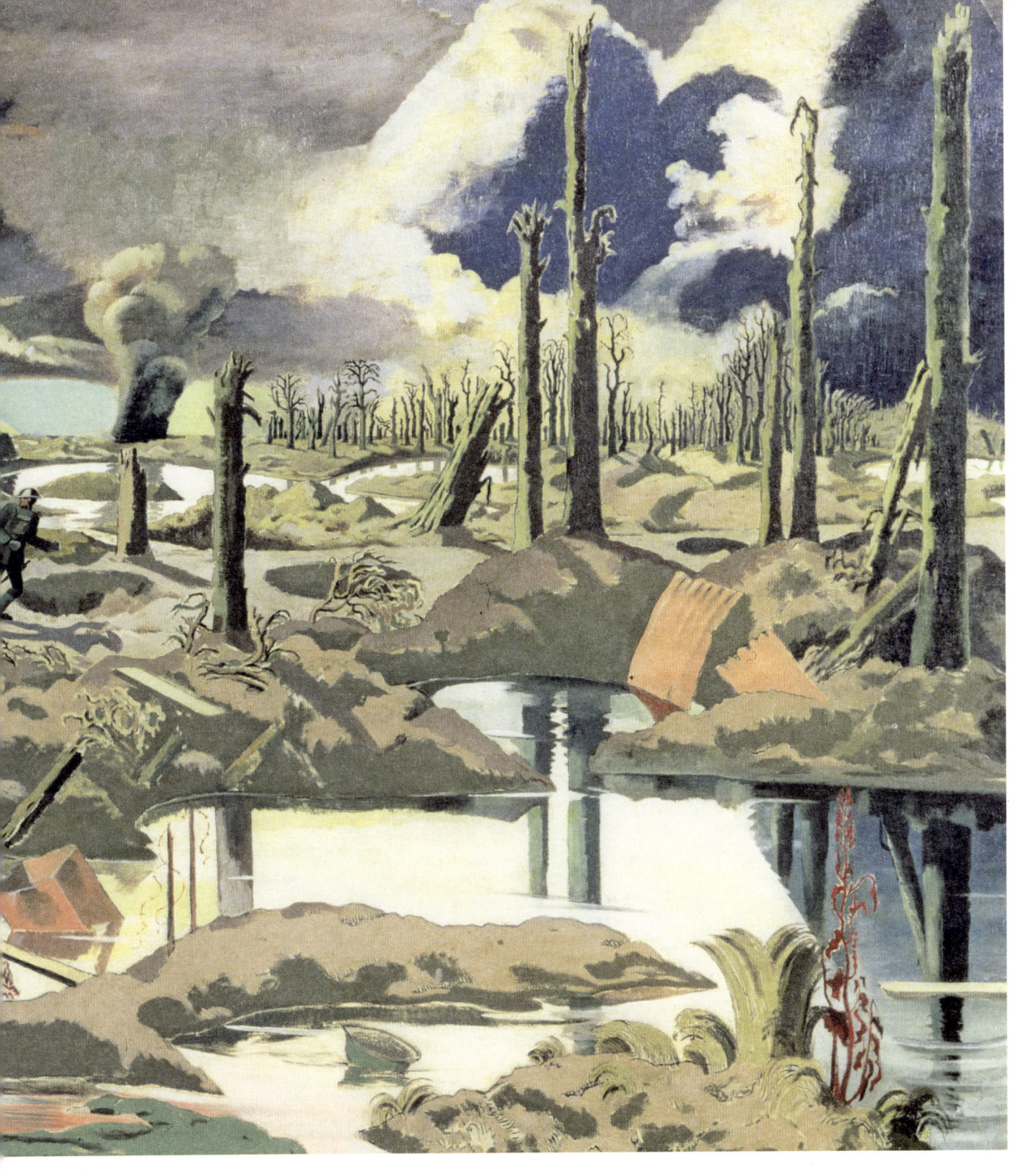

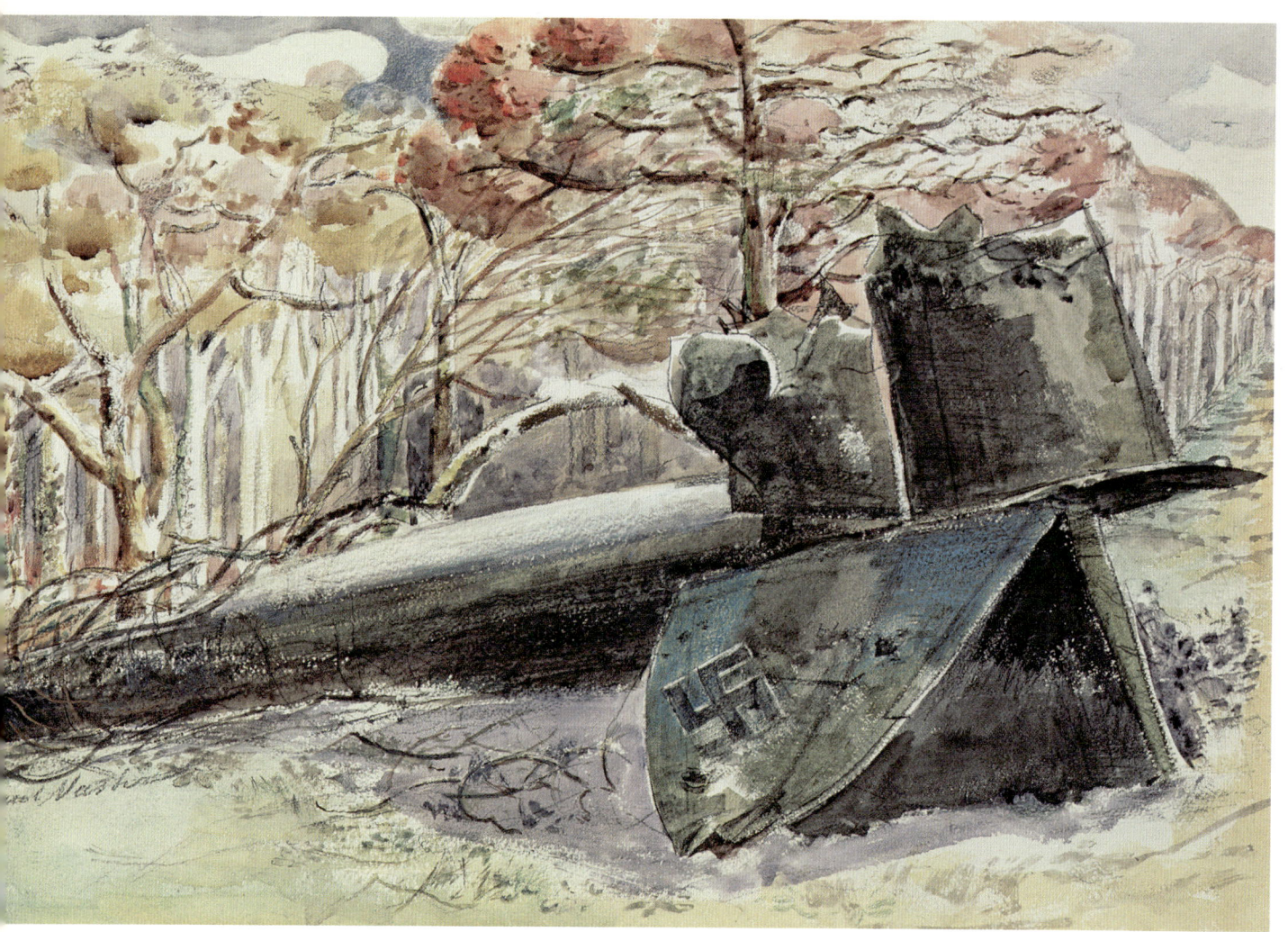

Bomber in the Wood, 1940
Ink and watercolour on paper, 38.5 x 56.6 cm (15 x 22¼ in)
• Leeds Art Gallery

The incongruity of a warplane wreck in a picturesque and peaceful English woodland setting clearly caught Nash's imagination. It also struck a chord with his Surrealist sense of a subconscious dimension intruding absurdly into our conscious life.

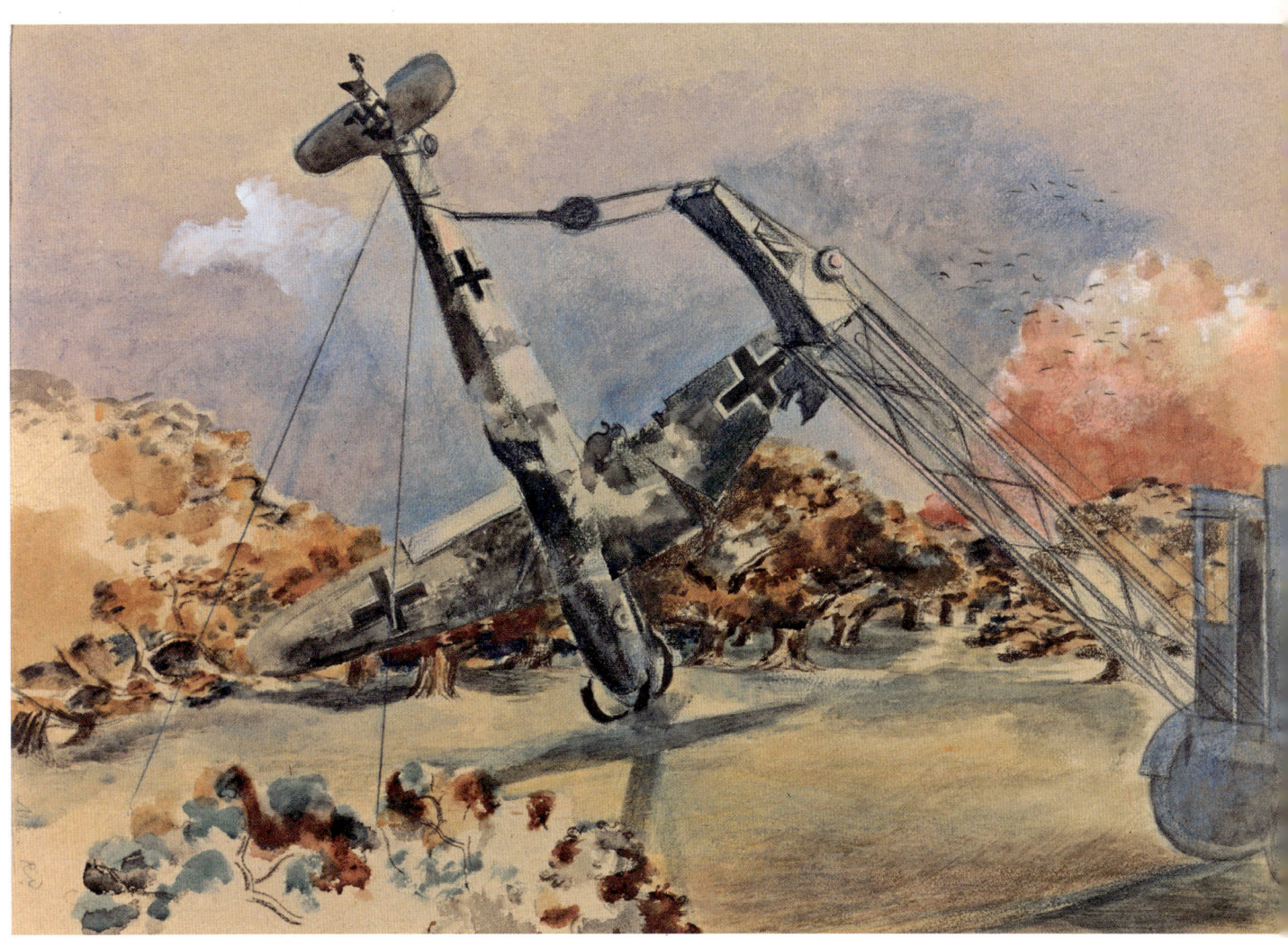

The Messerschmitt in Windsor Great Park, 1940
Pencil, chalks and watercolour on paper, 40 x 57.8 cm (15¾ x 22¾ in)
• Tate Britain, London

In this extraordinary work, a crashed German fighter does duty as a 'found object', its relation to its surroundings only made more complex by the crazy position in which it is captured.

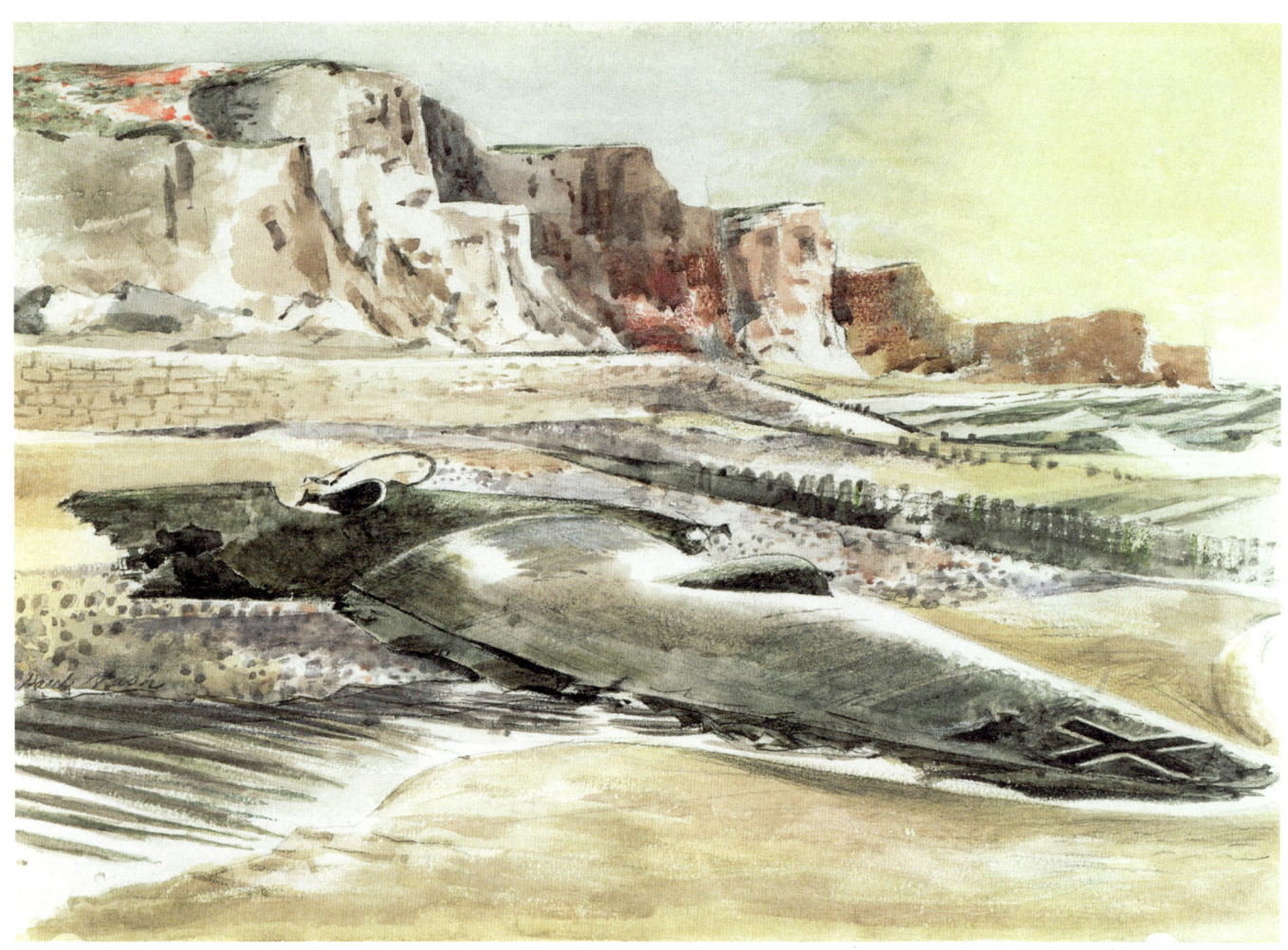

The Raider on the Shore, 1940
Watercolour with black crayon and brown pastel on paper,
40.1 x 58.5 cm (15¾ x 23 in)
• Art Gallery and Museum, Kelvingrove, Glasgow

Once a terrifying sight, this Heinkel 111 now lies broken, a find for beachcombers.
Nash was to paint a series of 'Raiders' pictures, all in their different ways underlining
the strange vulnerability of these monsters of the air.

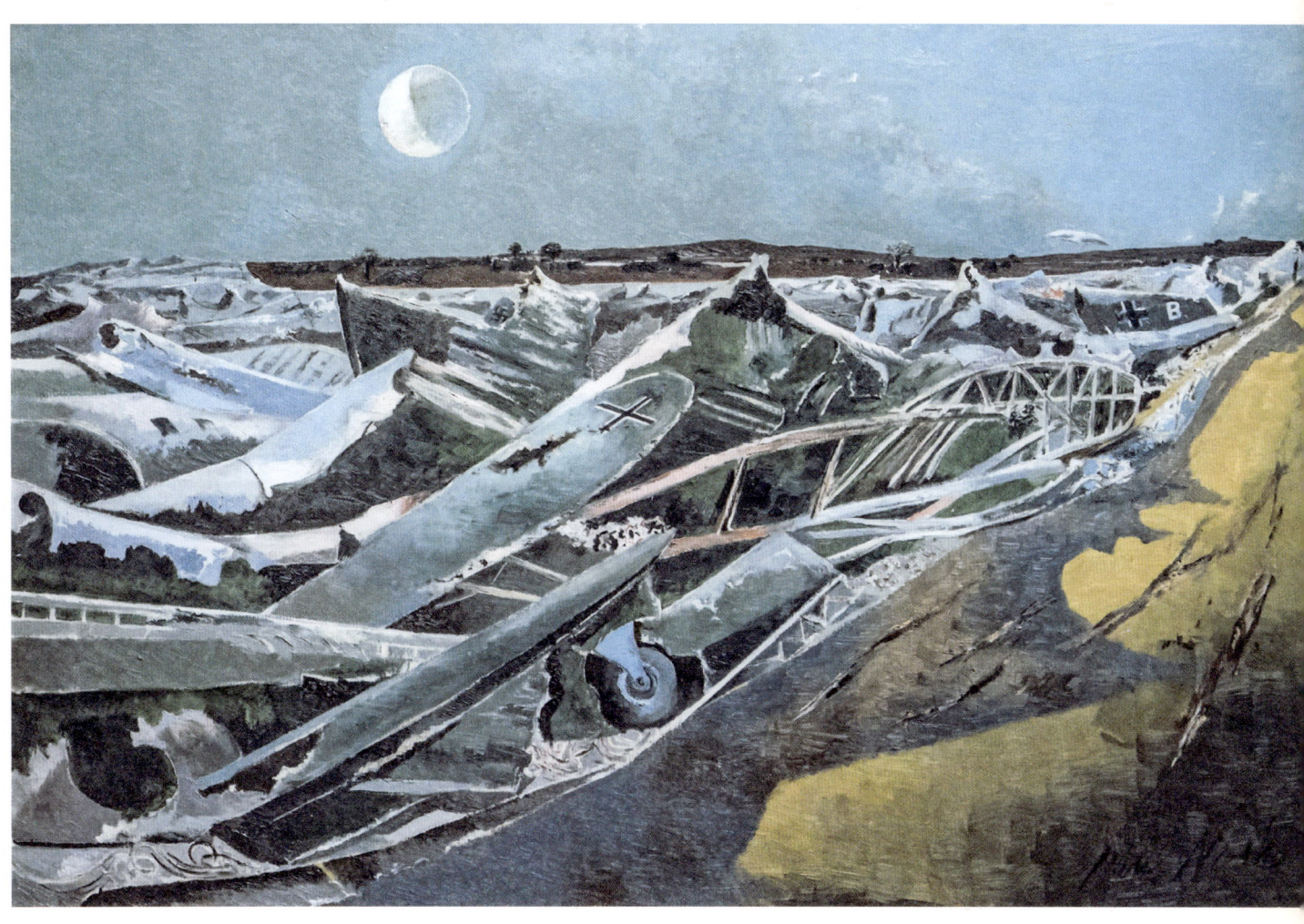

Totes Meer ('Dead Sea'), 1940–41
Oil on canvas, 101.5 x 152.5 cm (40 x 60 in)
• Tate Britain, London

A scrap-metal *Guernica*: a graveyard of wrecked aircraft stretches away like a heaving sea, whilst a white owl wings its way beneath a silver moon, in one of the most memorable paintings of the Second World War.

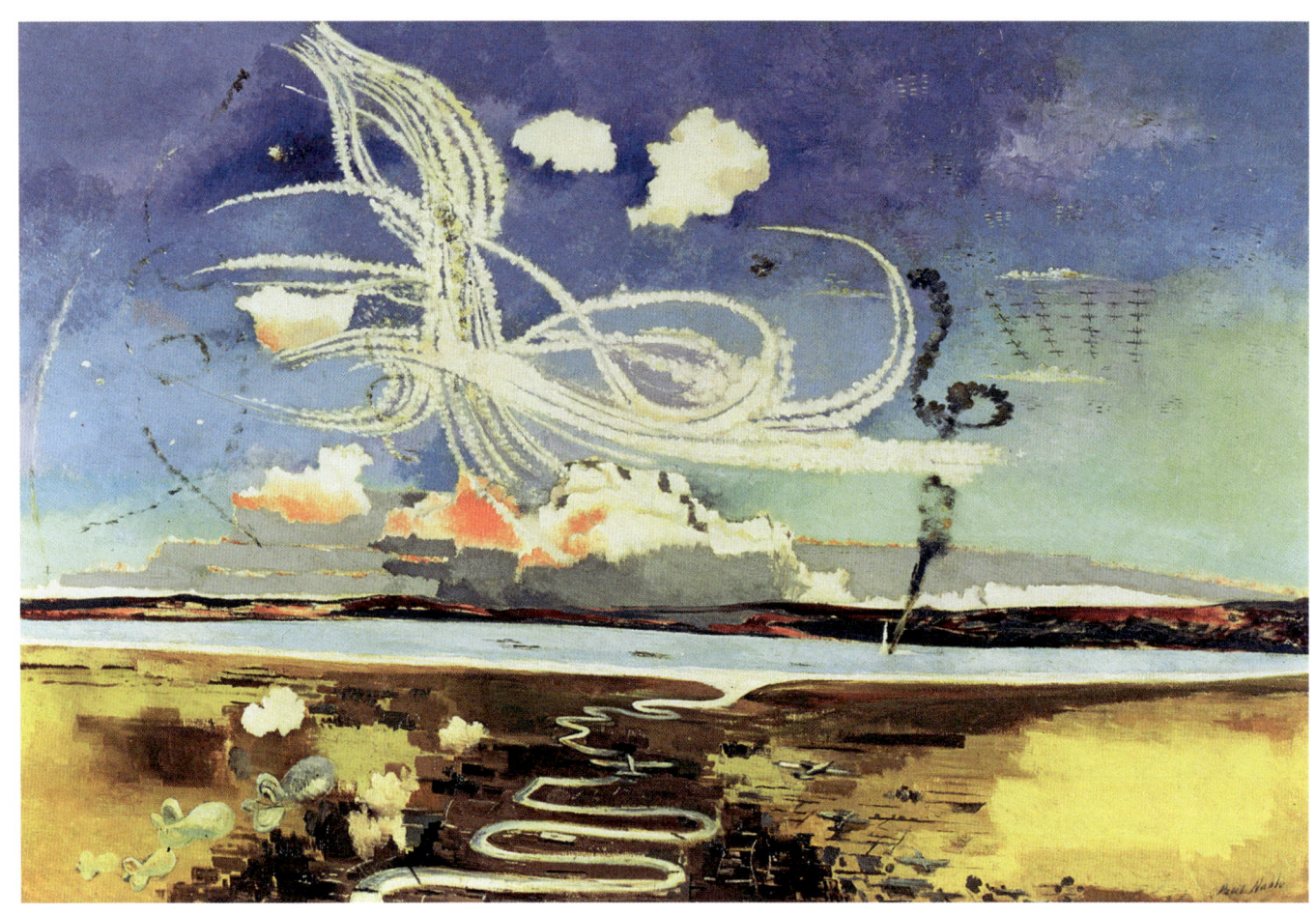

The Battle of Britain, 1941
Oil on canvas, 122.6 x 183.5 cm (48¼ x 72¼ in)
• Imperial War Museum, London

'Across the spaces of sky,' wrote Nash, 'trails of airplanes, smoke tracks of dead or damaged machines falling, floating clouds, parachutes, balloons. Against the approaching twilight new formations of the Luftwaffe threatening.'

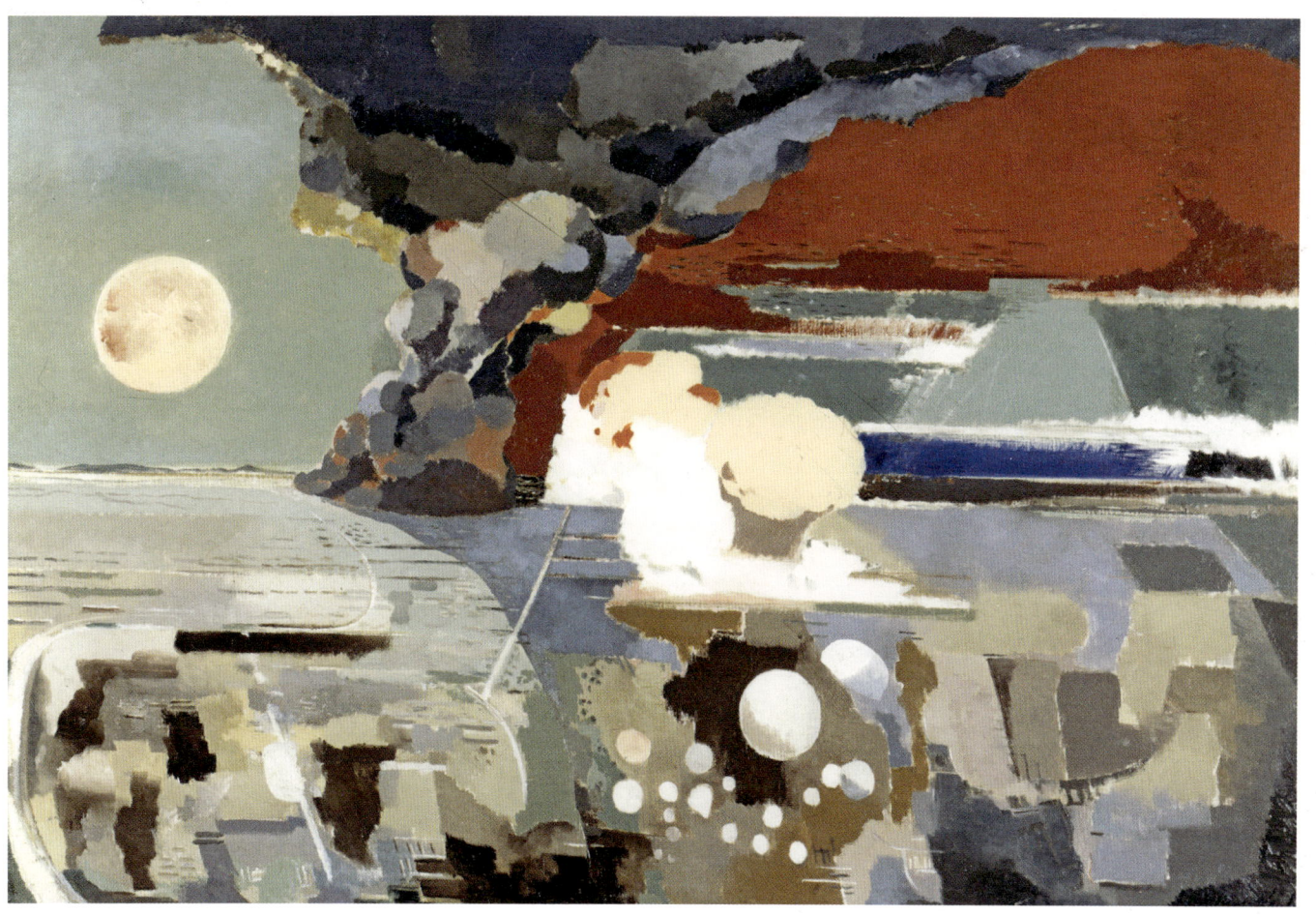

Battle of Germany, 1944
Oil on canvas, 122 x 182.8 cm (48 x 72 in)
• Imperial War Museum, London

The tide of war turned and the aggressor went down into an inferno of its own making. In this semi-Surrealist masterpiece, the scattered spheres seem to reflect the bomb bursts showering down upon a stricken city.

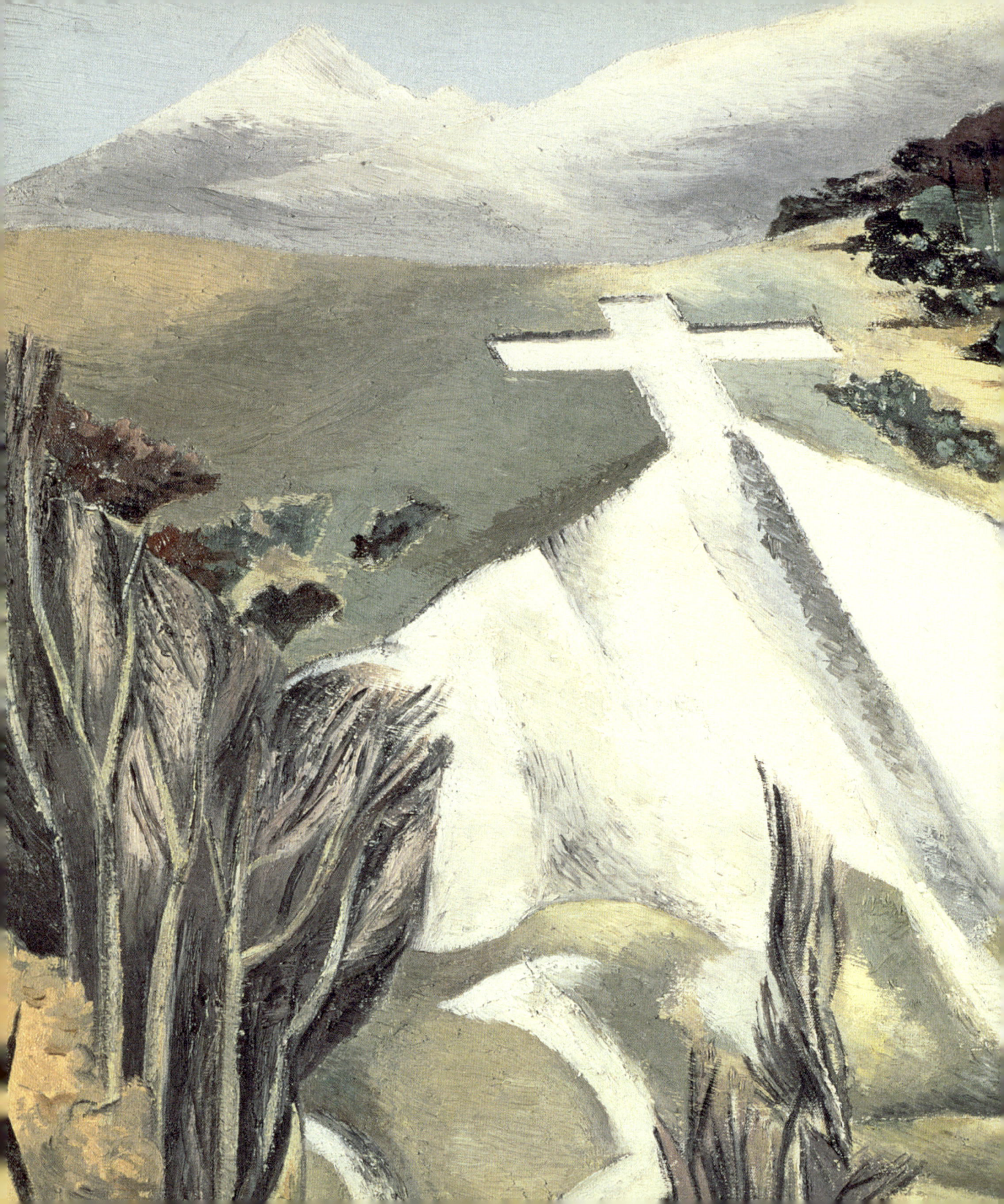

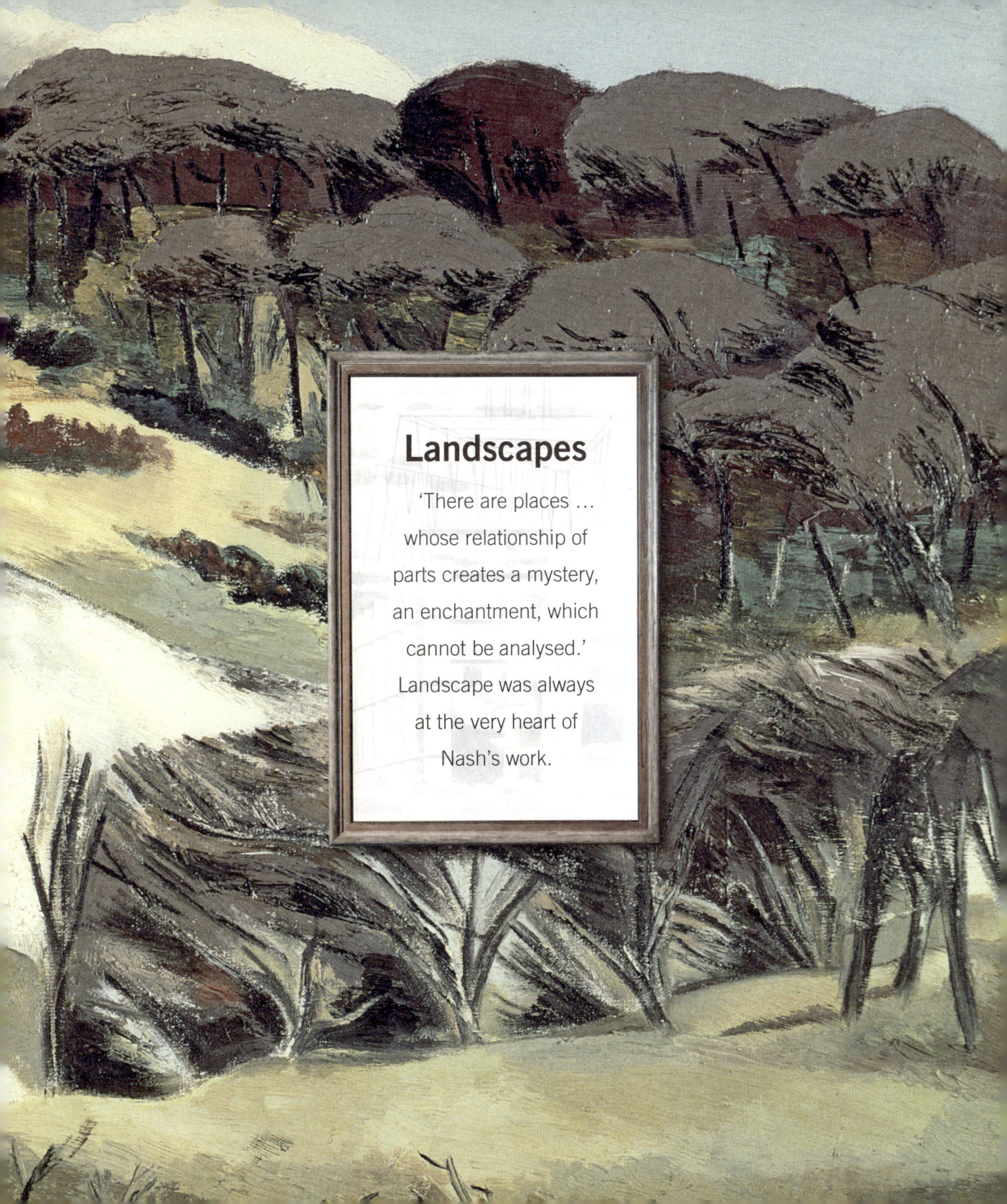

Landscapes

'There are places …
whose relationship of
parts creates a mystery,
an enchantment, which
cannot be analysed.'
Landscape was always
at the very heart of
Nash's work.

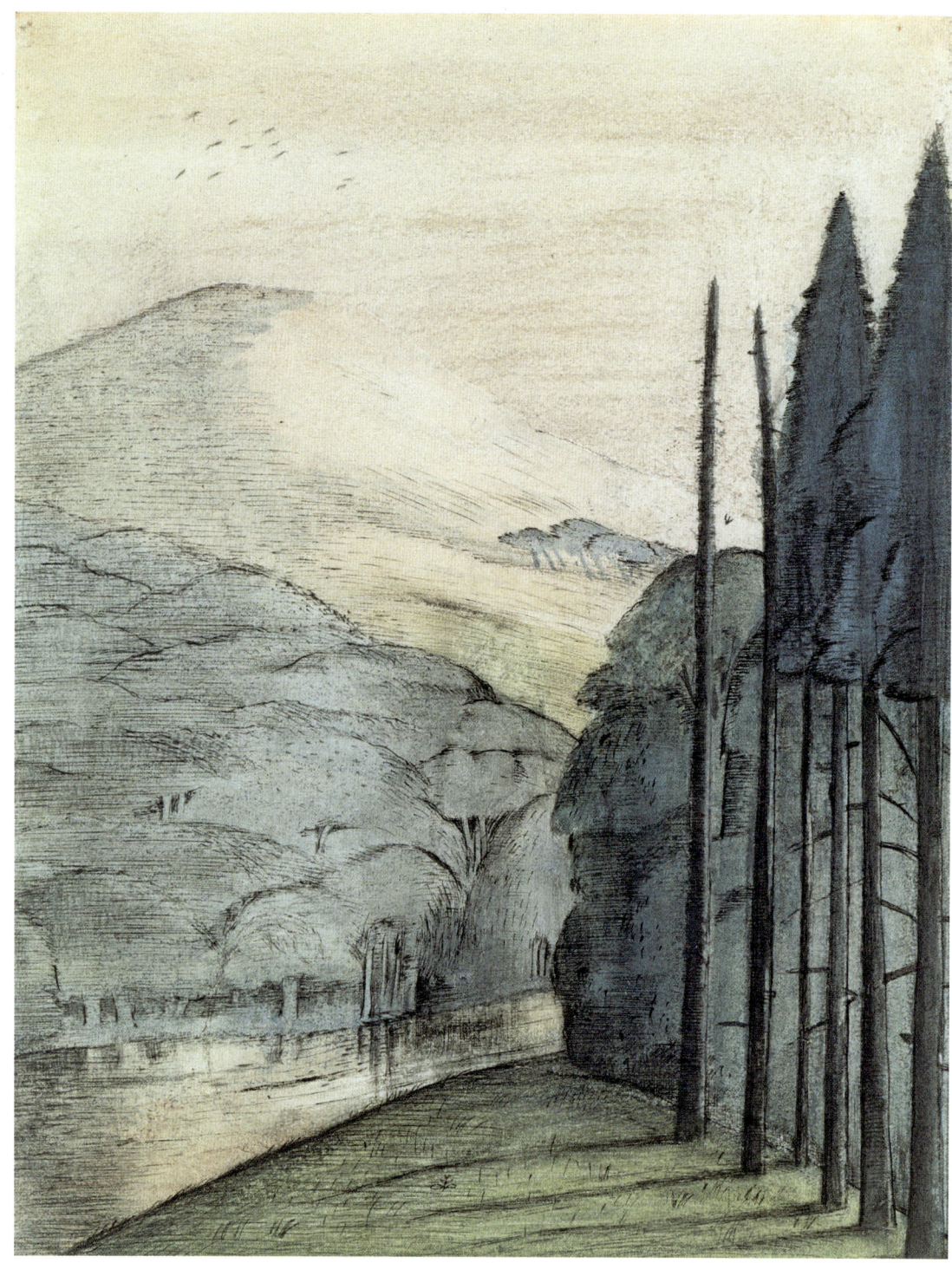

A Dawn, 1912
Ink, watercolour and chalk on paper, 38.5 x 31 cm (15 x 12¼ in)
• Private Collection

Trees 'dream' in the blue-grey light of an English dawn. You can almost see the silence; at the same time you can feel a certain restiveness in this peaceful, yet oddly disquieting scene.

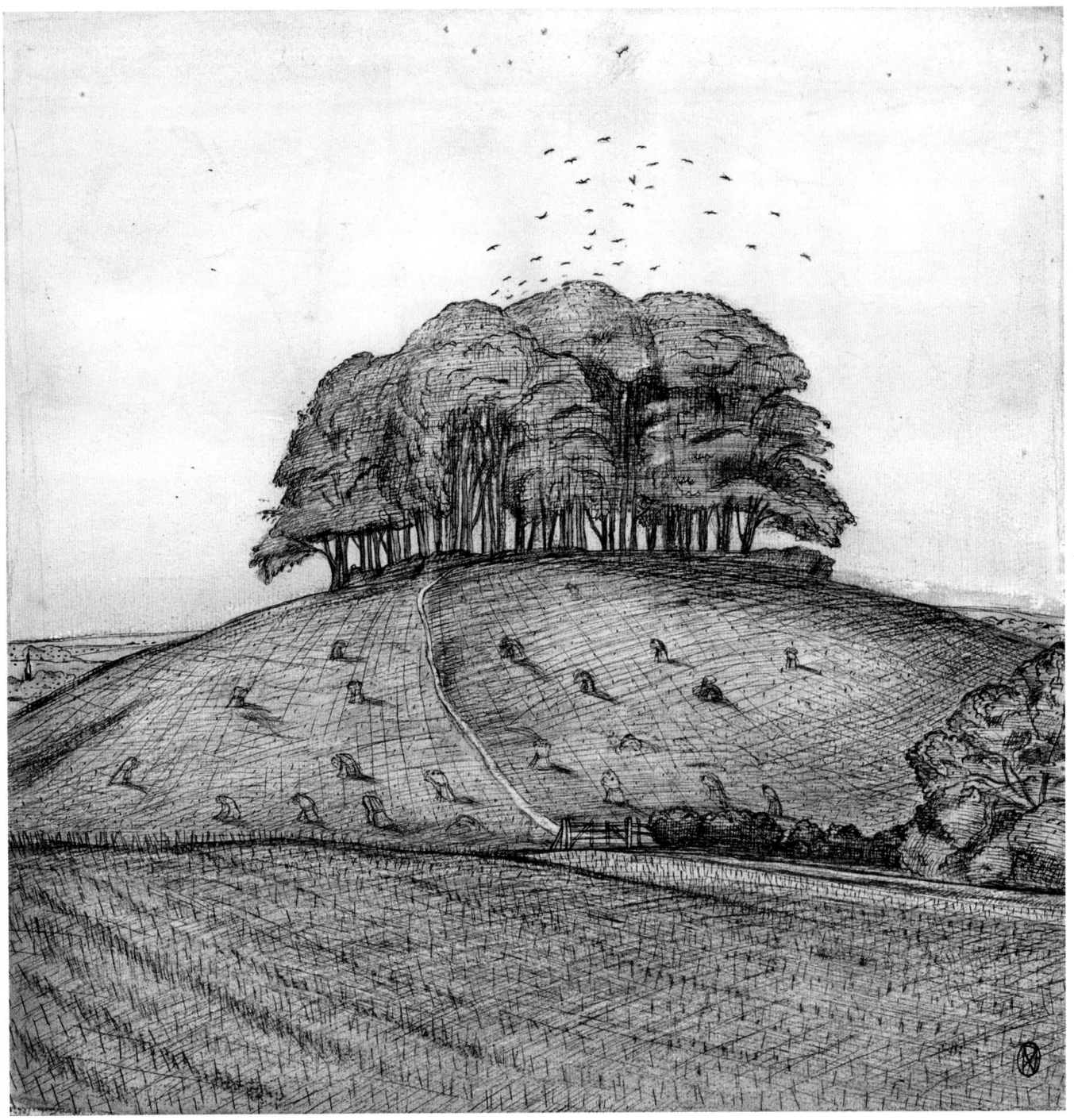

The Wood on the Hill, 1912
Ink, watercolour and chalk on paper
• Ashmolean Museum, Oxford

To the young Nash, the Wittenham Clumps comprised 'a beautiful, legendary country'.
Here, corn stooks stand like warriors, defending against all comers the lower slopes of
what had once been a prehistoric hill fort.

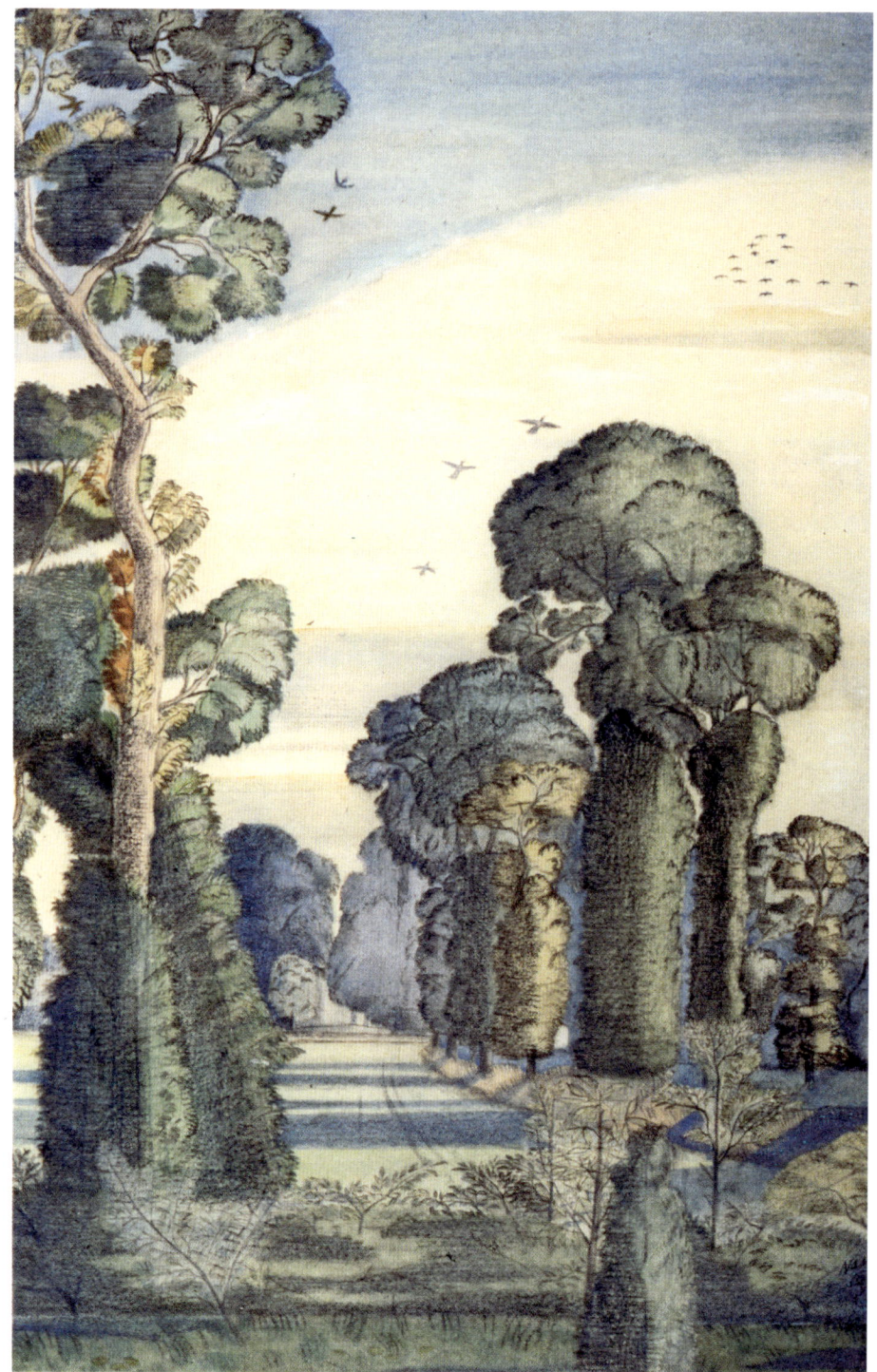

A Landscape at Wood Lane, 1913
Watercolour on paper, 56 x 37 cm (22 x 14½ in)
• Manchester Art Gallery

'Surrealism' was a decade away – even in the imagination of André Breton – but Nash was already able to find a sense of something ominously 'other' in the most apparently familiar scenes of Nature.

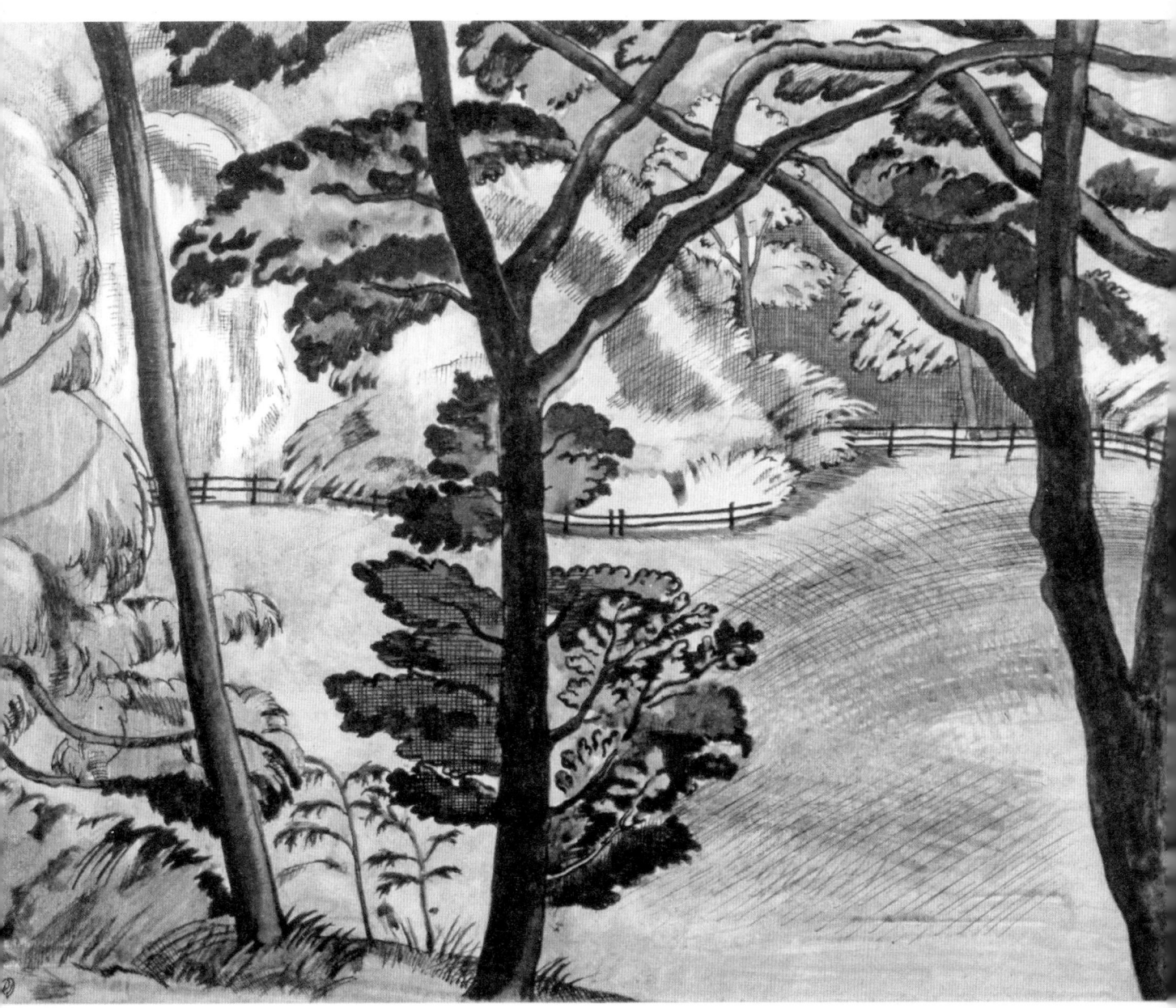

Edge of the Wood, 1914–15
Pen and ink and wash on paper, 35 x 42 cm (13¾ x 16½ in)
• Manchester Art Gallery

With its warm rose wash, this well-wooded landscape shows how cheerful and companionable the countryside could seem to the young Nash. Within a few months of its painting (near Silverdale, Lancashire), war was to break out.

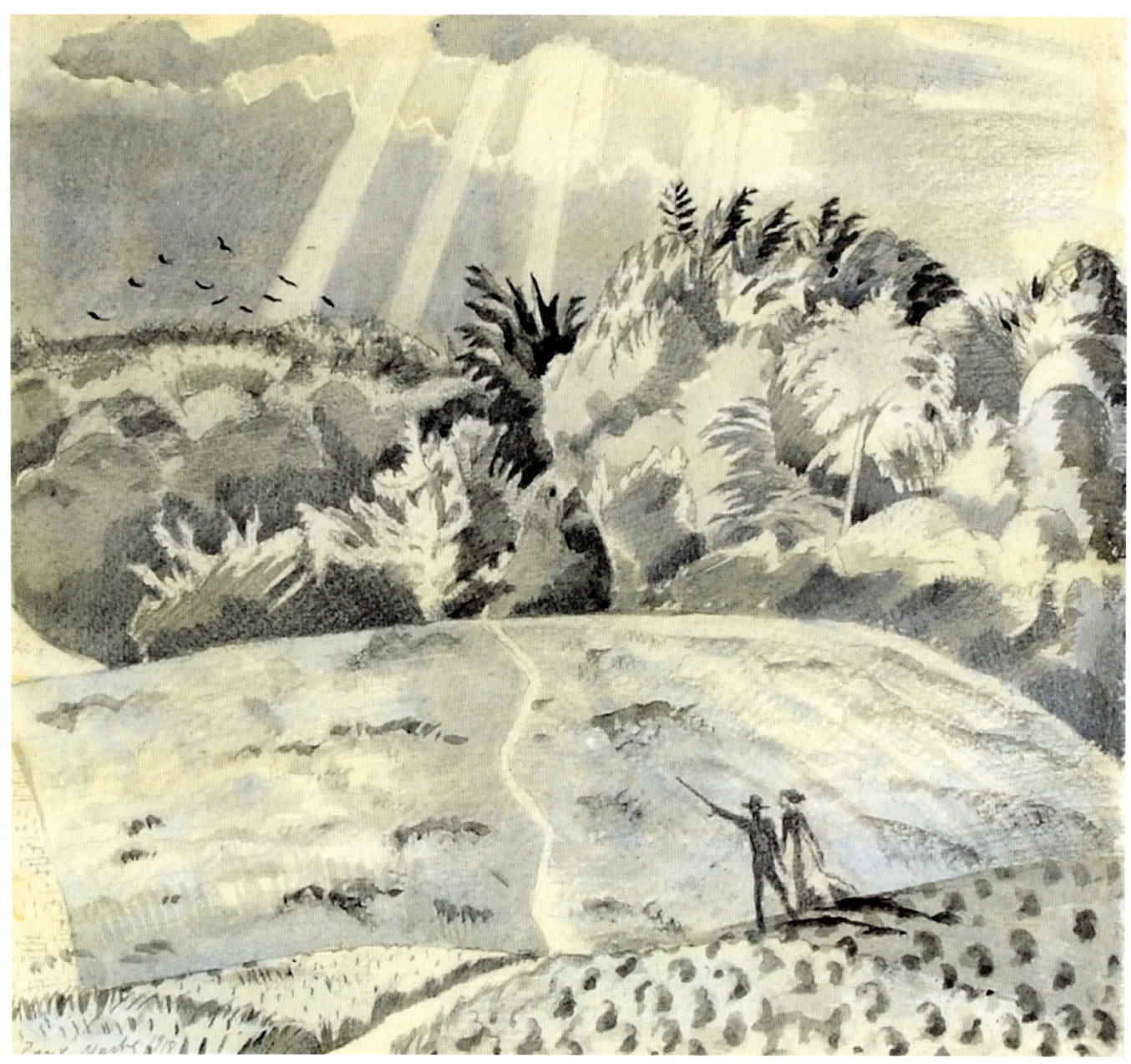

The Field Path, 1918
Ink on paper, 25.3 x 27.1 cm (10 x 10½ in)
• Tullie House Museum and Art Gallery, Carlisle

To view this consciously conventional, even wilfully naïve picture, you would never know that Nash's depictions of the Great War had ever been painted. That was the whole point, perhaps, but Nash would not be able to maintain his attitude of denial too much longer.

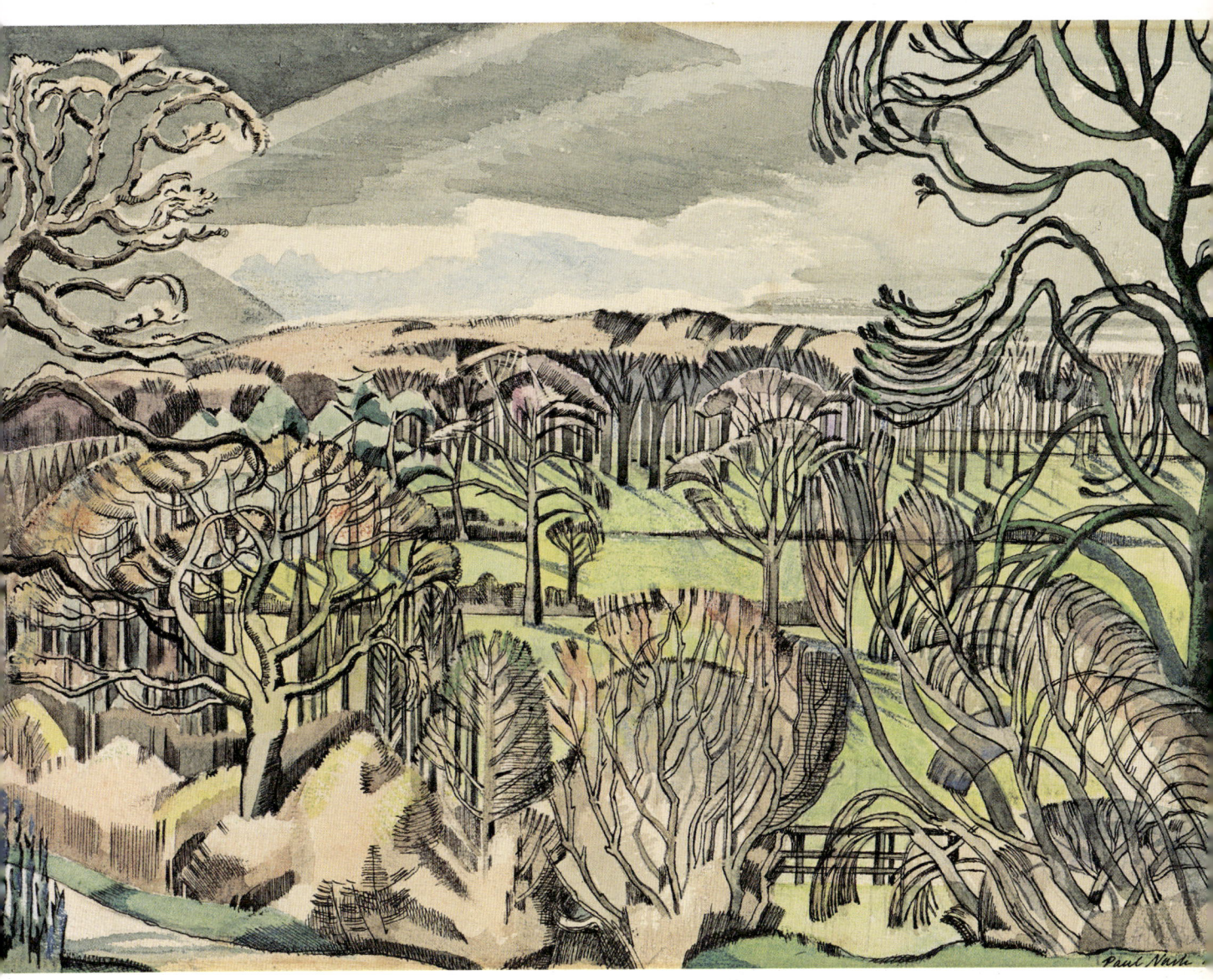

Landscape at Fulmer, Buckinghamshire, 1919
Pencil, pen and ink and watercolour on paper, 28 x 33 cm (11 x 14½ in)
• Private Collection

Storm clouds lour over a winter's scene of skeletal trees and tawny hilltops, with just a touch of green to liven the scene. Despite his efforts to find a psychological sanctuary here, the English countryside offered only cold comfort to an artist traumatised by his experiences in the War.

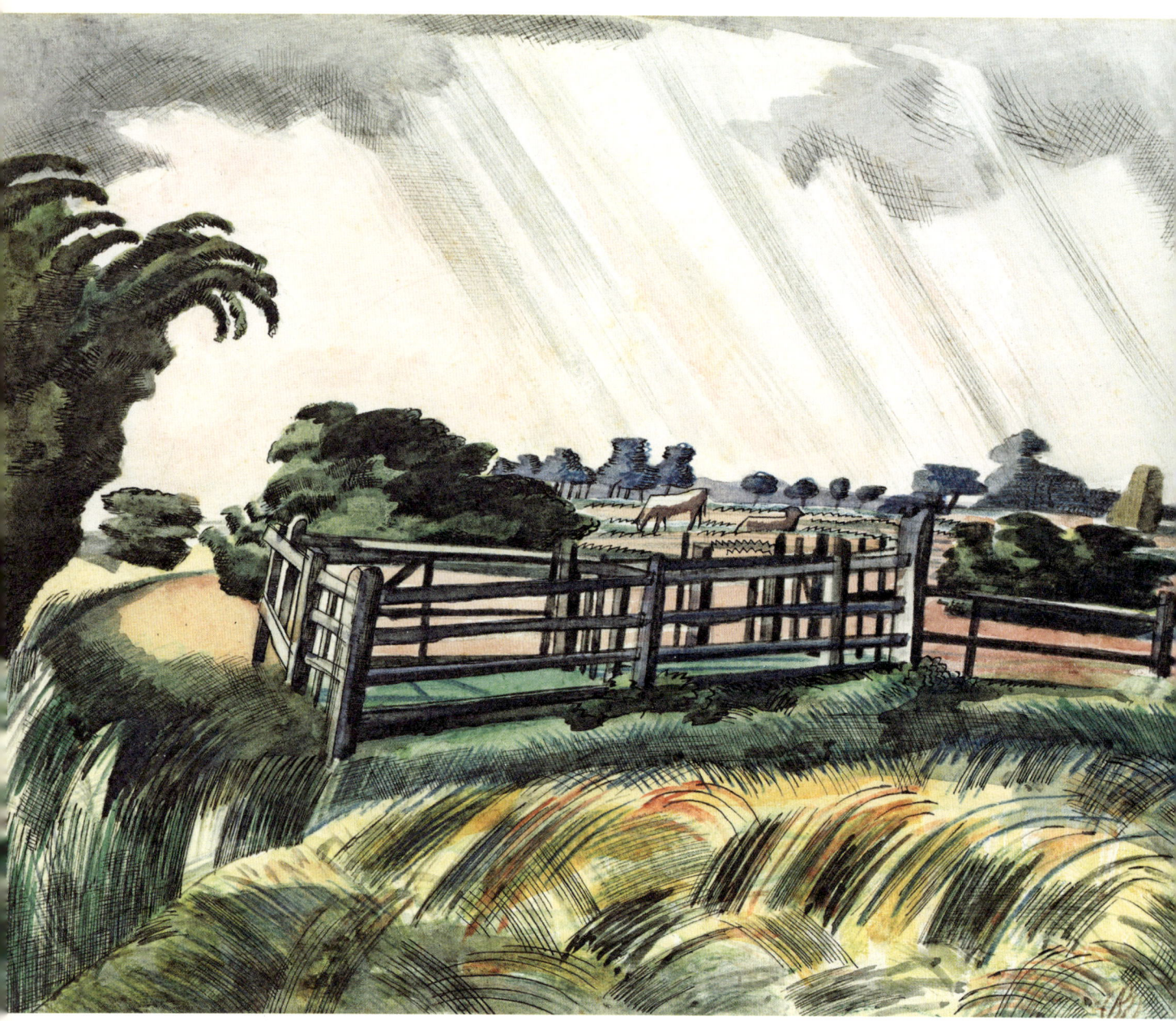

Sheepfold, Romney Marsh, 1920
Watercolour with pen and ink, 23.5 x 29.8 cm (9¼ x 11¾ in)
• Private Collection

If trees were 'people', in this painting they are potentially malevolent: the one on the left seems to claw its way into the scene above reedy tussocks that sway like angry waves.

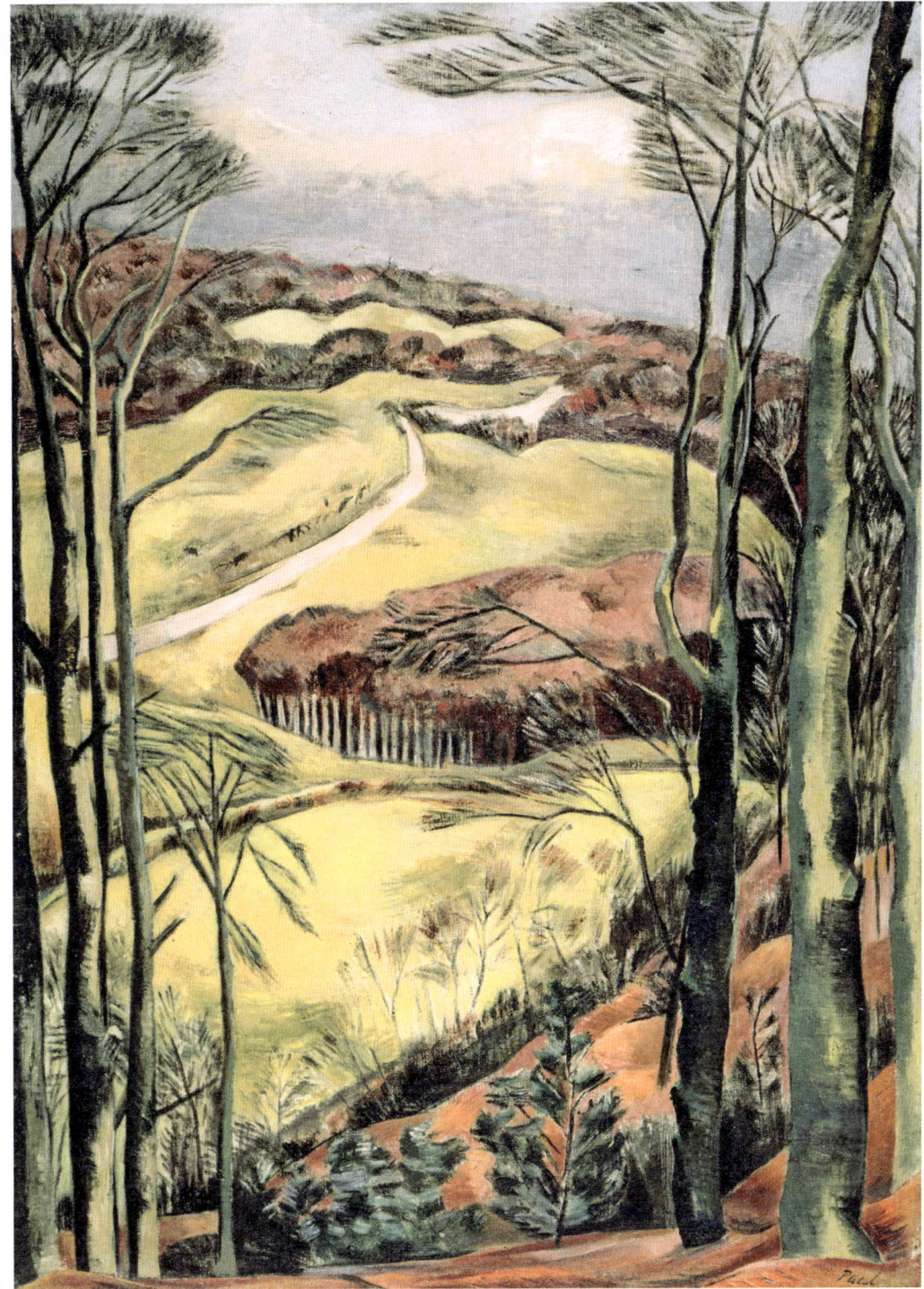

Berkshire Downs, 1922
Oil on canvas, 76 x 55.5 cm (30 x 22 in)
• National Galleries of Scotland, Edinburgh

The War had contaminated everything, it could sometimes seem: what 'should' be a peaceful scene here dons khaki, its fields and woods apparently wearing camouflage fatigues, while trees stand stiff like sentries in the foreground.

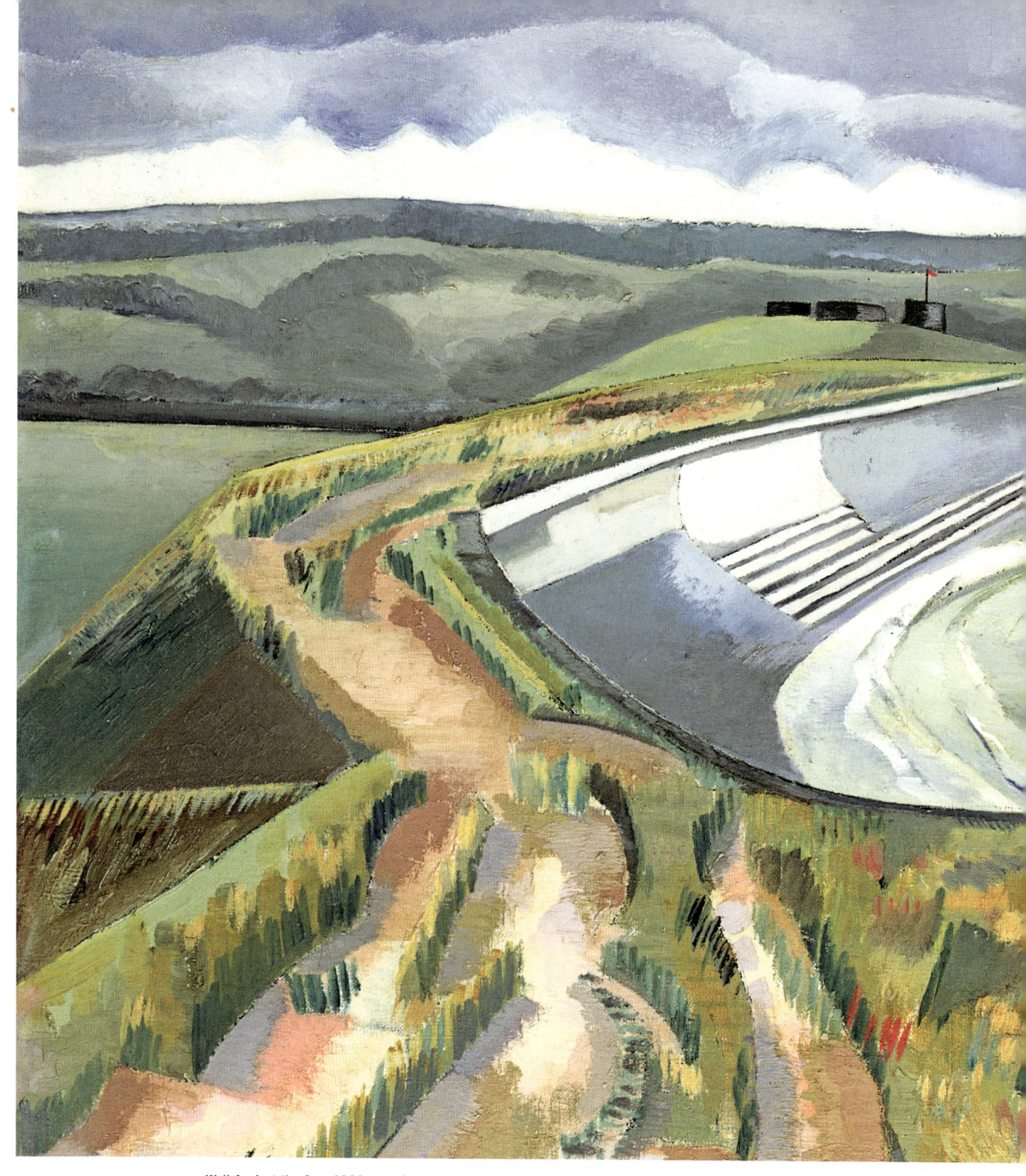

Wall Against the Sea, 1922
Oil on canvas • Private Collection

Nash saw war wherever he looked, even in the ceaseless, ageless assault of the waves upon the concrete rampart raised up in defence of the little Kent town of Dymchurch. He liked to walk along this wall at night.

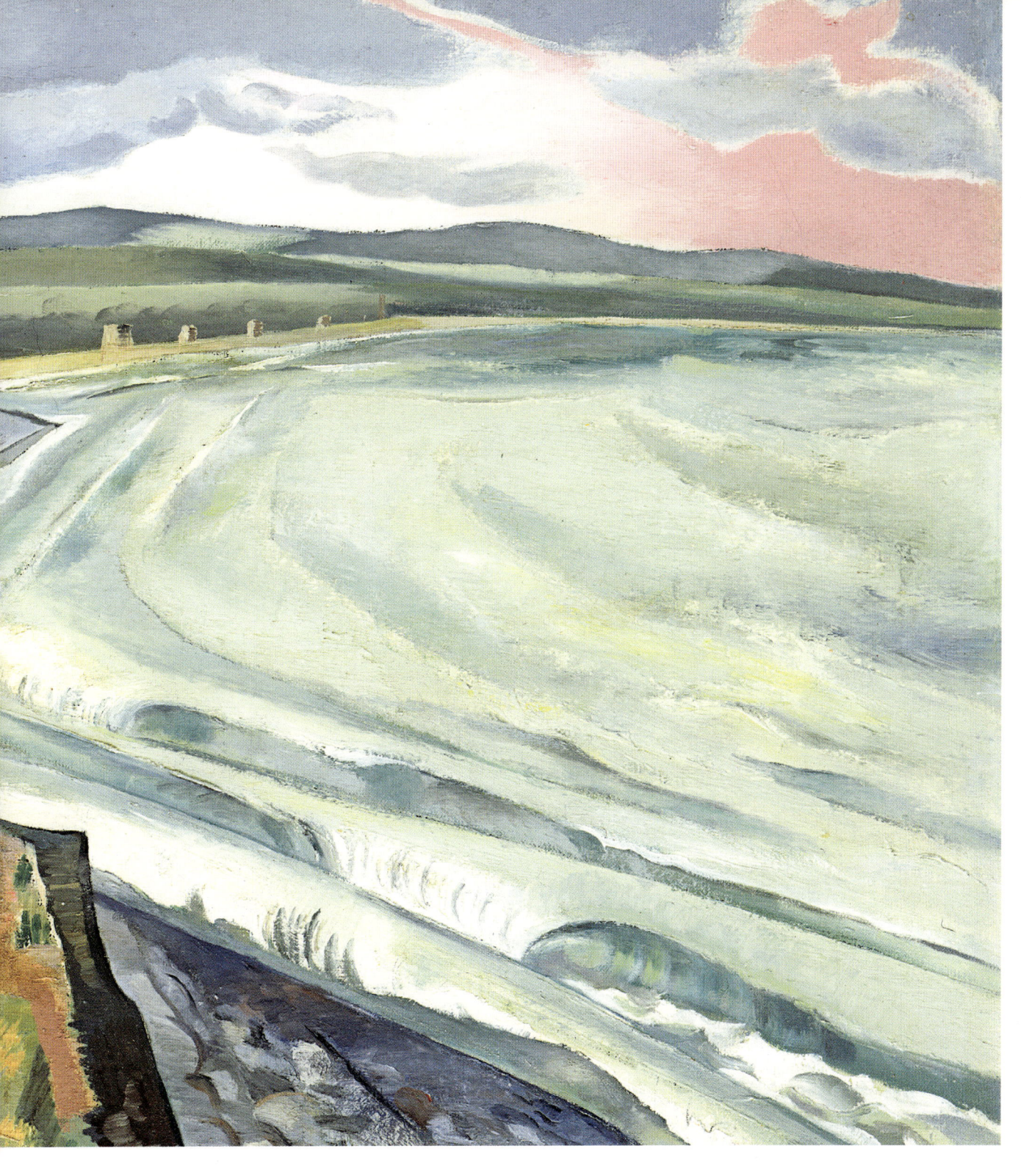

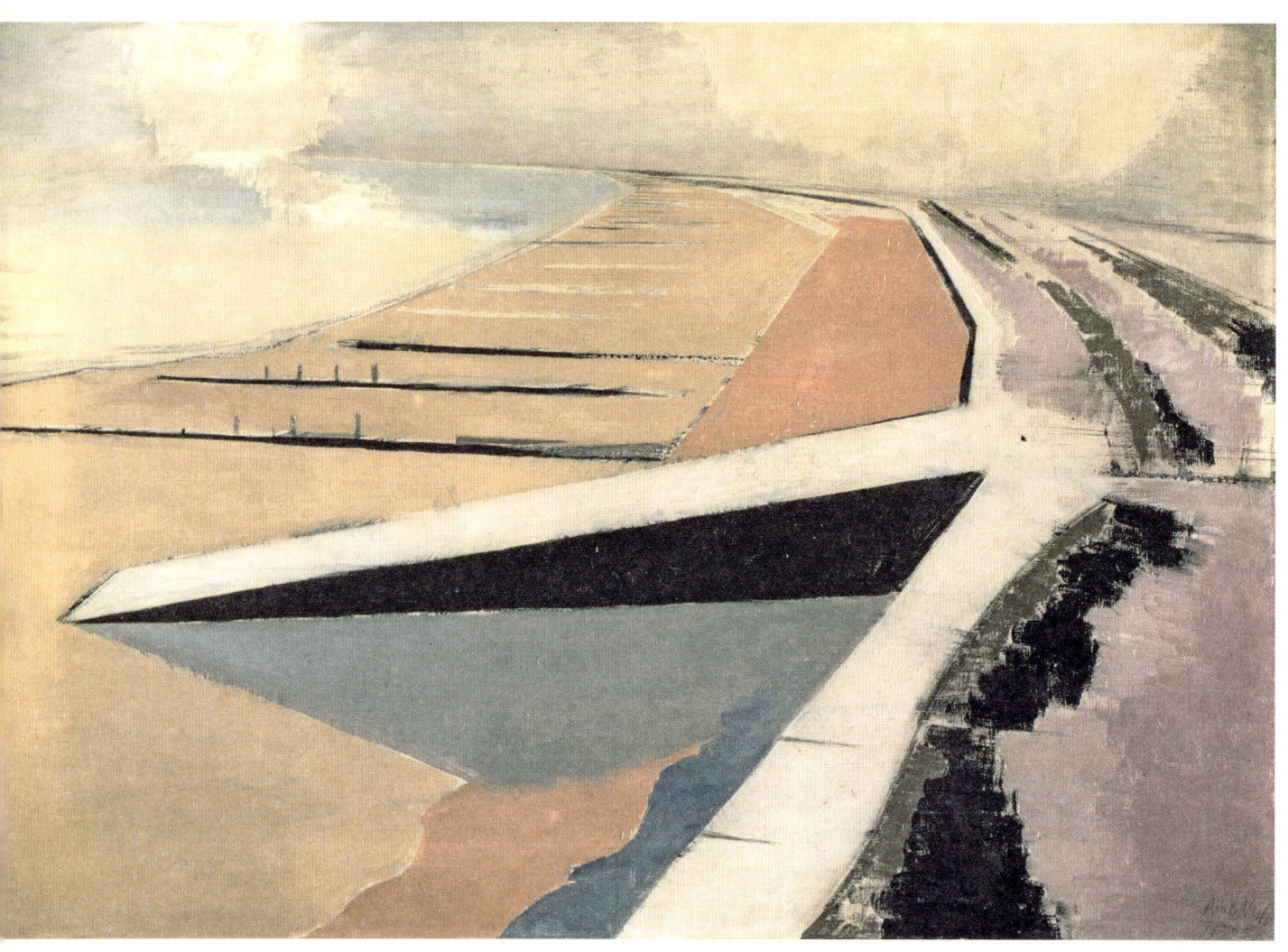

The Shore, 1923
Oil on canvas, 62.2 x 94 cm (24½ x 37 in)
• Leeds Museums and Galleries

Dymchurch becomes Cézanne-on-Sea in this stunning work, the cold clarity of the geometric forms set off by the warmth of the palette of pinks and tans. This was an early attempt by Nash to be both 'British' and 'Modern'.

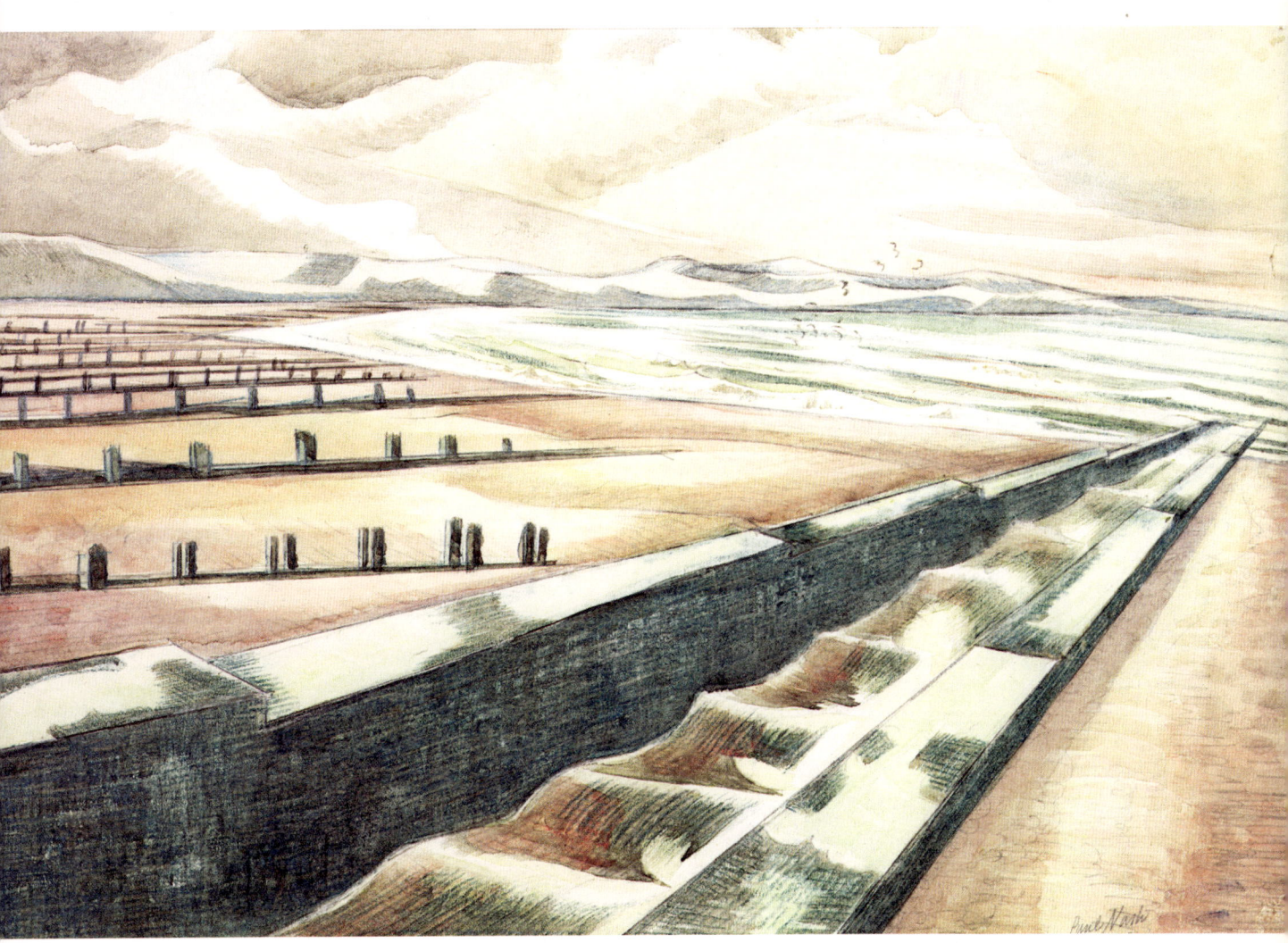

Channel and Breakwater, 1923
Watercolour, pencil and wax crayon on paper, 62.2 x 94 cm
(24½ x 37 in) • Harris Museum and Art Gallery, Preston

Are there signs of a slowly lifting mood in works like this from 1923? The tide may be well out, the beach bare and empty along this seafront, but the entire scene is awash with the pink of daybreak or dusk.

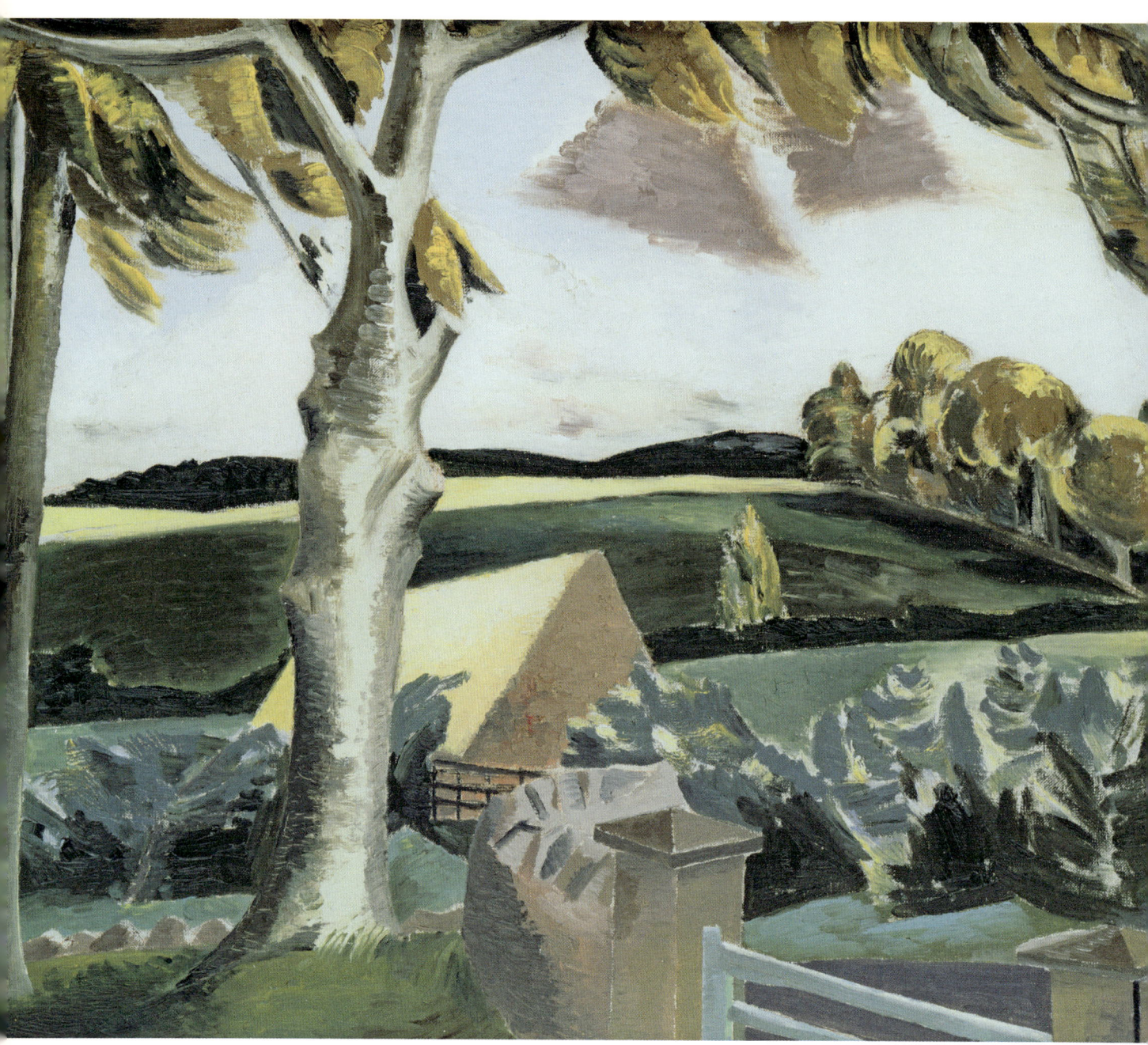

Cumberland Landscape, 1924
Oil on canvas, 51 x 61 cm (20 x 24 in)
• Private Collection

This scene is believed to have been painted at Bankshead, Brampton, near Carlisle, where Nash's friends Ben and Winifred Nicholson lived. This is about as far north (or west) as he ever really ventured: he was always very much an 'English' artist.

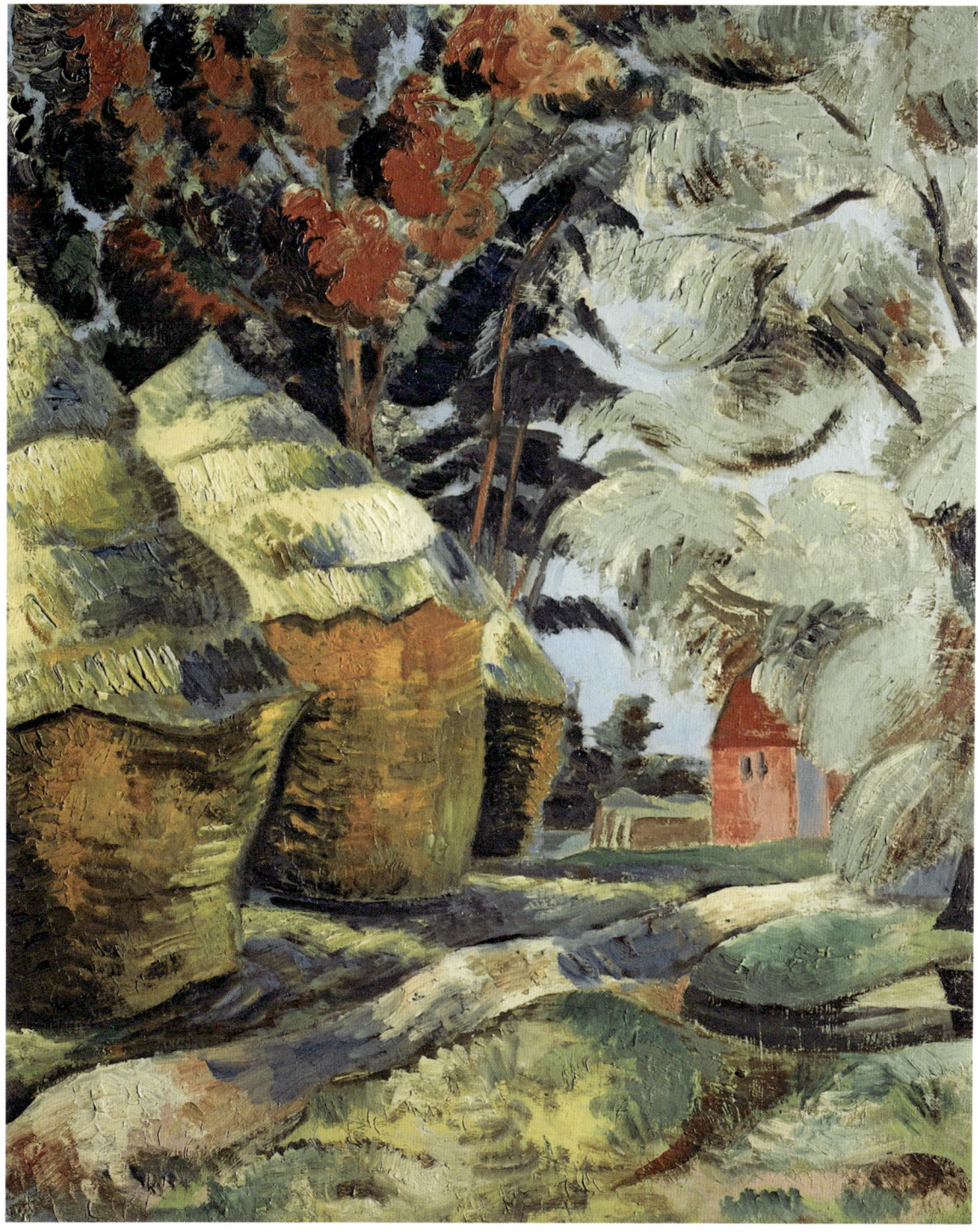

The Stackyard, 1925
Oil on canvas, 60.5 x 50.5 cm (23¾ x 19¾ in)
• Herbert Art Gallery and Museum, Coventry

These haystacks, big and bulbous, anticipate the abstract cylinders of later works such as *Equivalents for the Megaliths* (1935). First, though, it is the warmth of the work that strikes us, as well as the feathery delicacy with which foliage and grass are captured.

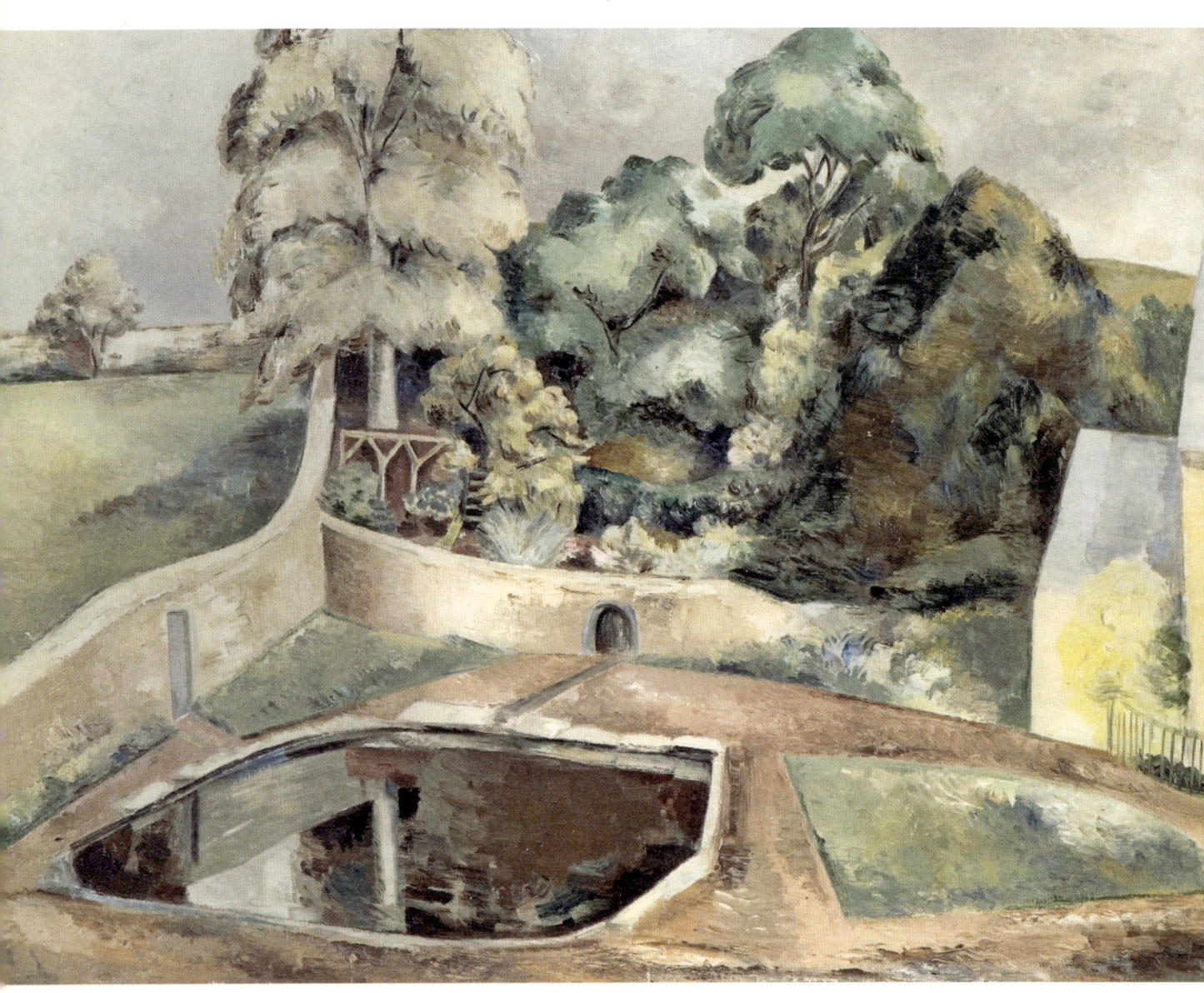

The Pond at Souldem, 1926
Oil on canvas, 71 x 92 cm (28 x 36¼ in)
• Wolverhampton Art Gallery

This strange – even proto-Surrealist – work is a weird dream of trees and their reflections, the grey one in the eponymous pond, the green in the little patch of lawn beside it.

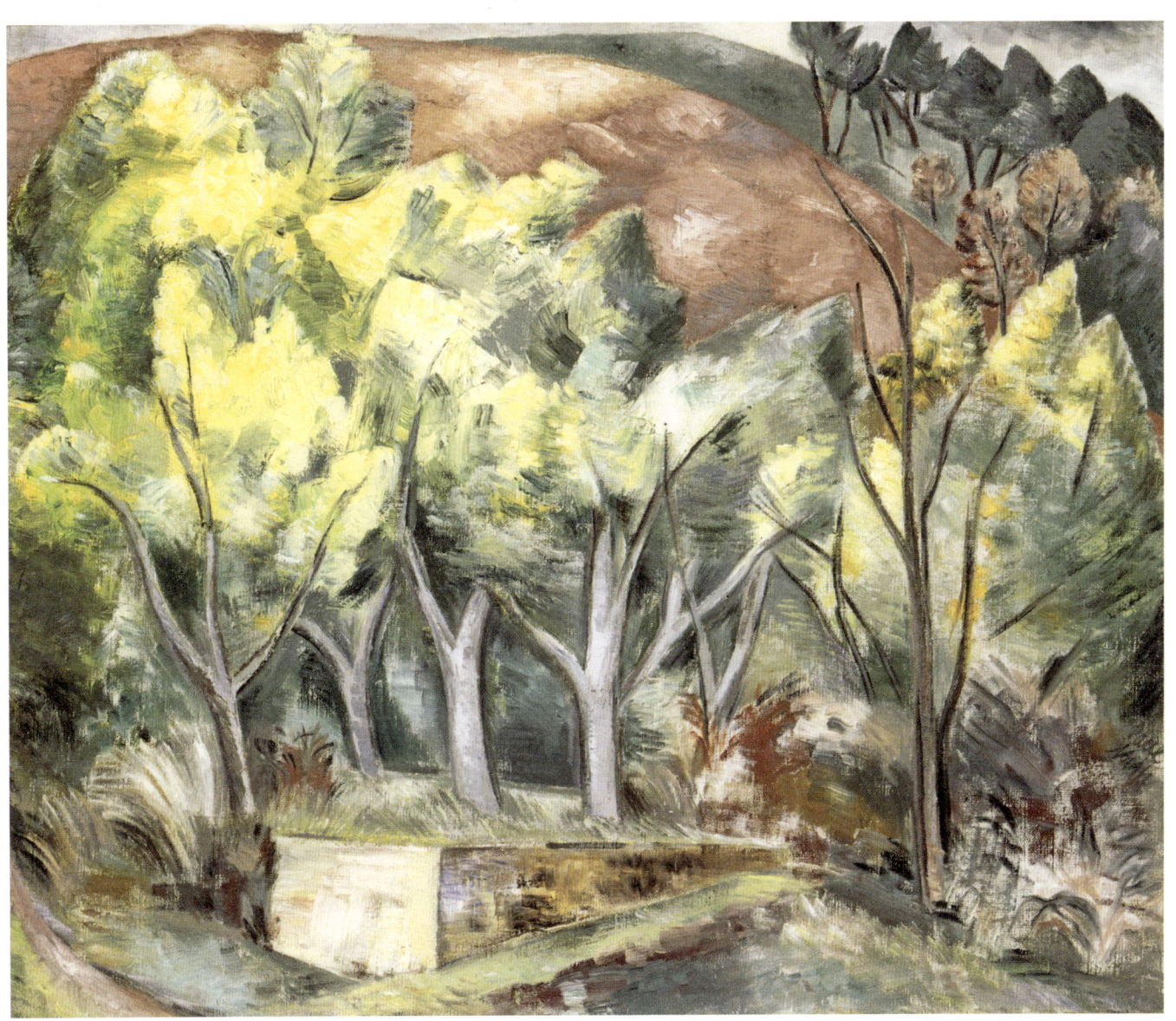

Mimosa Wood, 1926
Oil on canvas, 54.1 x 65.2 cm (21¼ x 25¾ in)
• Art Gallery of New South Wales, Sydney

By now Nash felt ready to revisit France – at least the Riviera. This explosion of yellows and greens is the view Margaret and he had from their window when they were staying in Cros-de-Cagnes, Nice.

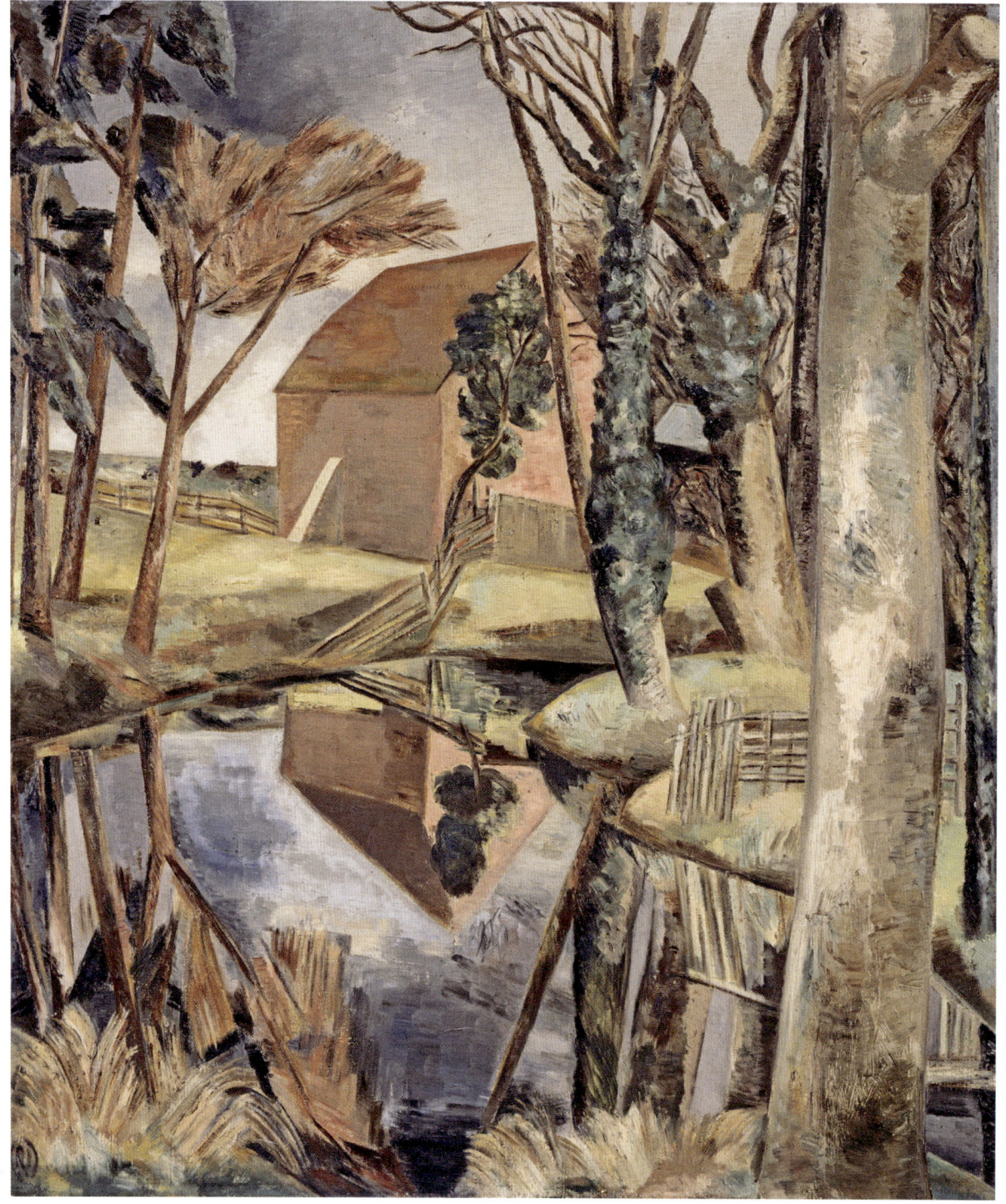

Oxenbridge Pond, 1927–28
Oil on canvas, 99.7 x 87.6 cm (39¼ x 34½ in)
• Birmingham Museum & Art Gallery

The landscape, with its physical features, was just the start of Nash's vision. The reflection in the water here hints at the existence of an alternative, if intangible, dimension beyond our own.

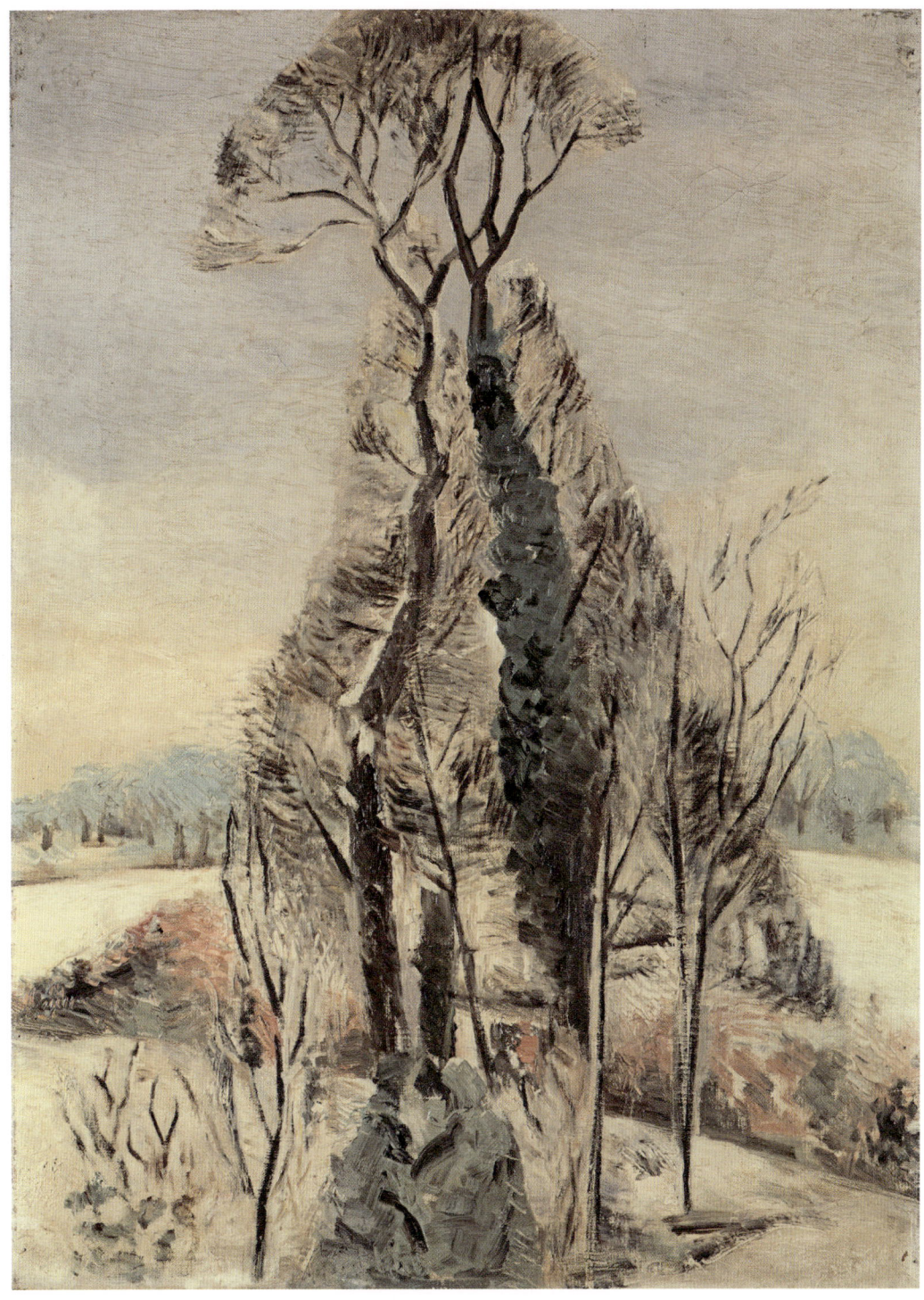

Iver Heath, Buckinghamshire – Snow, 1927–28
Oil on canvas, 82.5 x 64 cm (32½ x 25¼ in)
• Museums Sheffield

A study in structure. The bare branches cross-hatch the icy air, the trees here tracing out a tripod structure; paradoxically, even as they appear to fall inwards, a sort of pyramid rears up out of the snow.

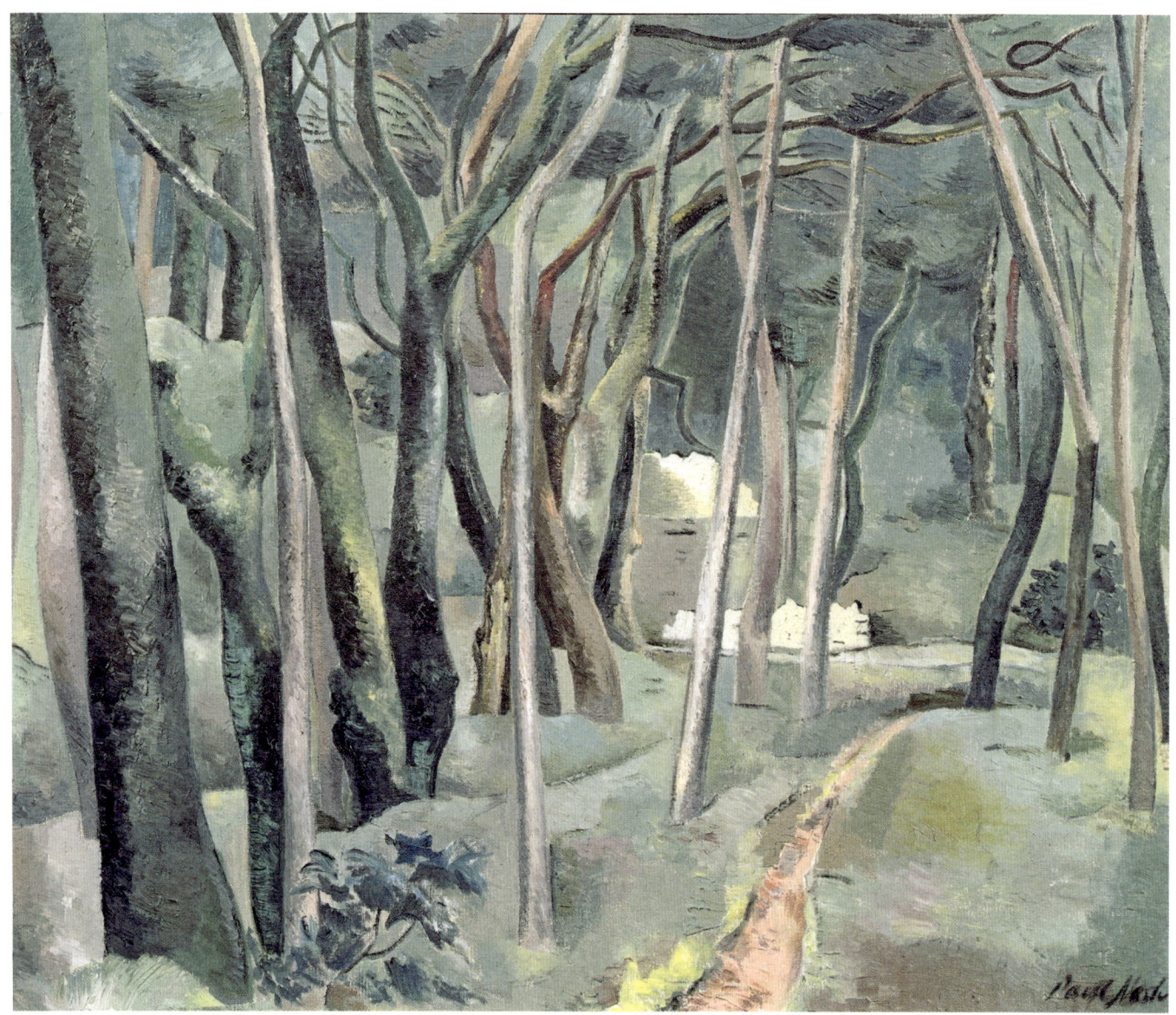

The Forest, 1930
Oil on canvas, 63.5 x 76.2 cm (25 x 30 in)
• Private Collection

Surrealism by stealth, perhaps: the scene is light and colourful enough, but there is nevertheless an insistence about the way the trees crowd in upon the narrow, winding path that is oddly disconcerting.

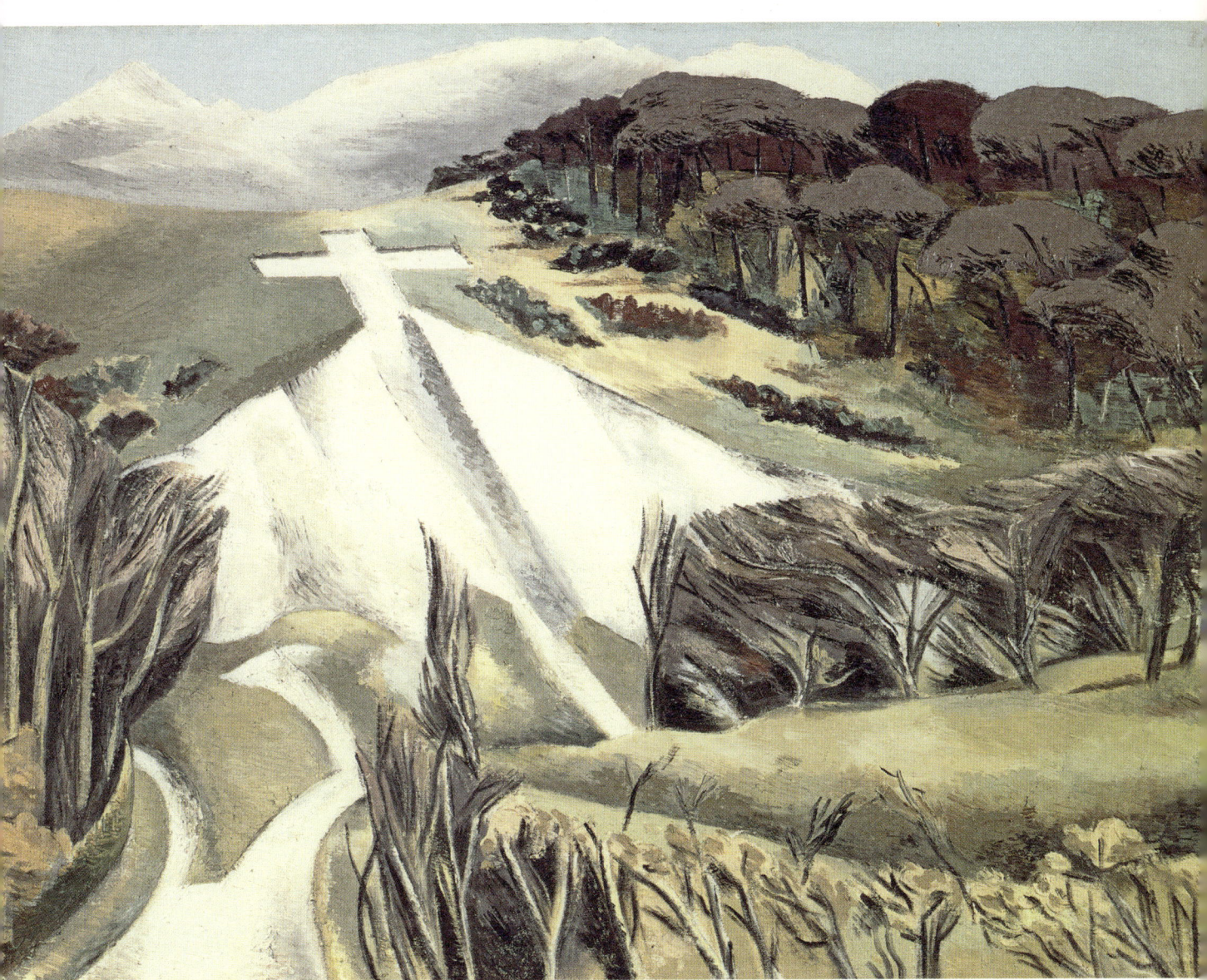

Whiteleaf Cross, 1931
Oil on board • Whitworth Art Gallery, Manchester

Reflecting as it does the jagged white clouds along the far horizon, the white of the exposed chalk appears to create a picture-within-a-picture; an alternative artwork in which other thoughts and other realities might exist.

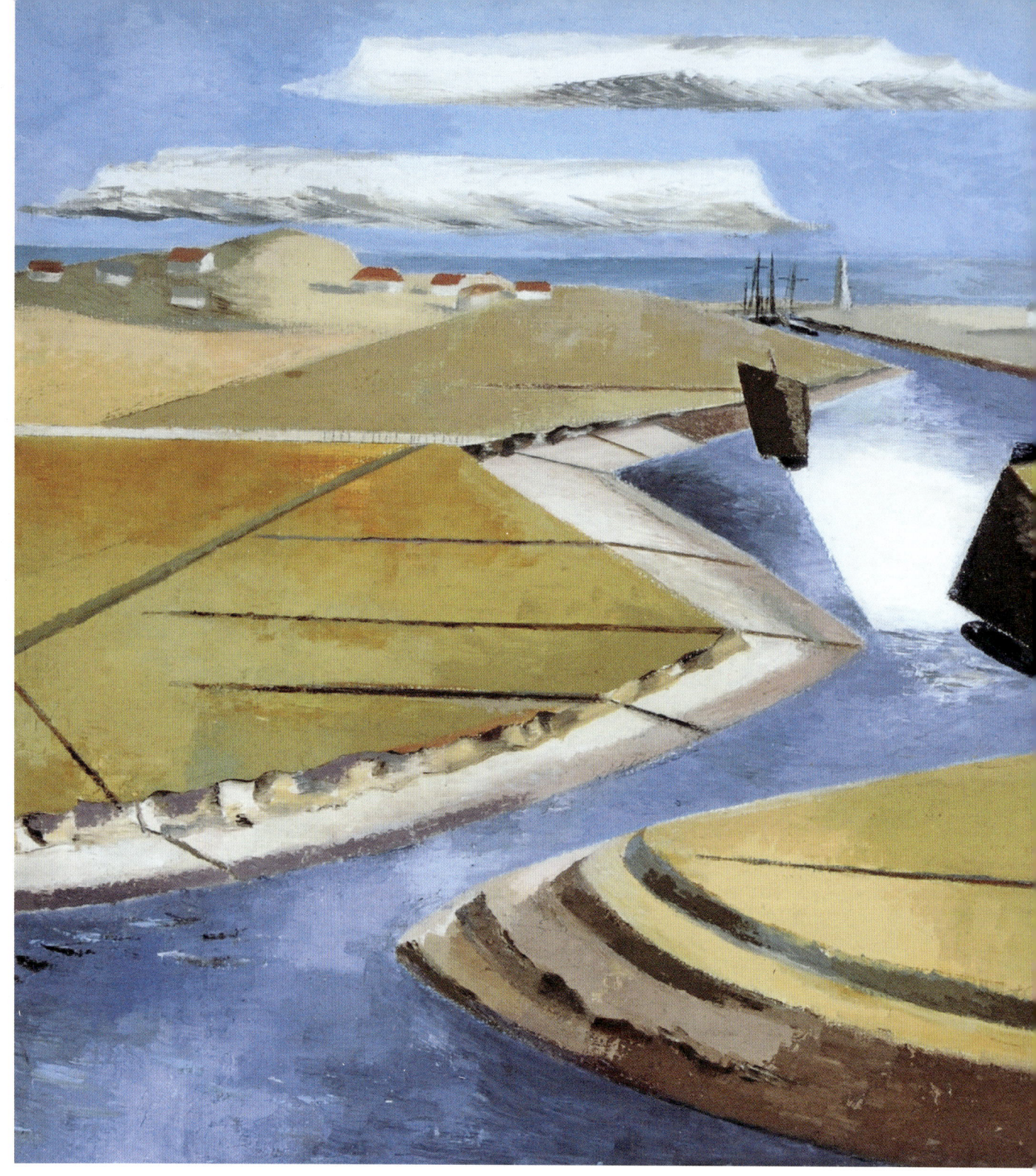

The Rye Marshes, 1932

Oil on canvas, 69 x 113 cm (27 x 44½ in)

• Ferens Art Gallery, Hull

'Everywhere you go, you can be sure of Shell.' Commercial art at its 'finest', this painting was commissioned by Jack Beddington, publicity director for the oil company, who subsequently used this bright and cheerful picture in Shell's promotional material.

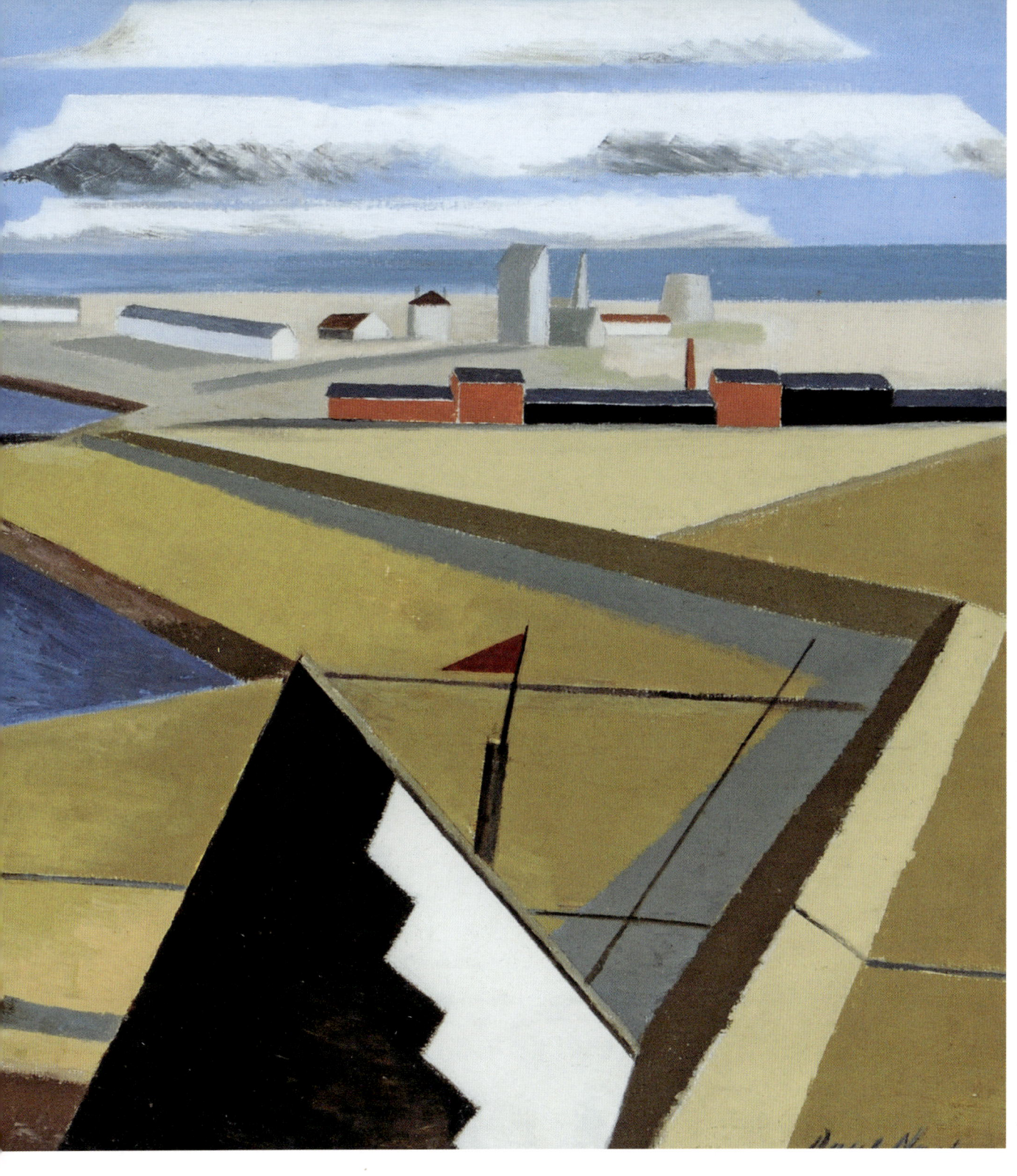

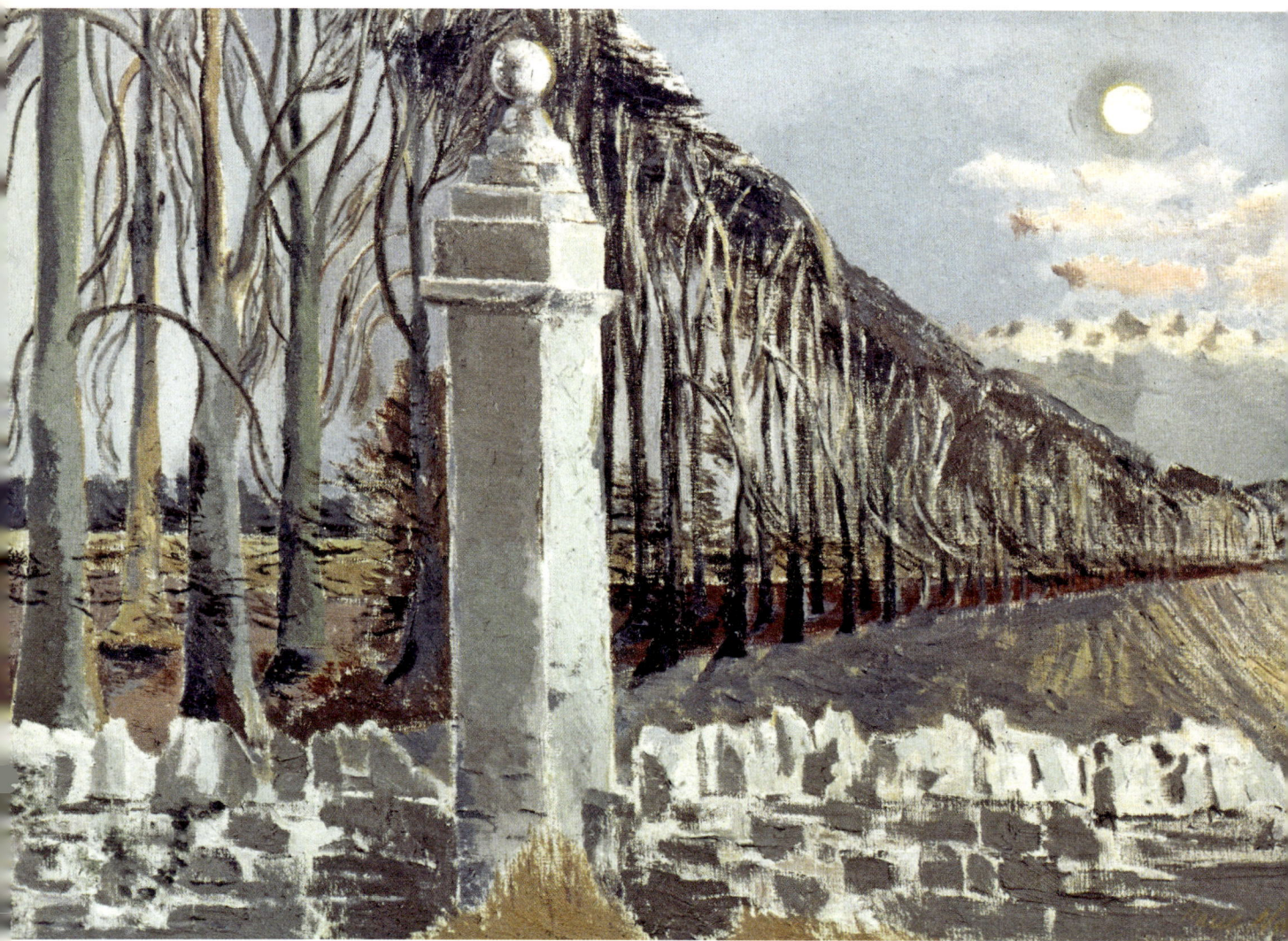

Pillar and Moon, 1932–42
Oil on canvas, 50.8 x 76.2 cm (27 x 44½ in)
• Tate Britain, London

'The pale stone sphere on top of the ruined pillar faces its counterpart the moon, cold and pale and as solid as stone. No legend or history attaches to such a picture; its drama is inherent in the scene.'

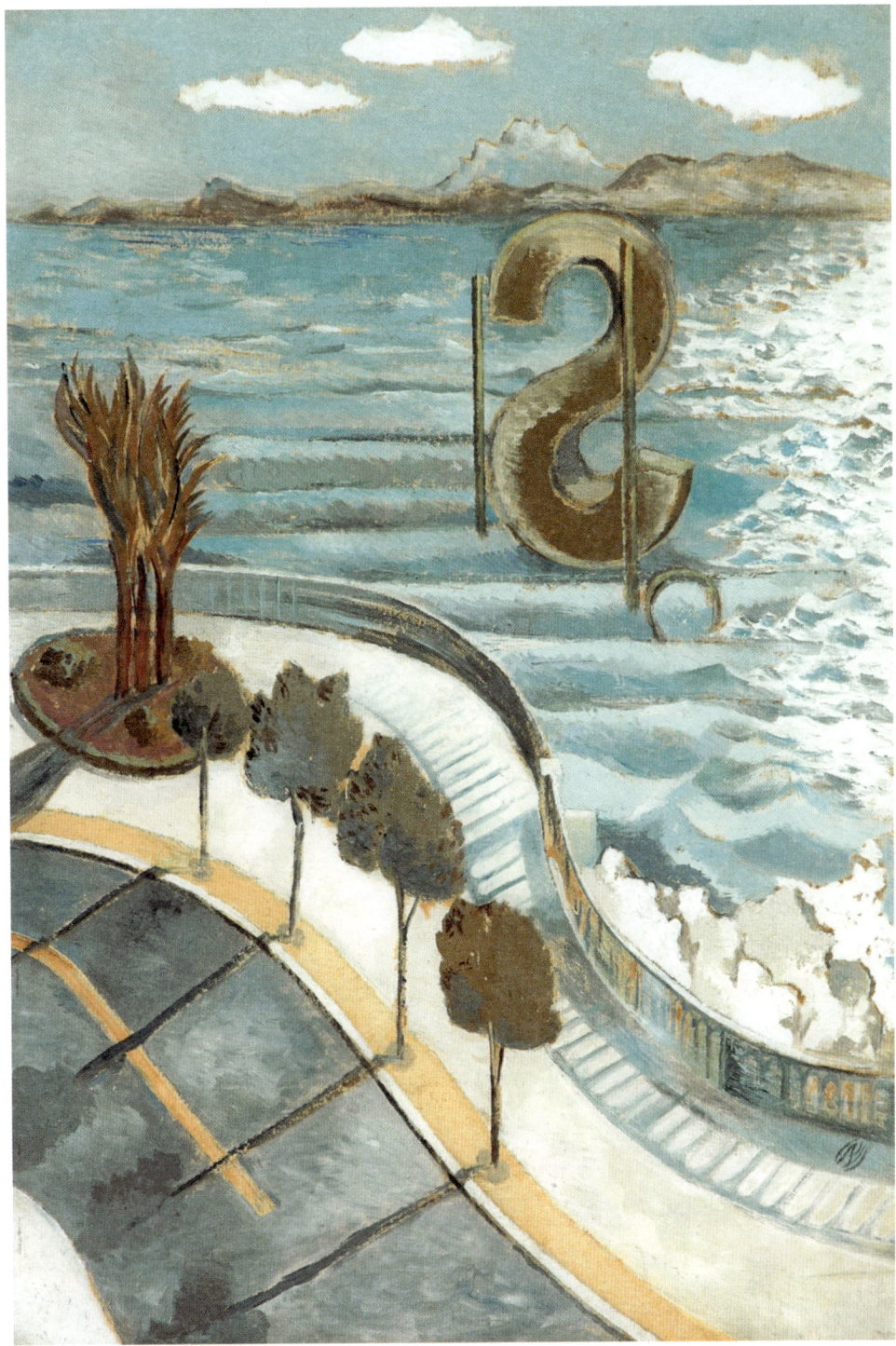

View from a Window, Nice, 1934
Oil on board, 63.5 x 46 cm (25 x 18 in)
● Bradford Art Galleries and Museum

What is the 'S' (which we see from behind) for? 'Surrealism'? It does not seem impossible, nor does anything else more likely suggest itself. Nash by this time was avowedly experimenting with Breton's approach – and where better to do that than in France?

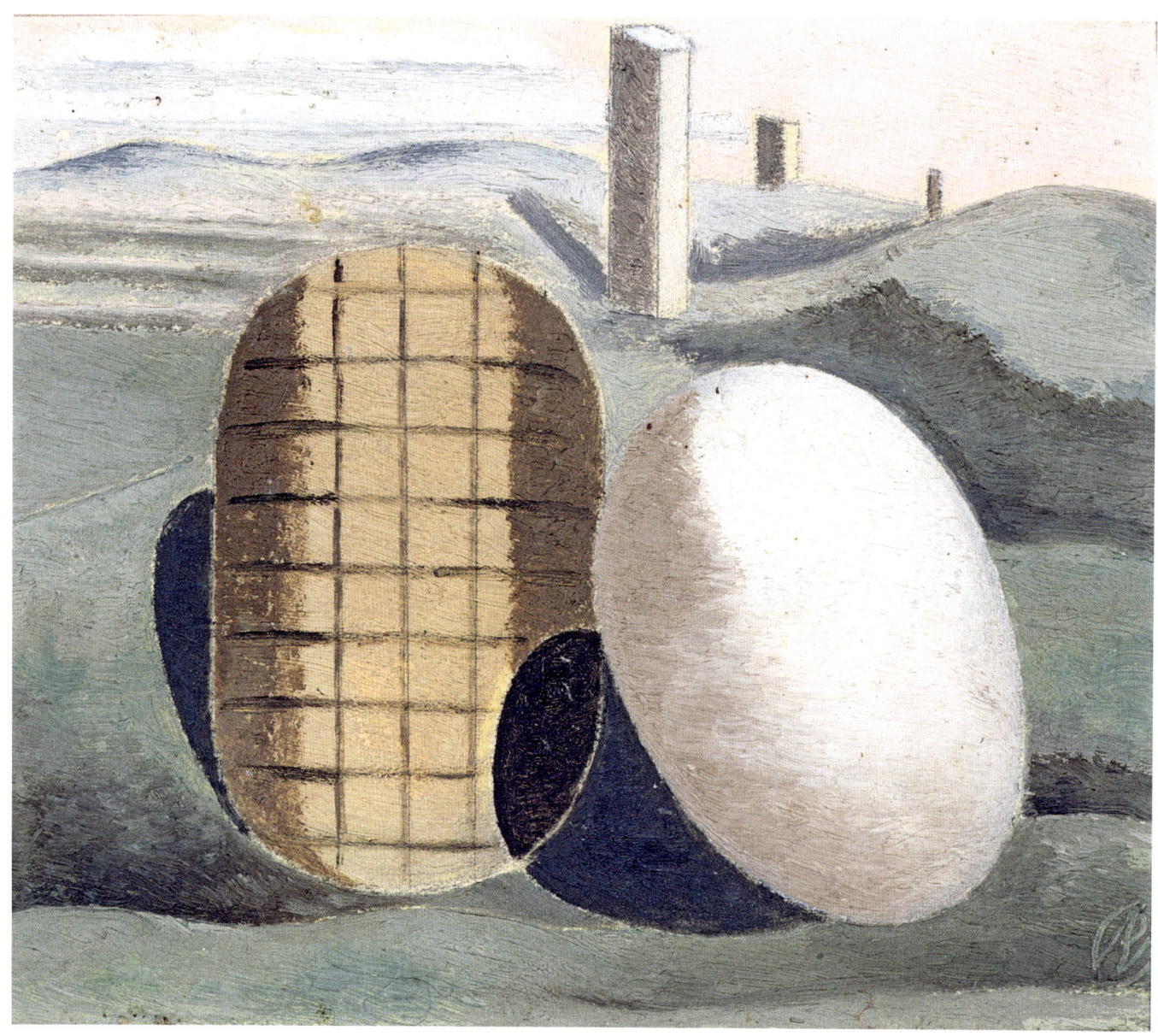

Landscape Composition (Objects in Relation), 1934
Tempera on hardboard, 13 x 15.5 cm (5 x 6 in)
• Pallant House Gallery, Chichester

Even when he ventured into abstraction, Nash persevered in his never-ending quest to explore the 'mystery', the 'enchantment' he had noticed since his boyhood in the 'relationship of parts'. This had always been the basis of his love of landscape.

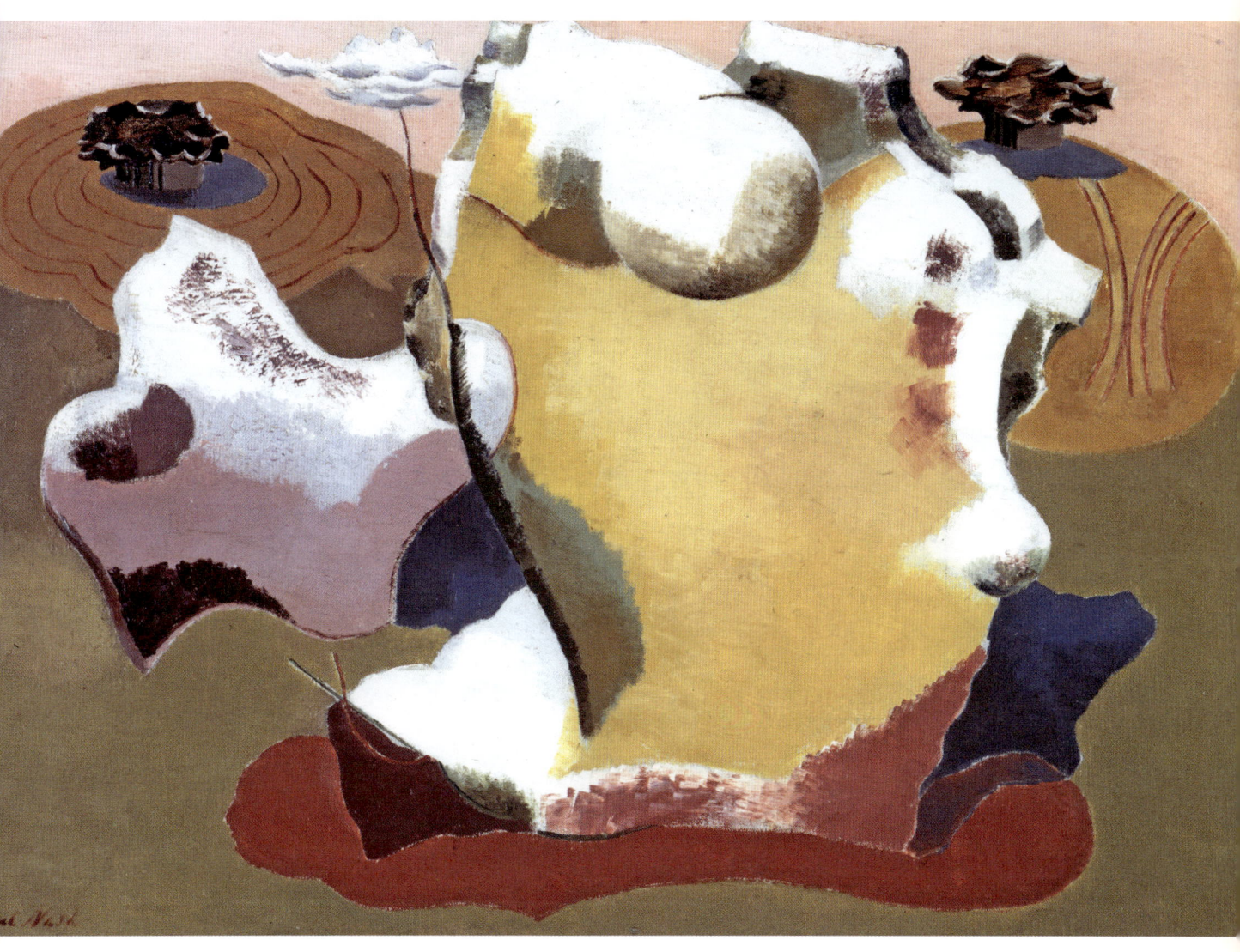

Landscape of the Megaliths, 1934
Oil on canvas, 49.5 x 73.2 cm (19½ x 28¾ in)
• British Council of Visual Arts, London

This extraordinary work, painted on the Riviera, was inspired by Nash's first visit to the standing stones at Avebury. It is semi-abstract, a prehistoric synthesis, incorporating in the background the twin mounds of Wittenham Clumps.

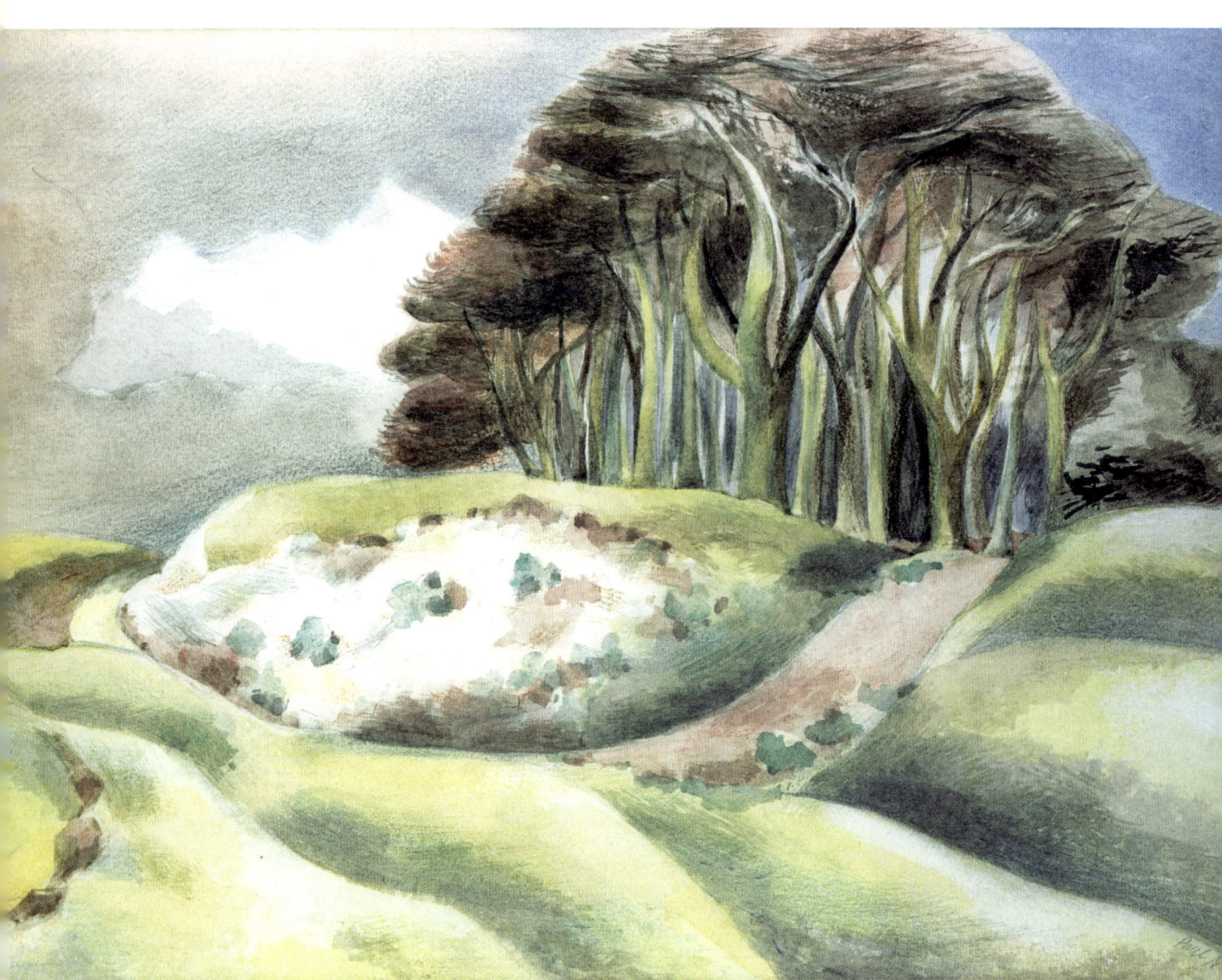

Wittenham, 1935
Watercolour on paper, 29 x 39 cm (11½ x 15½ in)
• Pallant House Gallery, Chichester

'Ever since I remember them the Clumps had meant something to me,' Nash recalled. He was to return to them in his painting over and over again. Here the contours of the tree crowns complement the curves of the ground.

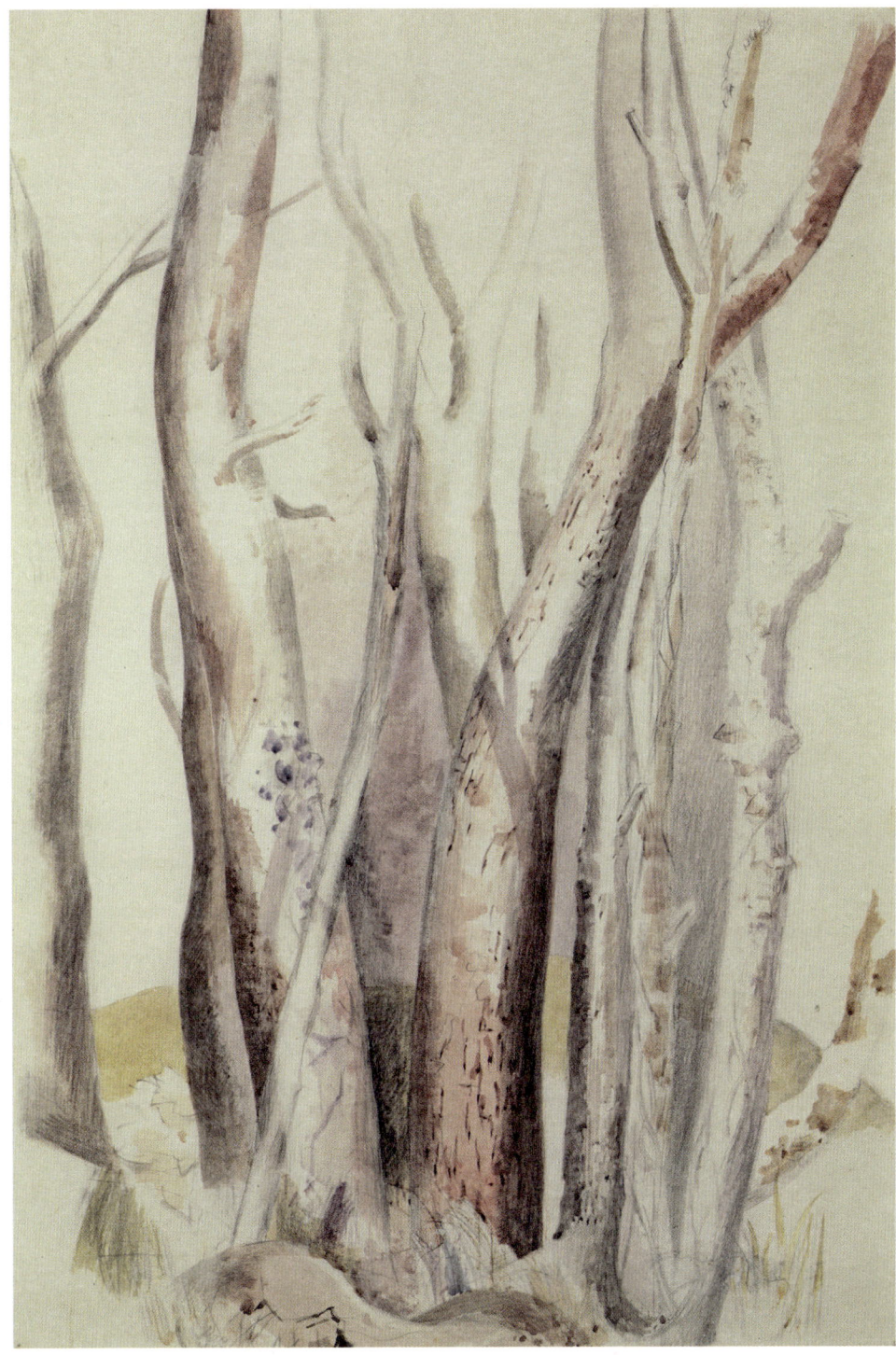

Study of a Wooded Landscape, 1935
Watercolour and pencil on paper, 54.5 x 37 cm (21½ x 14½ in)
• Private Collection

If trees were people for Nash, they were not just individuals but social beings as well:
he was fascinated by their interrelations both with one another and with the world.

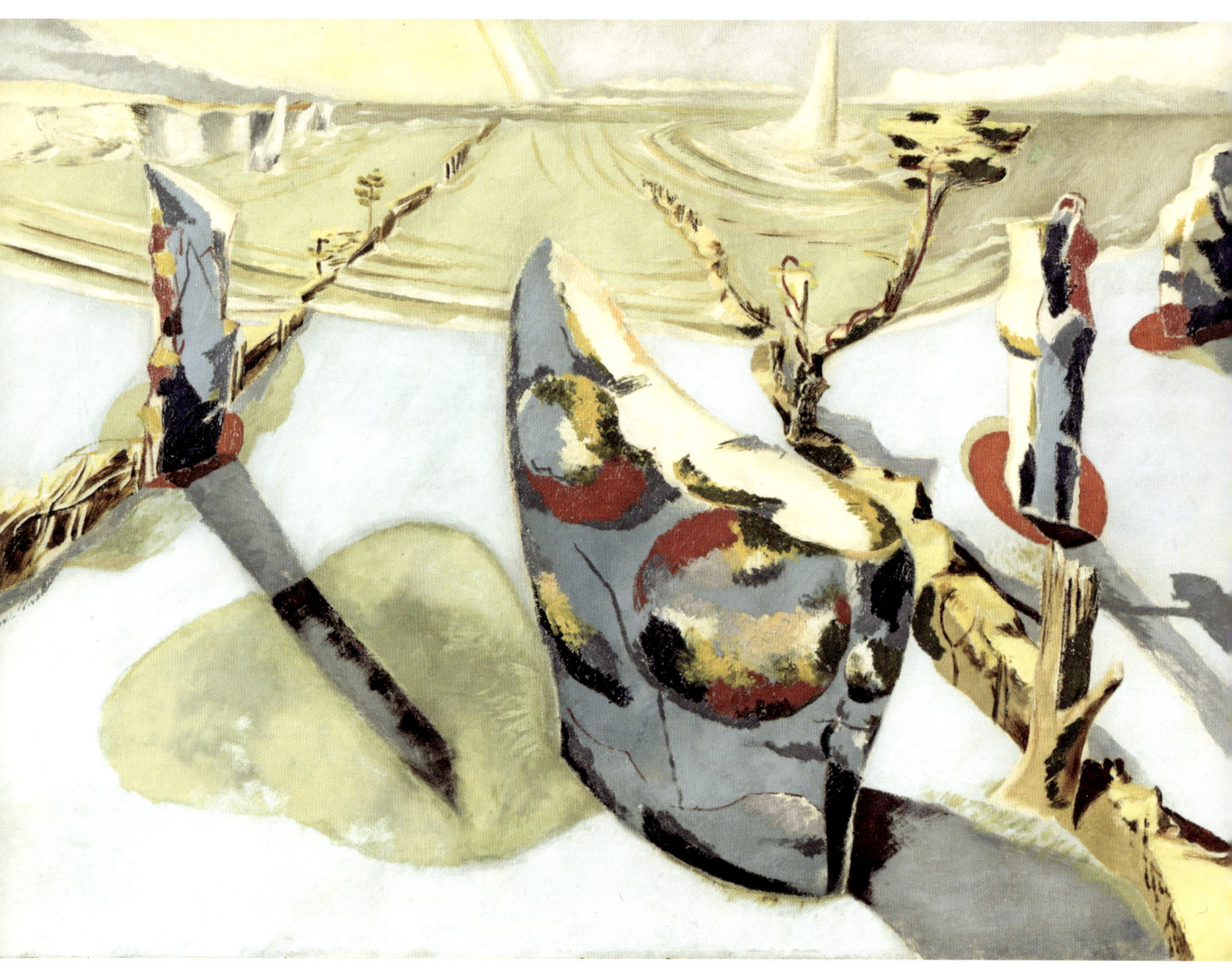

Circle of the Monoliths, 1937–38
Oil on canvas, 78.8 x 104.1 cm (31 x 41 in)
• Leeds Art Gallery

Avebury as you have never seen it before – as no one had, indeed, in 5,000 years.
These monoliths exist in relation not only to each other and their environment, but
also to the subconscious mind and feelings of the artist.

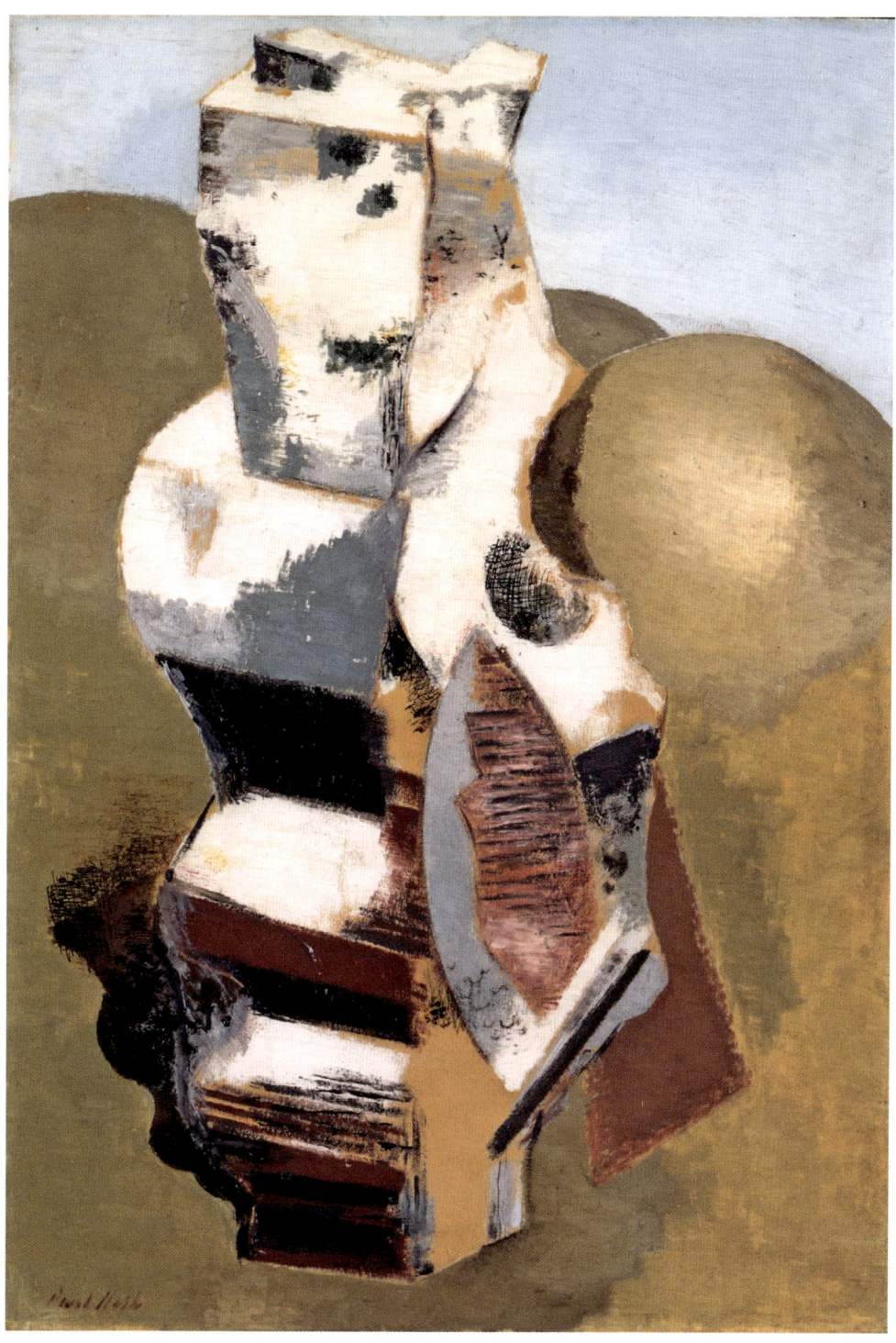

Druid Landscape, c. 1938
Oil on cardboard, 58.5 x 40.5 cm (23 x 16 in)
• British Council of Visual Arts, London

A 'stone circle' it may have been, but Avebury was made up of hundreds of individual monoliths, each with its own distinctive shape and stature, its own weathered, lichen-coloured surface, its own agglomeration of fissures, cavities and bumps.

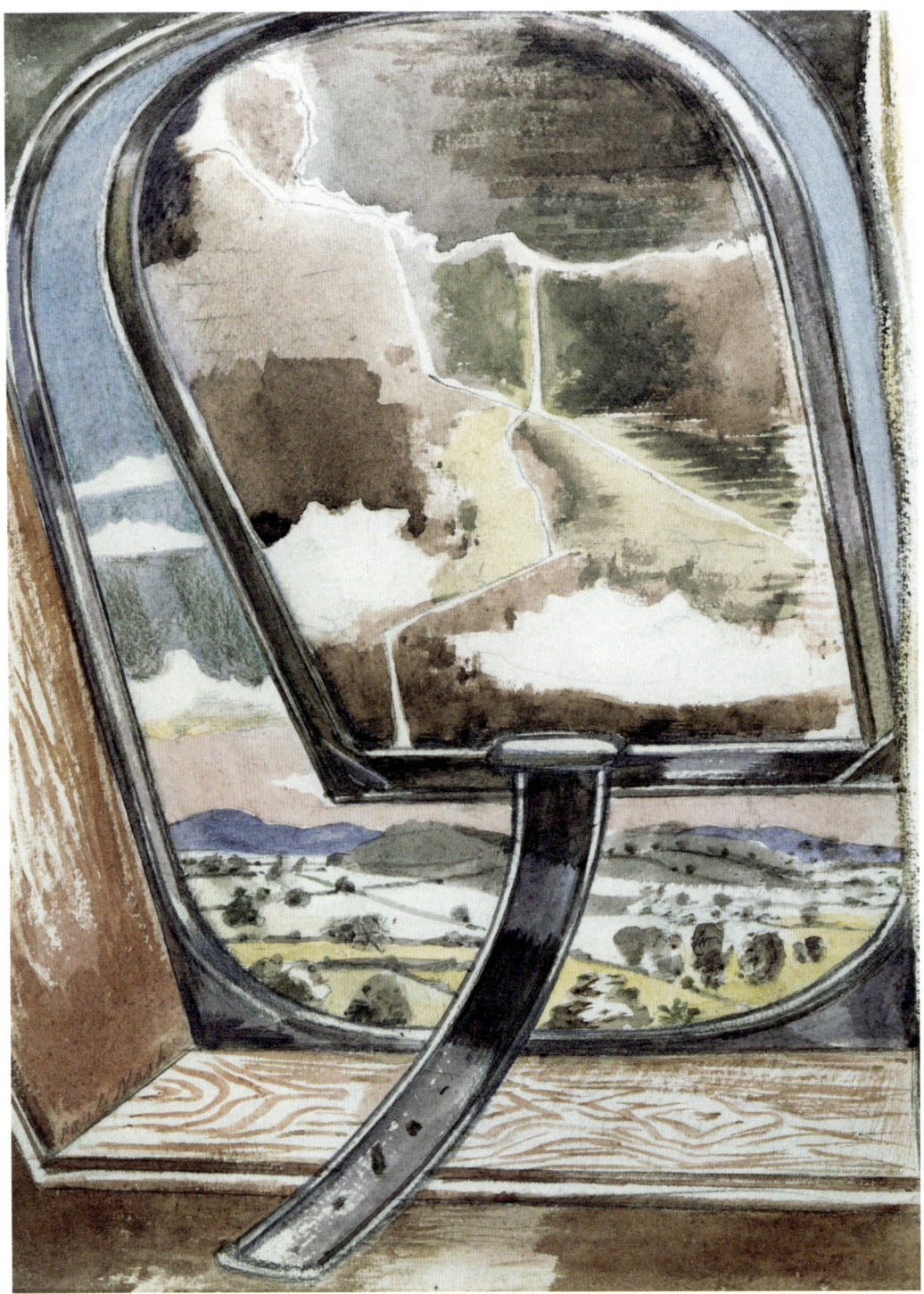

The Different Skies, 1939
Watercolour and pencil, 38.1 x 27.9 cm (15 x 11 in)
• Private Collection

There was always a mathematical aspect to Nash's more celebrated mystic side: if his vision of landscape always hinged on the interrelation of distinct figures, he was especially intrigued by the relations between different geometric planes.

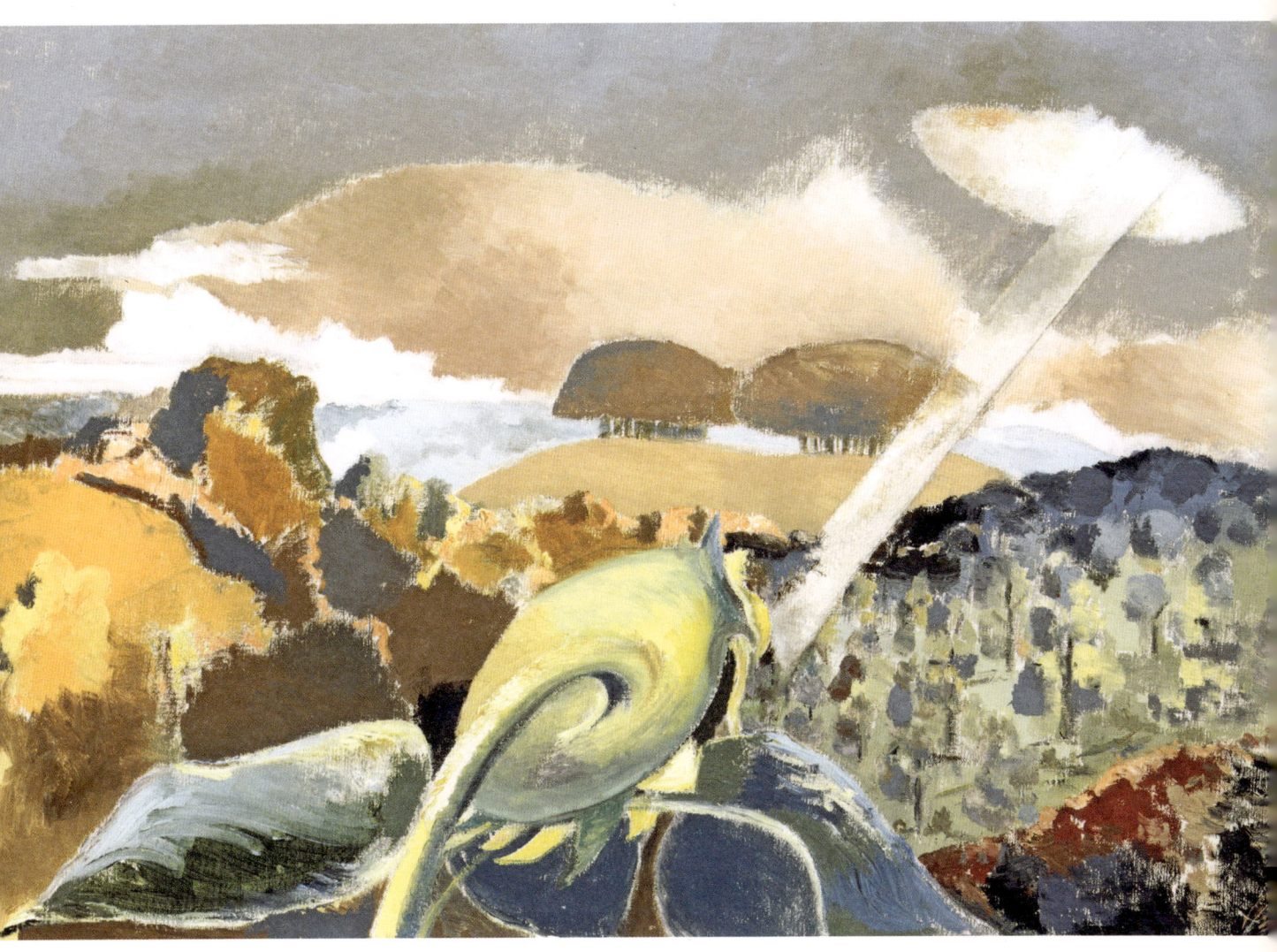

Sunflower and Sun, 1942
Oil on canvas, 51.1 x 76.5 cm (20 x 30 in)
• Art Gallery of New South Wales, Sydney

Sunflowers are stunning – as Van Gogh had noticed. Nash, though, like Blake before him, was less concerned with their intrinsic beauty than with their curious relationship with the sun, the longing with which they tracked it across the sky.

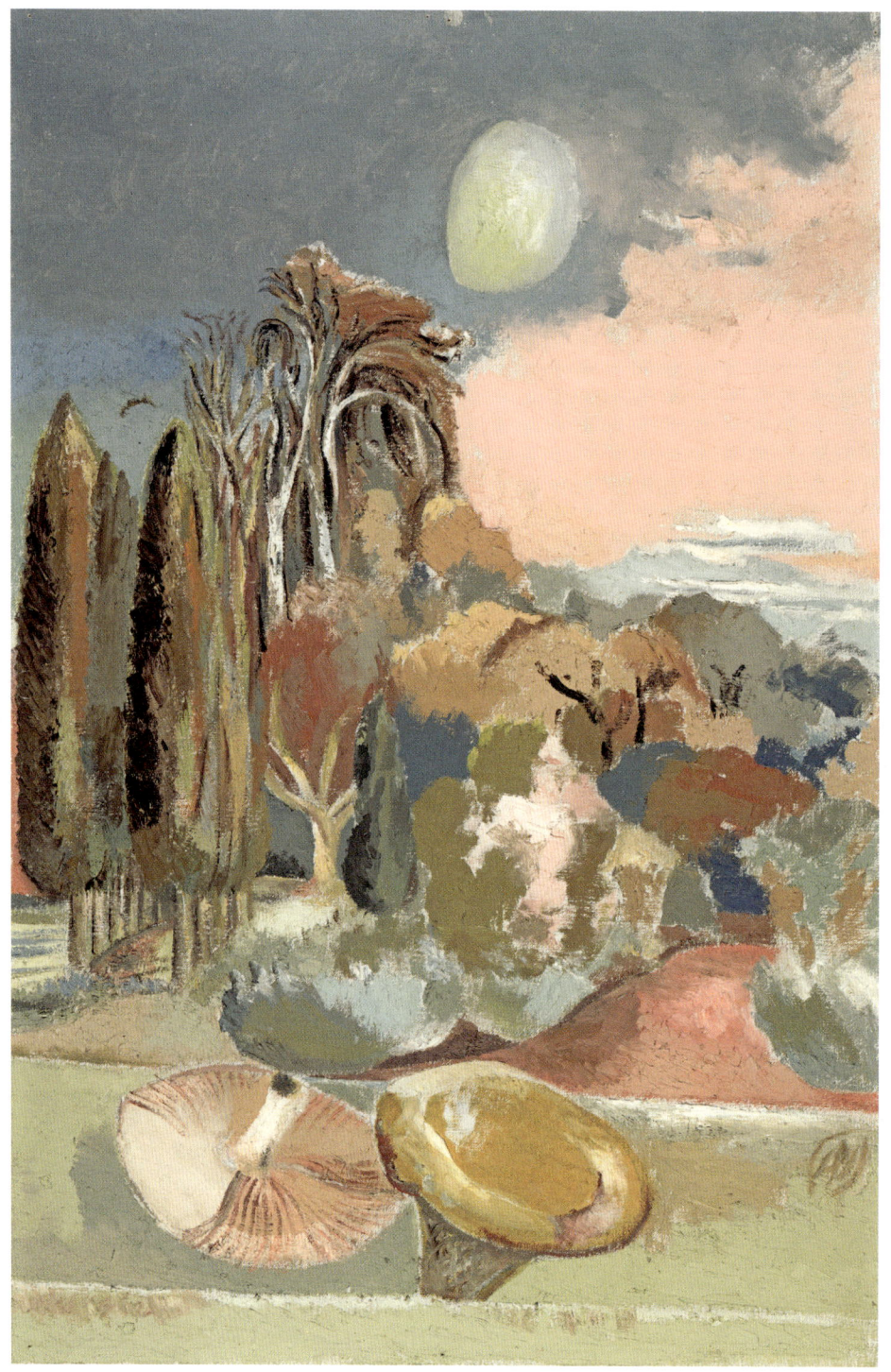

November Moon, 1942
Oil on canvas, 76.2 x 58.8 cm (30 x 23 in)
• Fitzwilliam Museum, Cambridge

Cypresses, ancient symbols of death, stand sentry in honour of the dying year. Beyond, the trees are crowned with browns and tans. In the foreground, the convolvulus flower complements the upturned mushroom. Autumn's produce, both reflect the changing moon above.

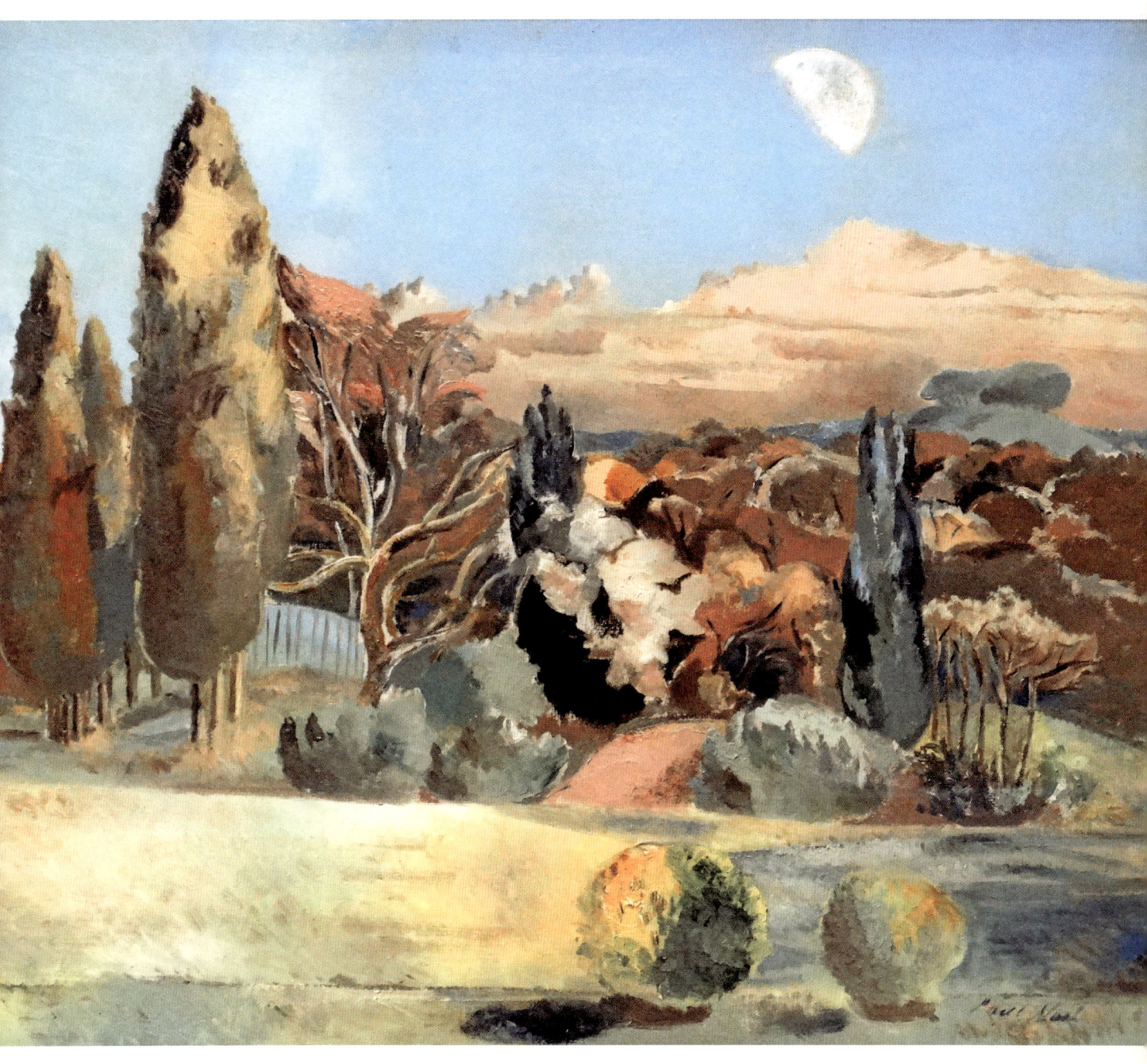

Landscape of the Moon's First Quarter, 1943
Oil on canvas, 63.3 x 71 cm (25 x 28 in)
• Birmingham Museum & Art Gallery

Wittenham Clumps rises in the distance, its silhouette stunted against alpine banks of cloud behind. The waxing moon, mirrored in the bushes in the foreground, bathes the entire scene in mystic light.

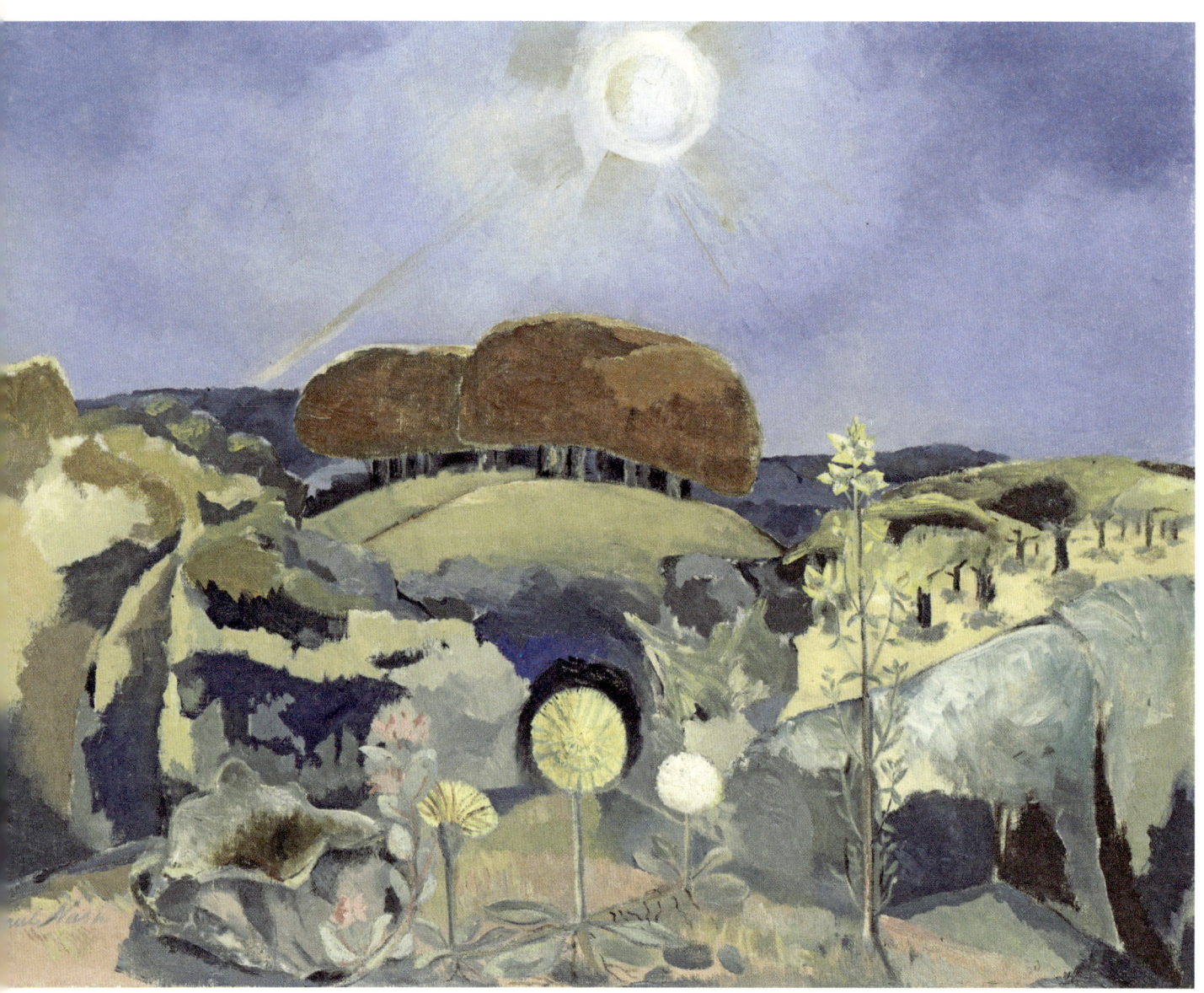

Landscape of the Summer Solstice, 1943
Oil on canvas, 76.2 x 58.8 cm (30 x 23 in)
• National Gallery of Victoria, Melbourne

Wittenham Clumps are illuminated here by the eerie light of the longest evening.
The silvery sphere of the moon is matched on the ground by the flossy-headed
flowers; trees rise like chestnut mushrooms from the rounded brow.

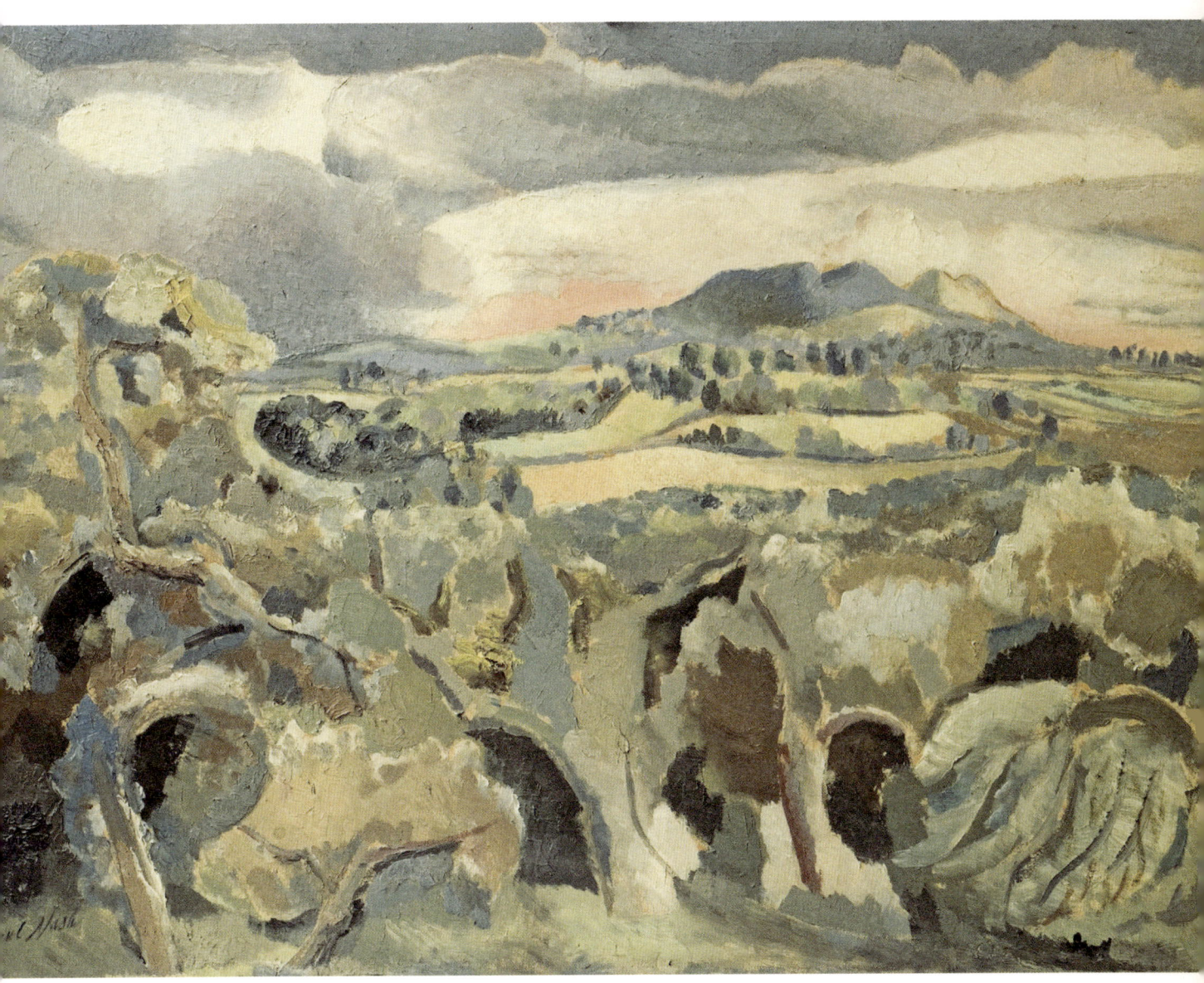

Landscape of the Malvern Distance, 1943
Oil on board, 55.9 x 76.2 cm (22 x 30 in)
• Southampton City Art Gallery

Nash often stayed at Sandlands, the Boar's Hill home of the artist-gardener Hilda Harrisson (1888–1972). He loved to look out in the evening, enjoying the views across to distant hills.

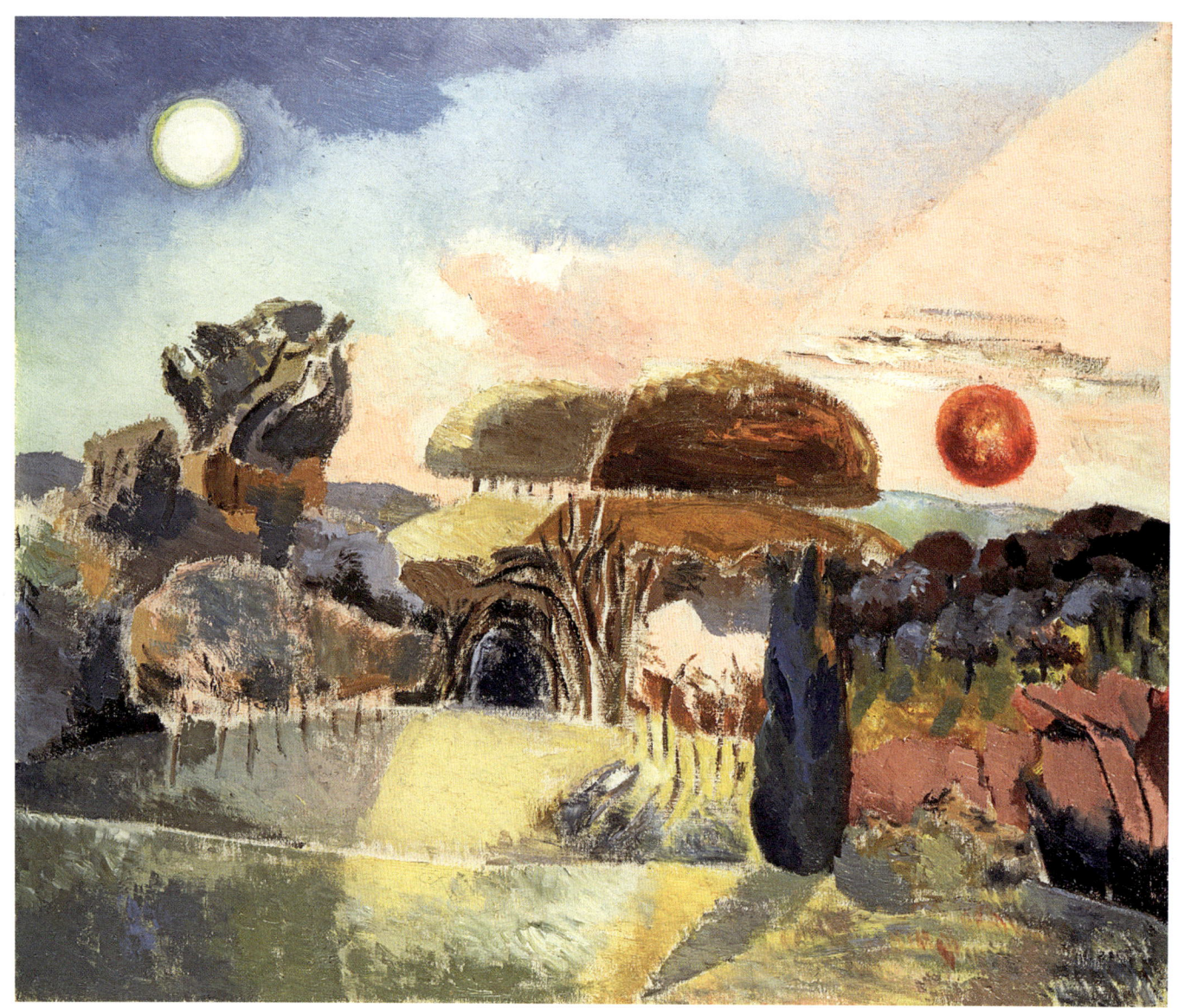

Landscape of the Vernal Equinox (III), 1944
Oil on canvas, 63.5 x 76.2 cm (25 x 30 in)
• Scottish National Gallery of Modern Art, Edinburgh

Nash liked to align himself with humankind and Nature's most ancient rhythms.
Here a setting sun and a rising moon share a sky at that enchanted moment which
marks the end of winter and the beginning of spring.

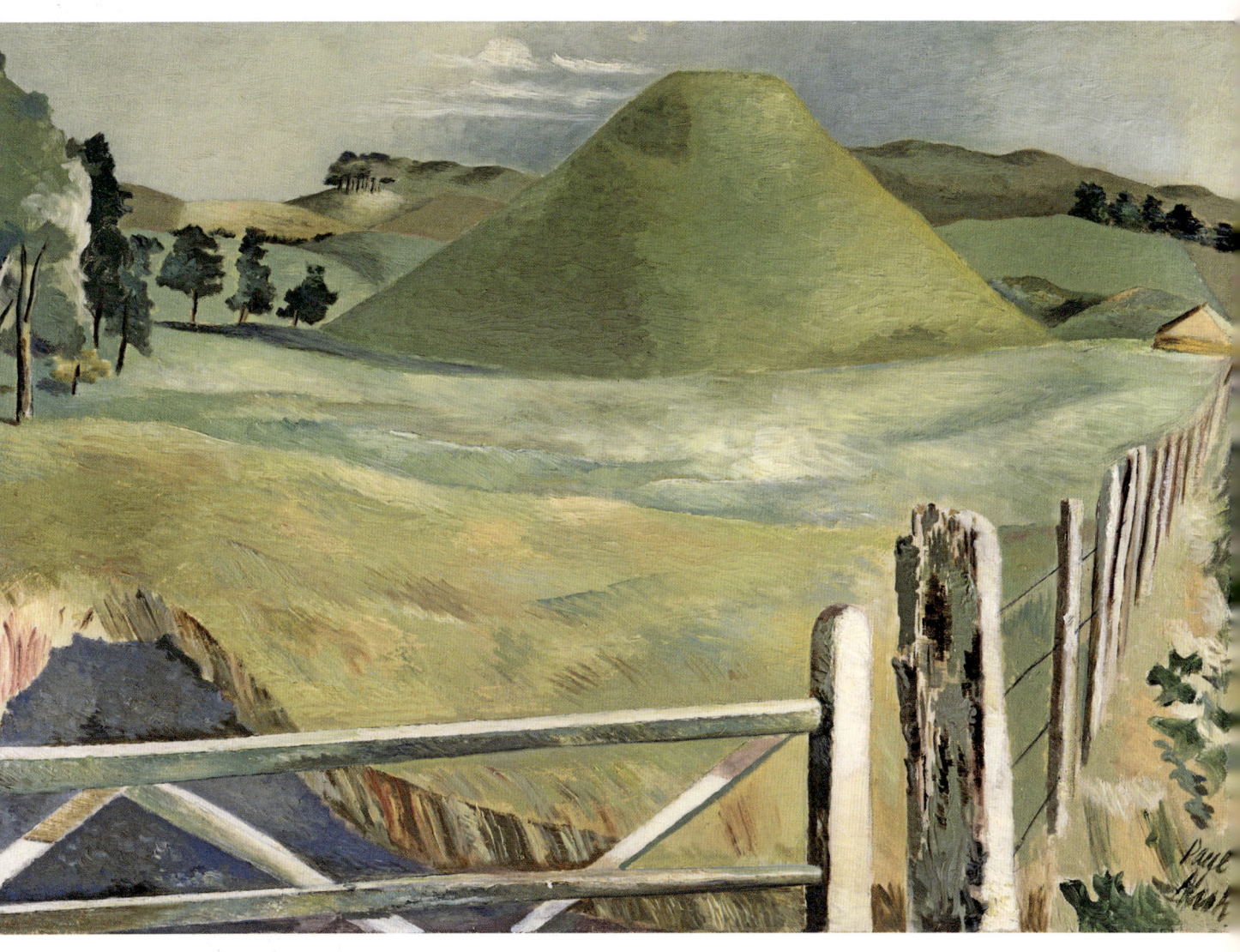

Silbury Hill, 1944
Oil on canvas, 50.8 x 72.3 cm (20 x 28½ in)
• Private Collection

Presumably a burial mound, its real purpose remains mysterious. It is certain, however, that this Wiltshire monument is a man-made hill. A human attempt to shape the 'natural' landscape, it was bound to attract Nash's attention

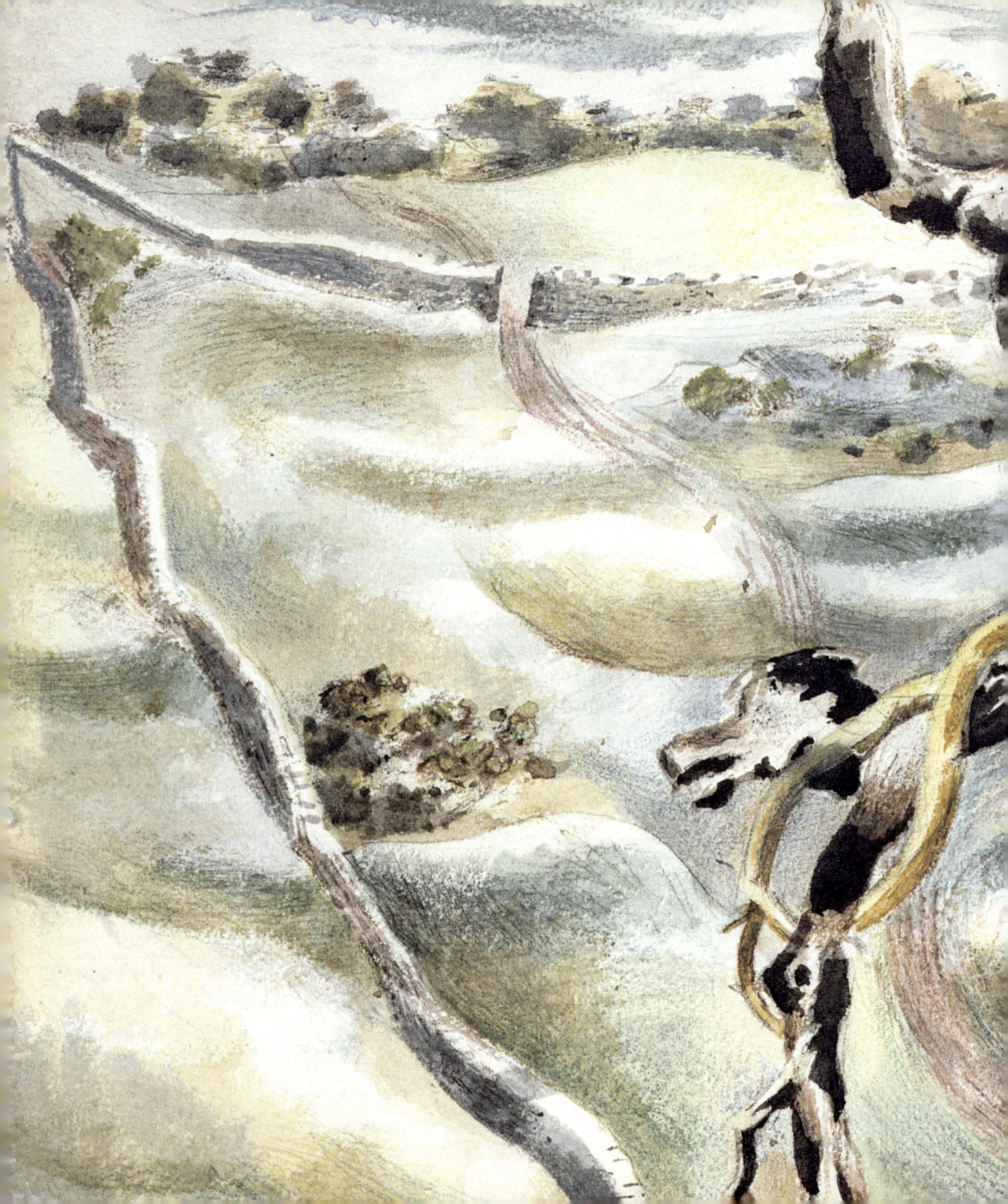

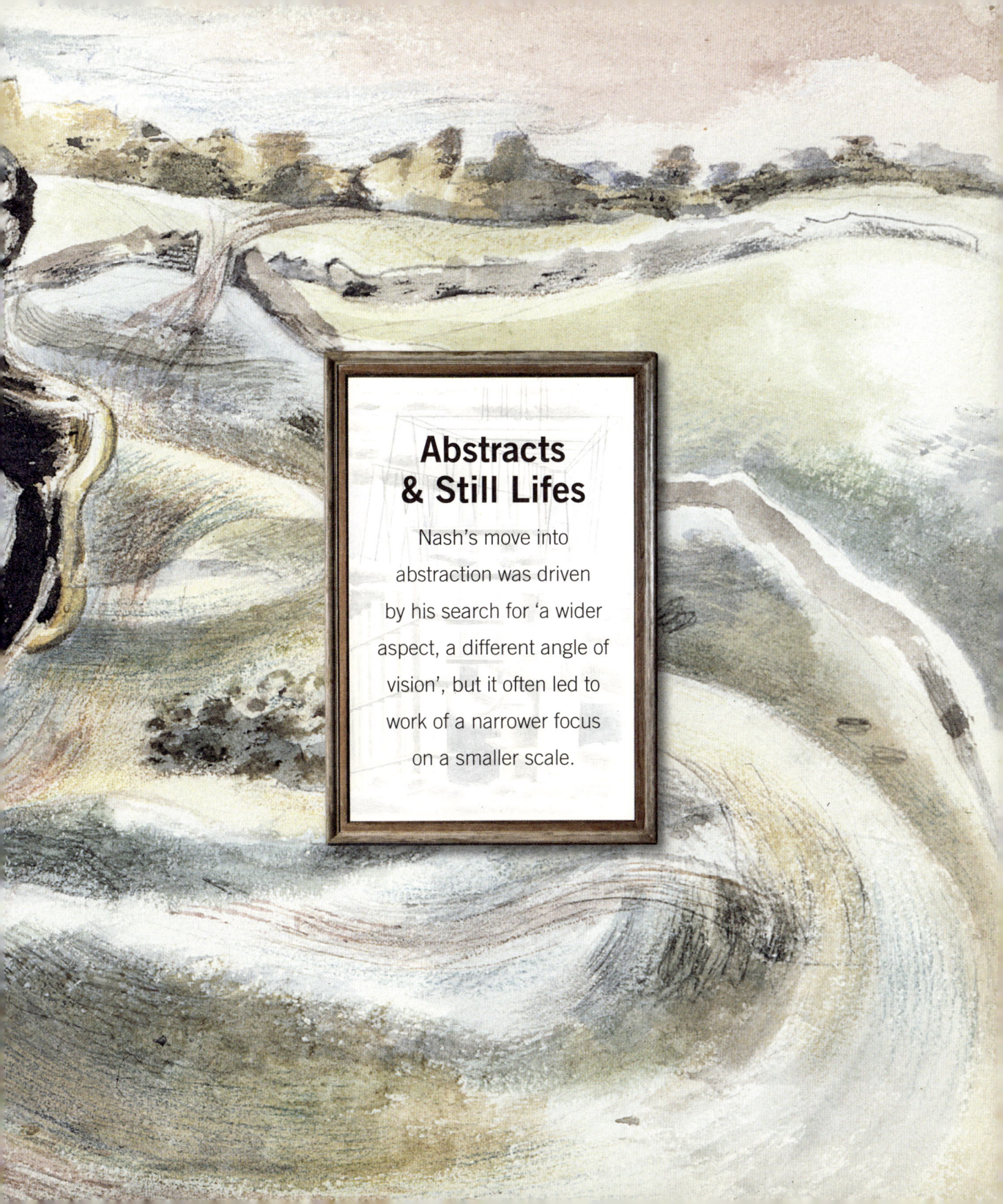

Abstracts
& Still Lifes

Nash's move into
abstraction was driven
by his search for 'a wider
aspect, a different angle of
vision', but it often led to
work of a narrower focus
on a smaller scale.

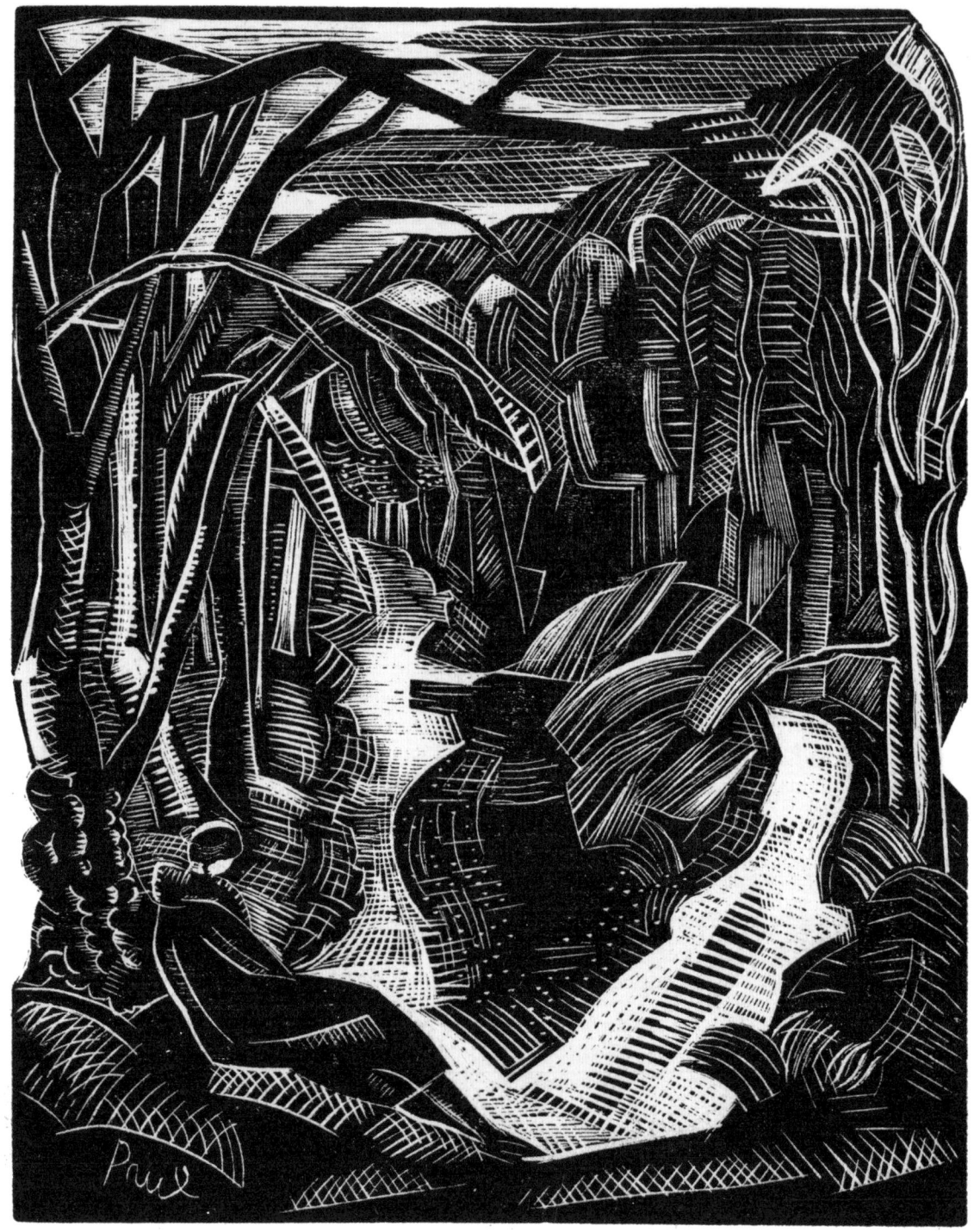

Au Bords du Bois, 1921
Wood engraving on paper
• Royal Albert Memorial Museum, Exeter

The First World War may have been over but Nash had not recovered. Behind this pensive-looking female figure, a dark and ominous wood extends. Nash saw engraving as therapeutic, a way of interacting more physically and immediately with his art.

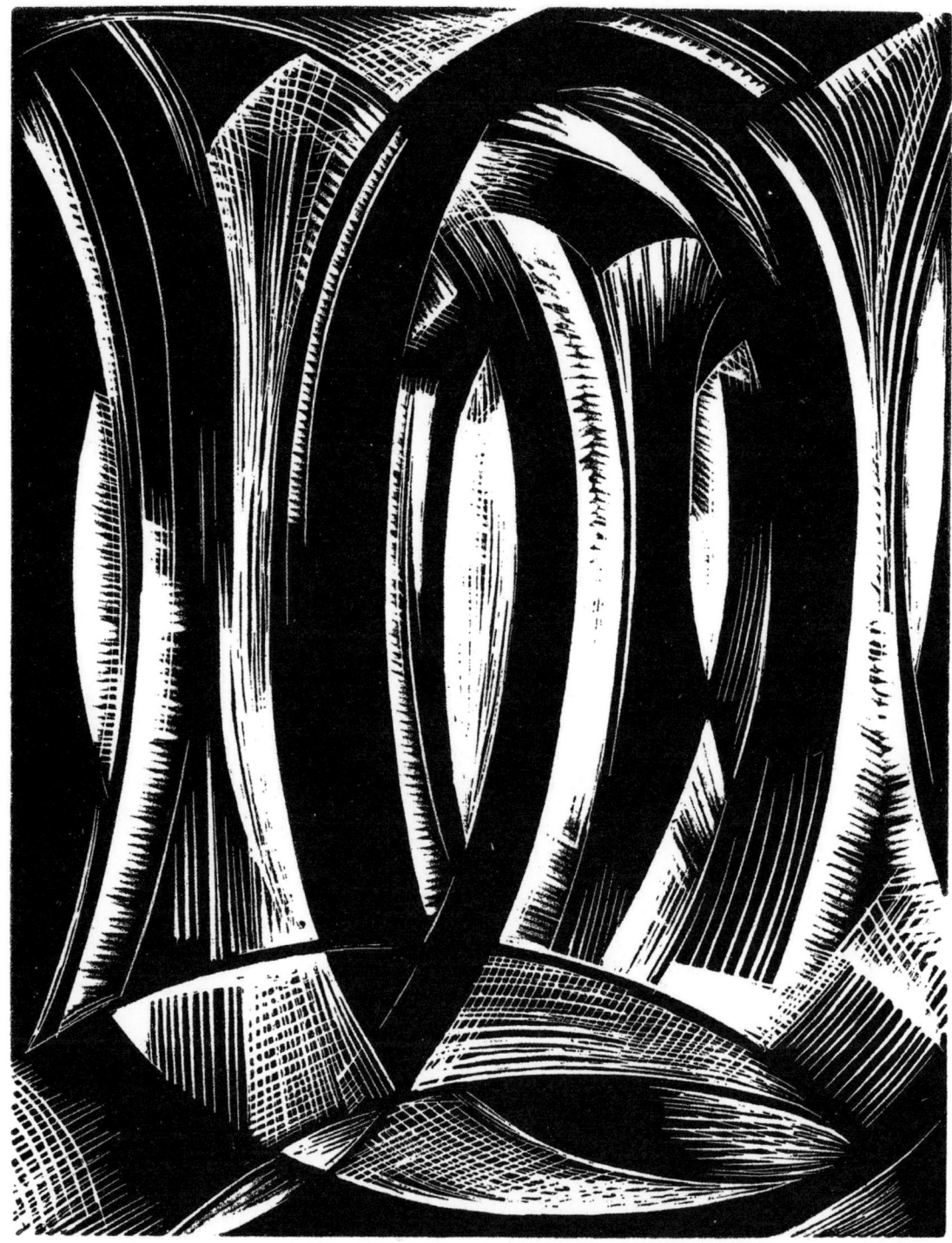

Book of Genesis (Heaven), 1924
Woodcut • Private Collection

Nash went back to the very roots of creativity in the dozen woodcuts he made to illustrate the first chapter of the Bible's Book of Genesis. This page shows the moment at which the heavens were separated from the earth.

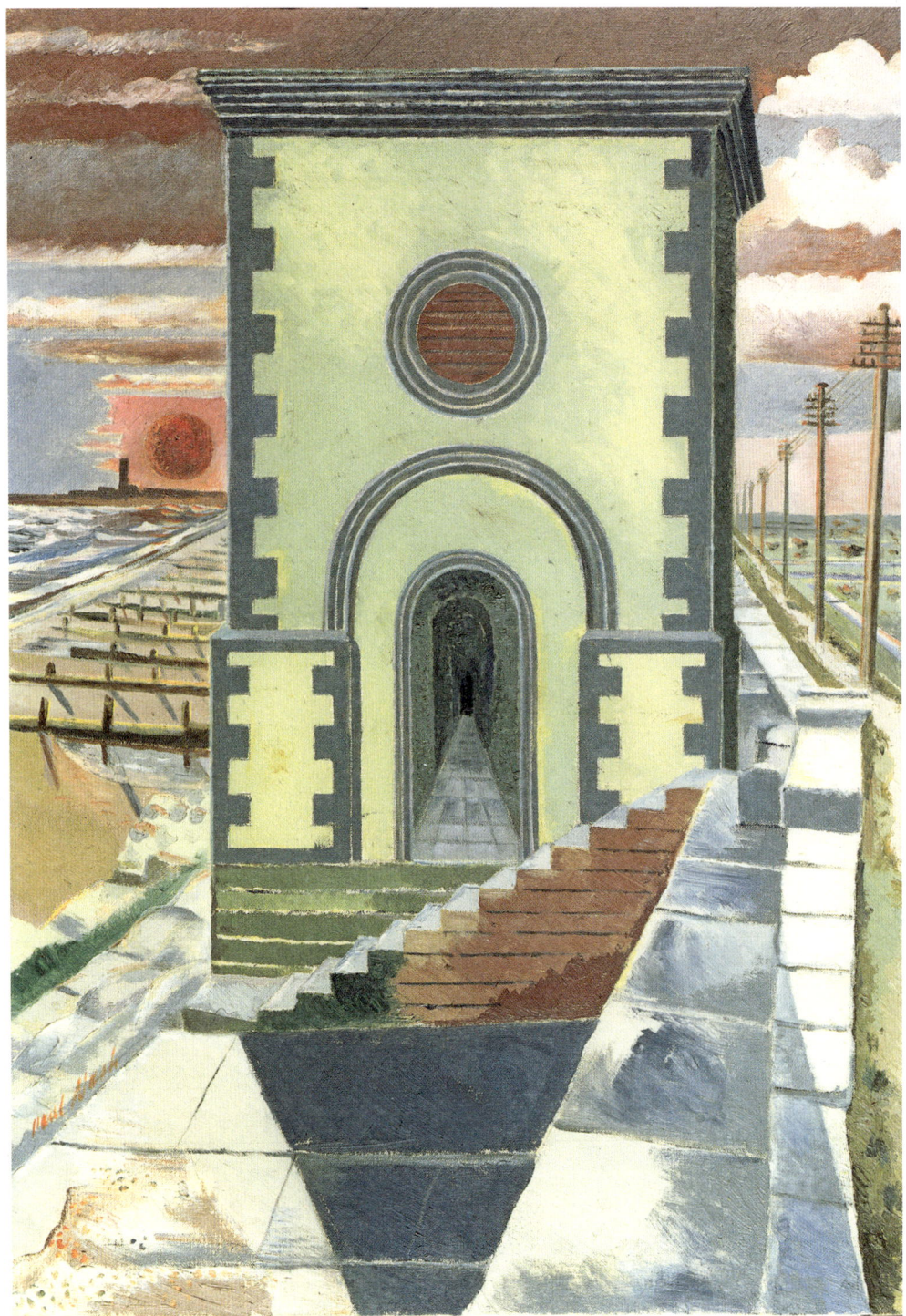

Nostalgic Landscape, 1923–38
Oil on canvas, 28 x 20 cm (11 x 7¾ in)
• New Walk Museum and Art Gallery, Leicester

Warm reds and terracottas here share a canvas with some distinctly sickly greens and greys. The 'pageant' of the past is no parade of happiness for Nash, nostalgia by no means necessarily comforting.

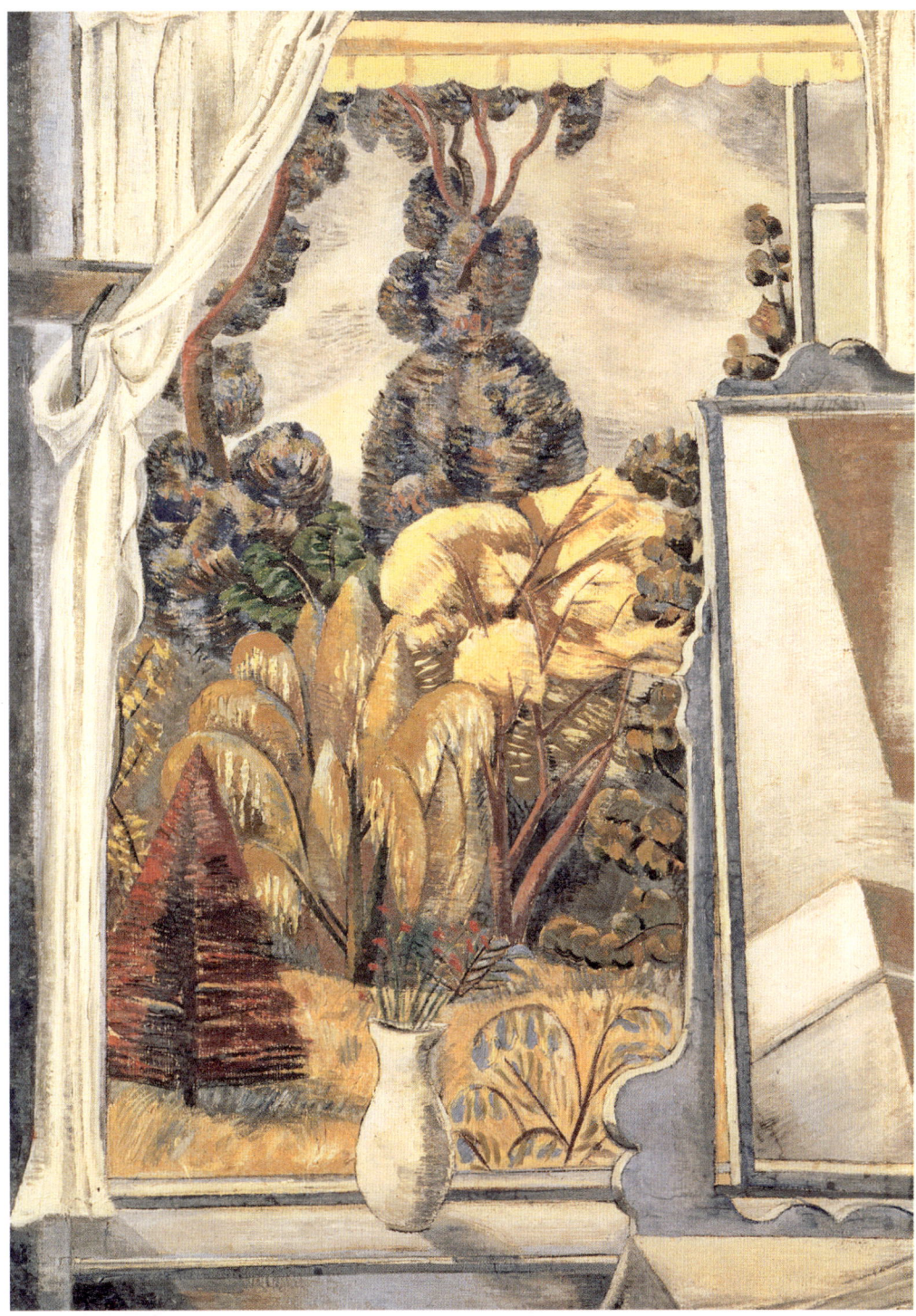

Mirror and Window, 1924
Oil on canvas, 76 x 56 cm (30 x 22 in)
• Private Collection

Boundaries made and broken: the mirror frames a picture within a picture, its hard-edged geometry jarring with the wavy natural forms of the woods outside, which are continuous with the flowers on the windowsill.

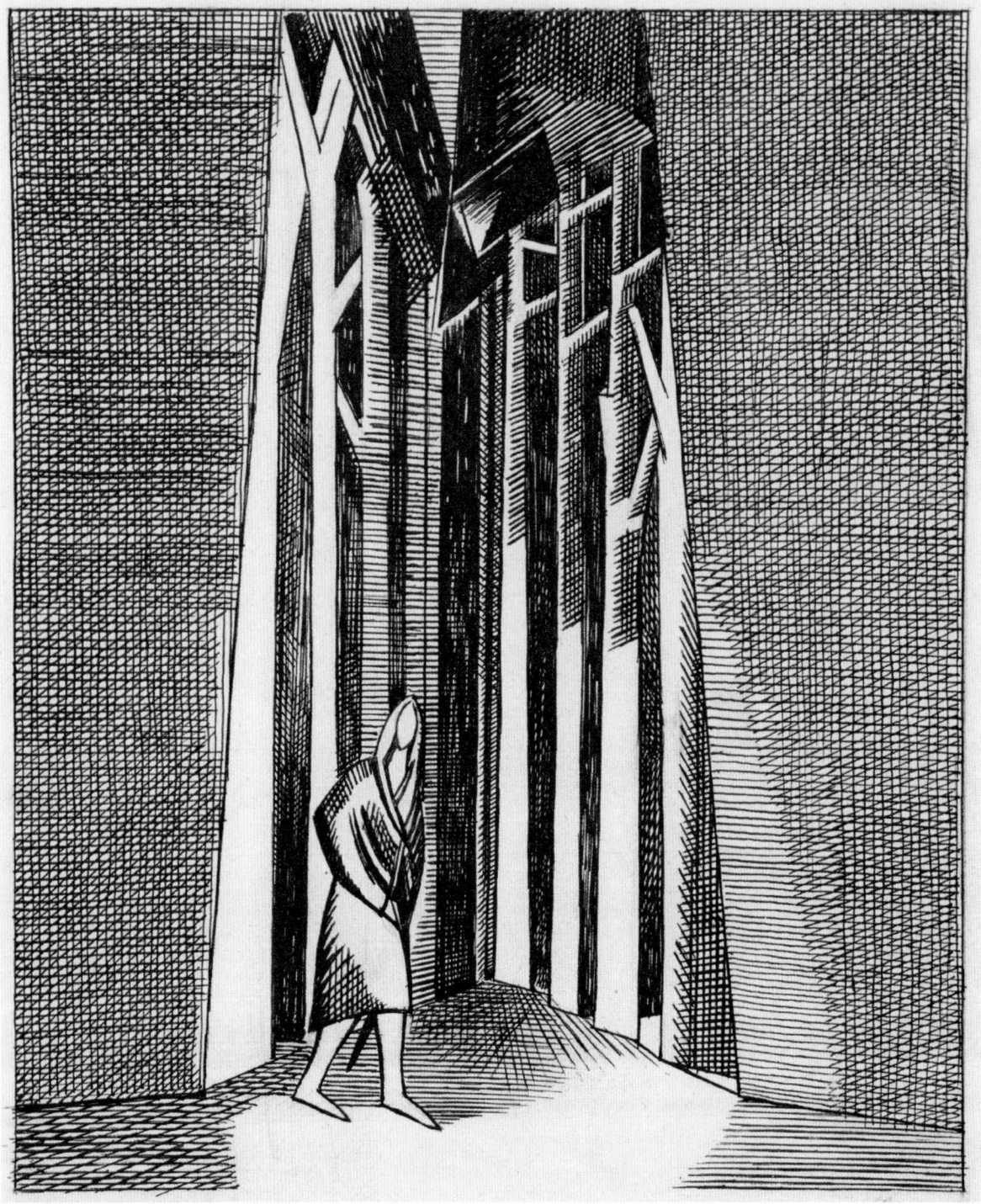

A Wood – Illustration for *King Lear*, Act II, Scene iii, 1926
Ink on paper, 35.8 x 20.5 cm (14 x 8 in)
• Private Collection

'I heard myself proclaim'd,/ And by the happy hollow of a tree/ Escap'd the hunt.' For Nash, as for Shakespeare's Edgar, a wood could be a refuge, however dark and frightening it might seem.

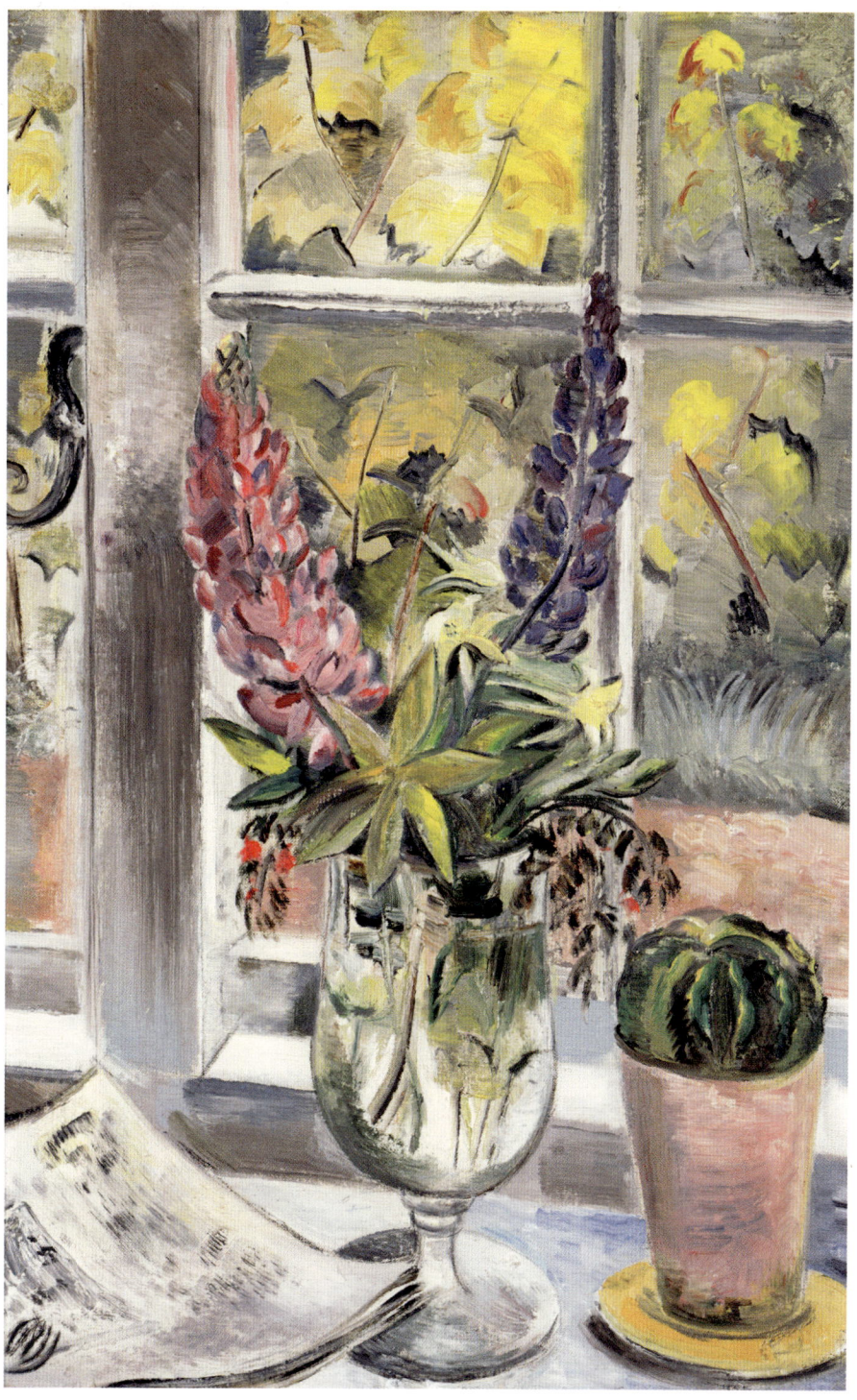

Lupins and Cactus, 1927
Oil on canvas, 61 x 41 cm (24 x 16 in)
• Private Collection

Nash kept returning to the window-set still life, and not just because it played off natural and geometric forms. He loved its liminality, the way it spanned the interior and outside realms, with different textures, shapes and scales.

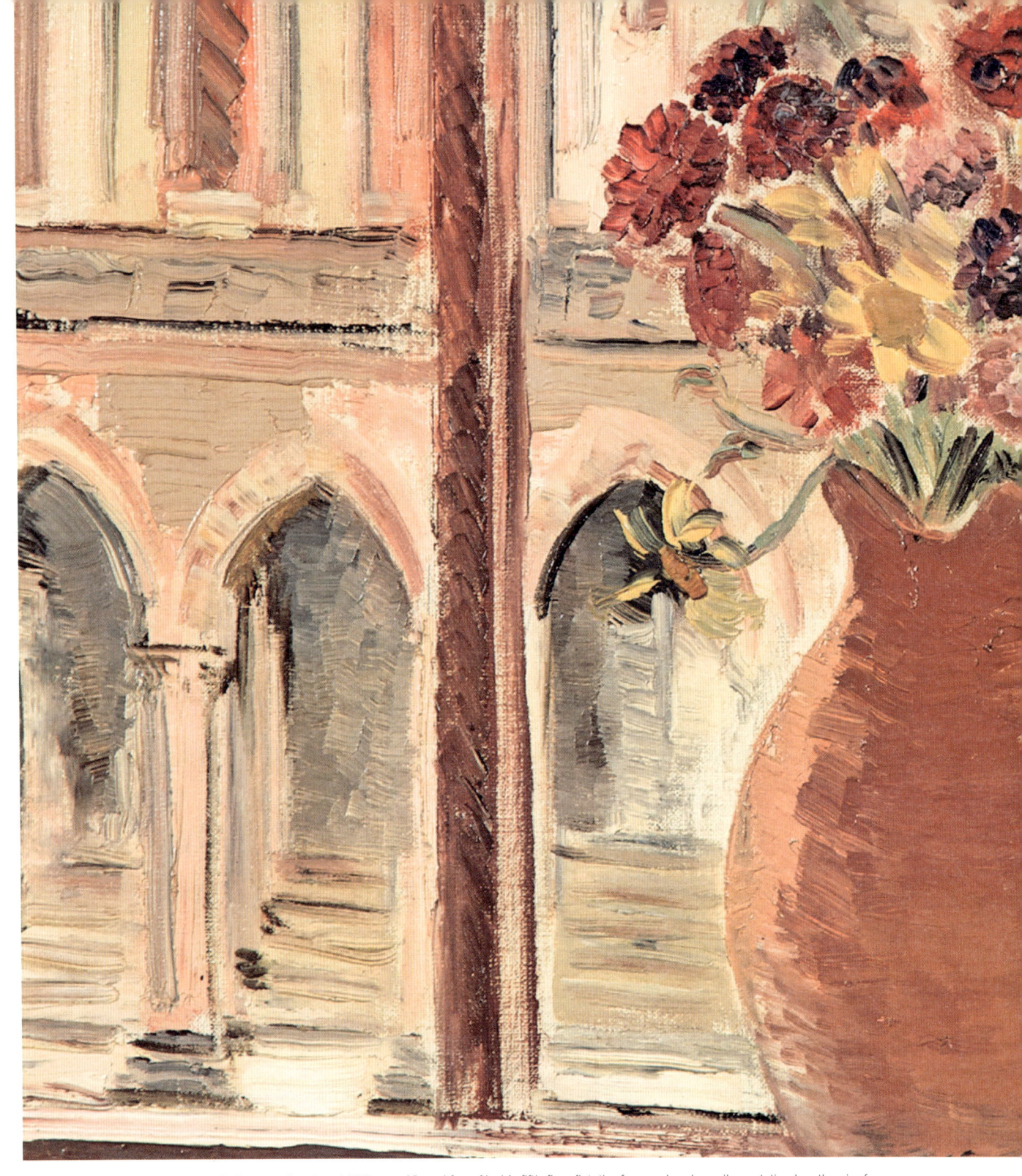

St Pancras, London, 1927
Oil on canvas, 41 x 60 cm (16 x 23⅗ in)
• Cheltenham Art Gallery and Museum: The Wilson

Viewed from Nash's fifth-floor flat, the famous London railway station has the air of an Italian *palazzo*. The reds and pinks of the flowers complement the colours of the terracotta vase and of the ornate brickwork in the background.

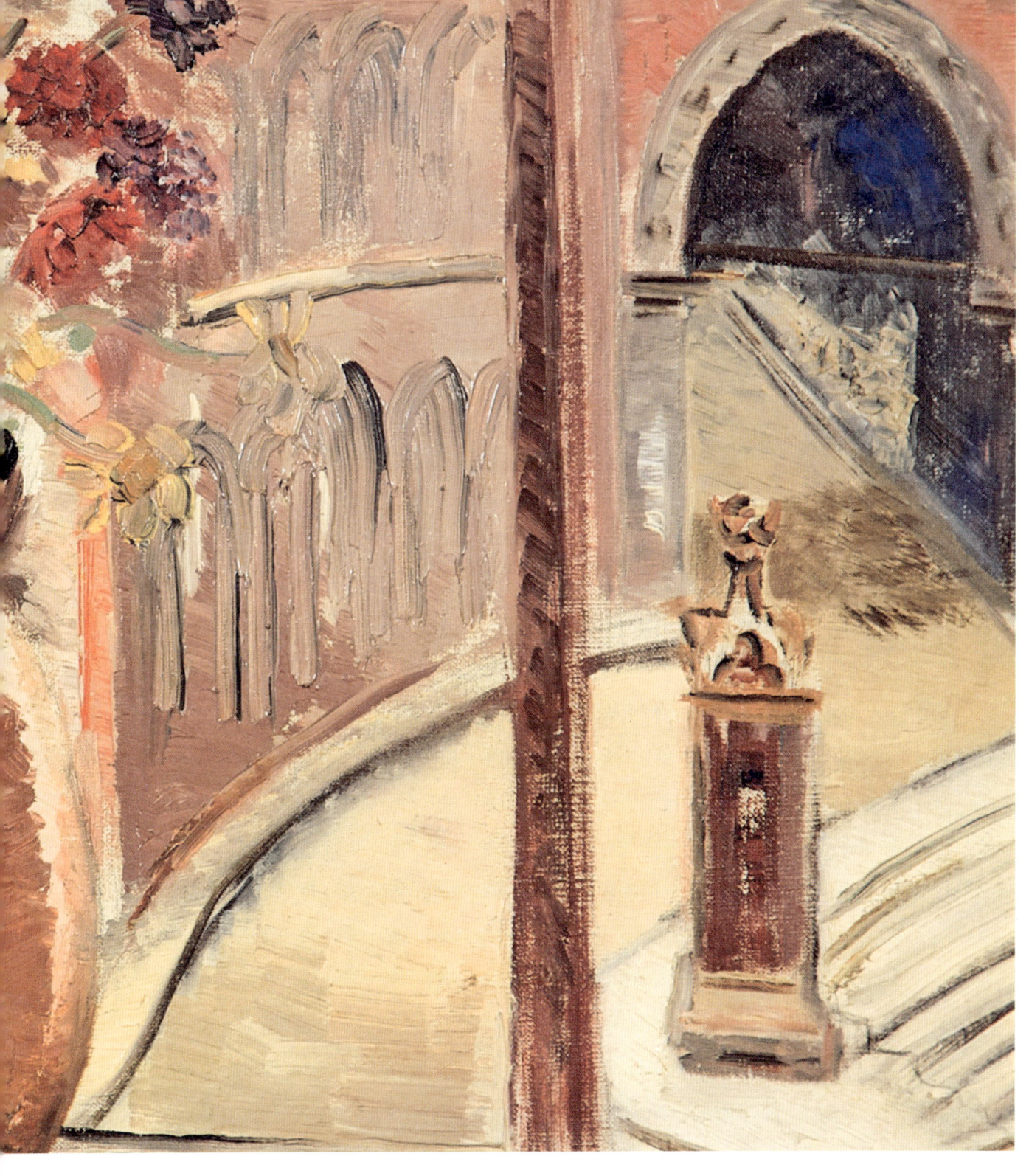

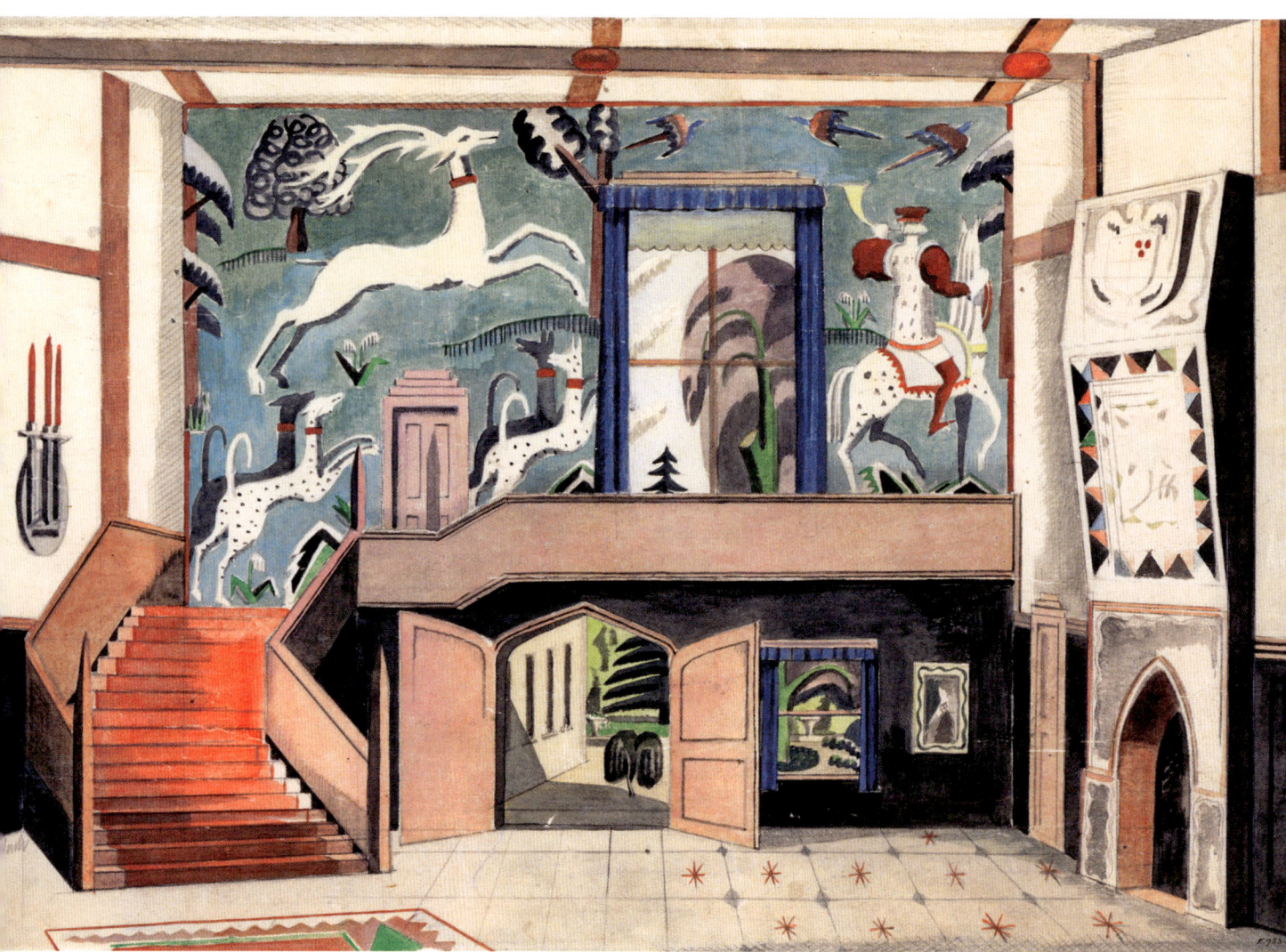

Interior Design, 1920s–30s   Again, the play of interior and exterior: here, however, it is not the woods beyond but the
Watercolour on paper • Private Collection   wall within which boasts its own heraldic hunting scene, the shadowed forms of the hounds
adding an unexpected realistic note.

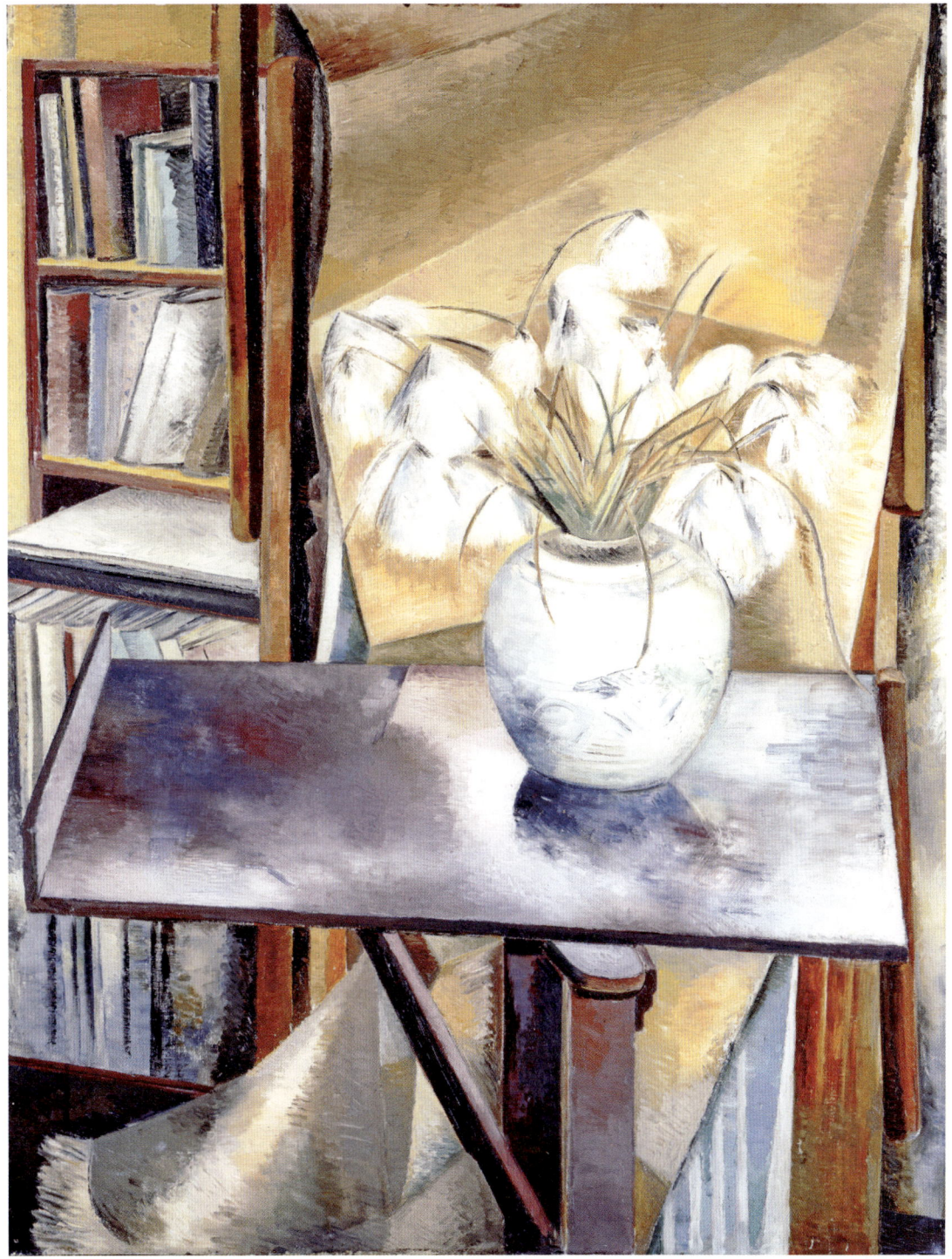

Still Life with Bog Cotton, 1927
Oil on canvas, 91.4 x 71.7 cm (36 x 28¼ in)
• Leeds Art Gallery

Not so much a still life as a stunning light show, the white cotton of the flower heads shine in the sun. The vase and table gleam beautifully, set off by a background of mahoganies and browns.

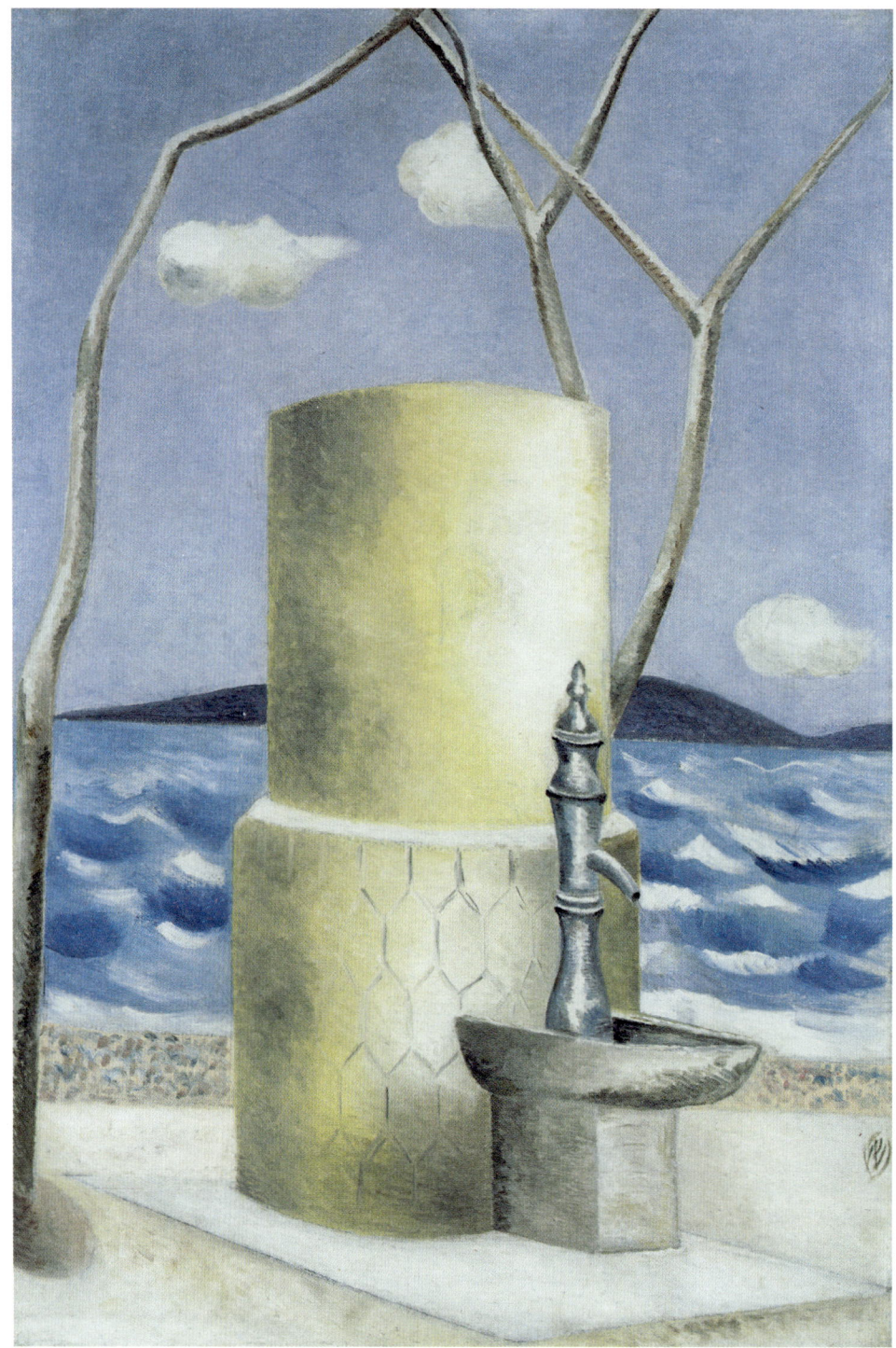

Plage, 1928
Oil on canvas, 72.8 x 49.5 cm (28½ x 19½ in)
• National Museum Wales, Cardiff

The all but abstract character of the tower at the centre of this painting, the unexplained fountain and the mysterious play of light all suggest the influence of Giorgio de Chirico's *Pittura Metafisica*.

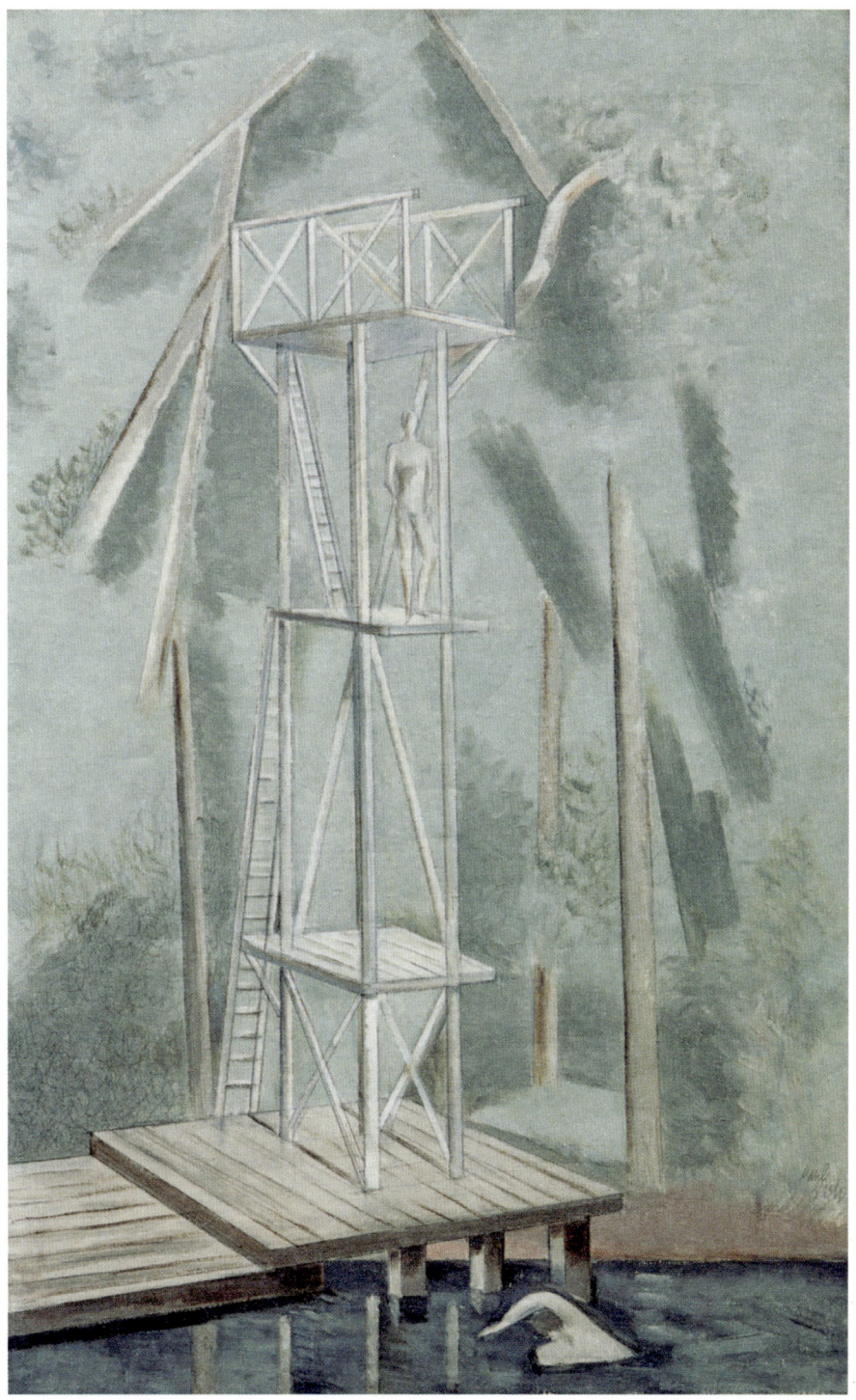

The Diving Stage, 1928
Oil and pencil on canvas, 84 x 53.5 cm (33 x 21 in)
• British Council of Visual Arts, London

A public swimming pool, it is said, became a biblical vision here. The intrepid divers clambering up and plunging down made Nash think of the white dream-angels ascending and descending Jacob's Ladder (Genesis 28:12).

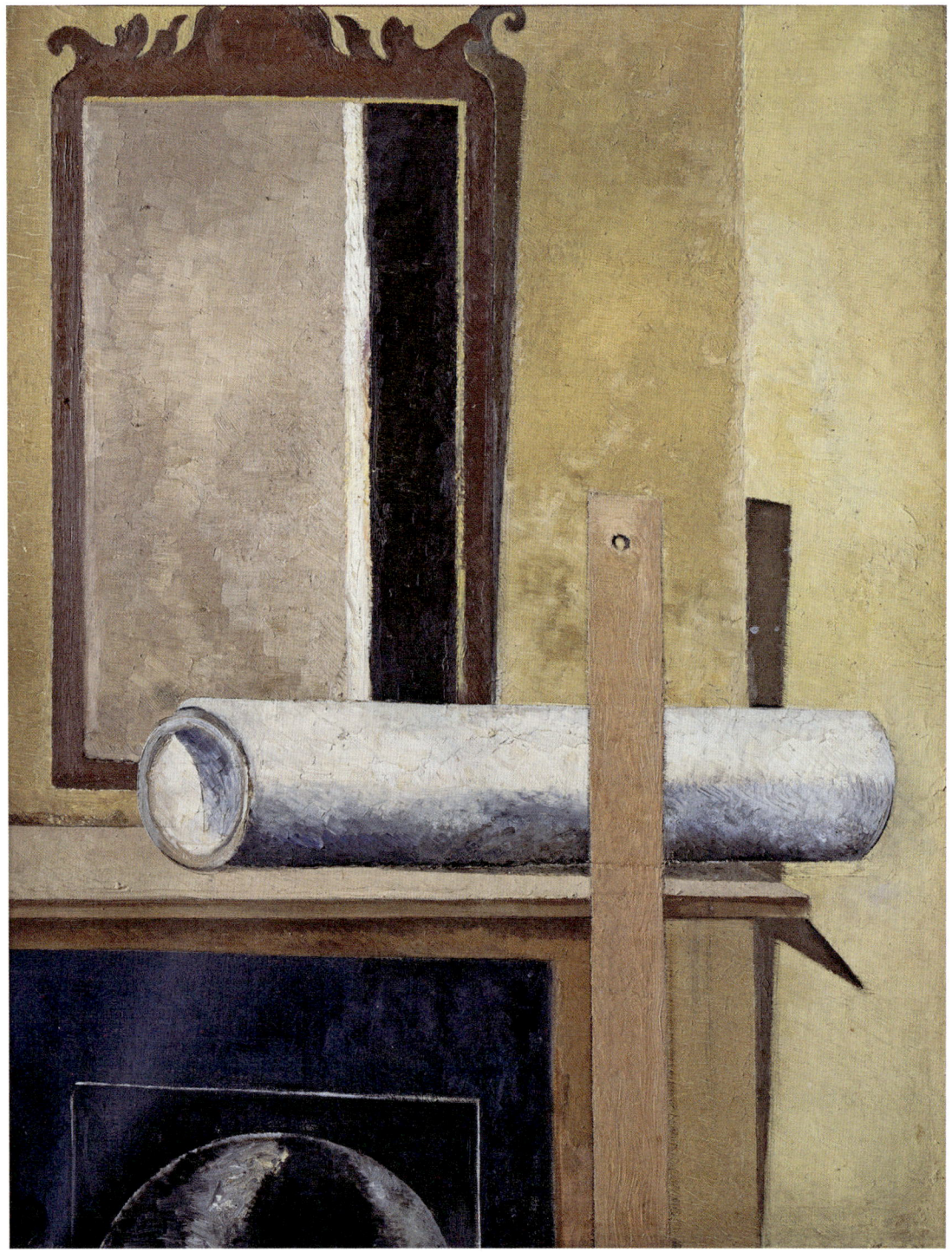

The Mantel-Piece, 1928
Oil on canvas, 91.4 x 71.1 cm (36 x 28 in)
• Private Collection

The mirror frame reflects items in the painting just as its glass reflects the room, giving a giddying sense of infinite regression. The rolled-up sheet and wooden lath remind us how mundane the materials of artistic inspiration are.

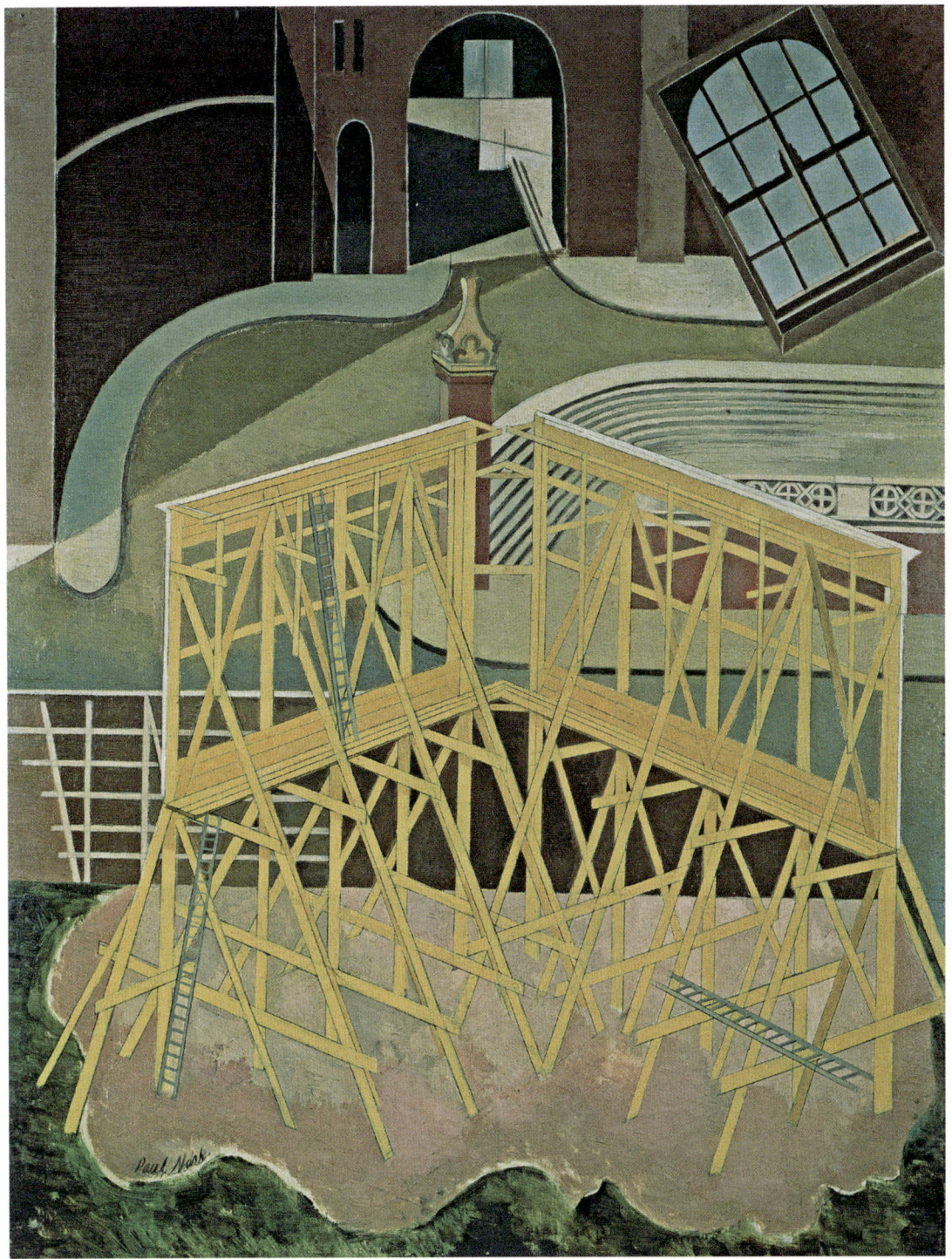

Northern Adventure, 1929
Oil on canvas, 92.7 x 71.6 cm (36½ x 28¼ in)
• Aberdeen Art Gallery and Museums

A surrealized version of the view we had in *St Pancras* (1927, *see* pages 100–01). The window here floats free as part of the picture; its eccentric orientation reminds us how arbitrary conventional 'realist' perspectives are.

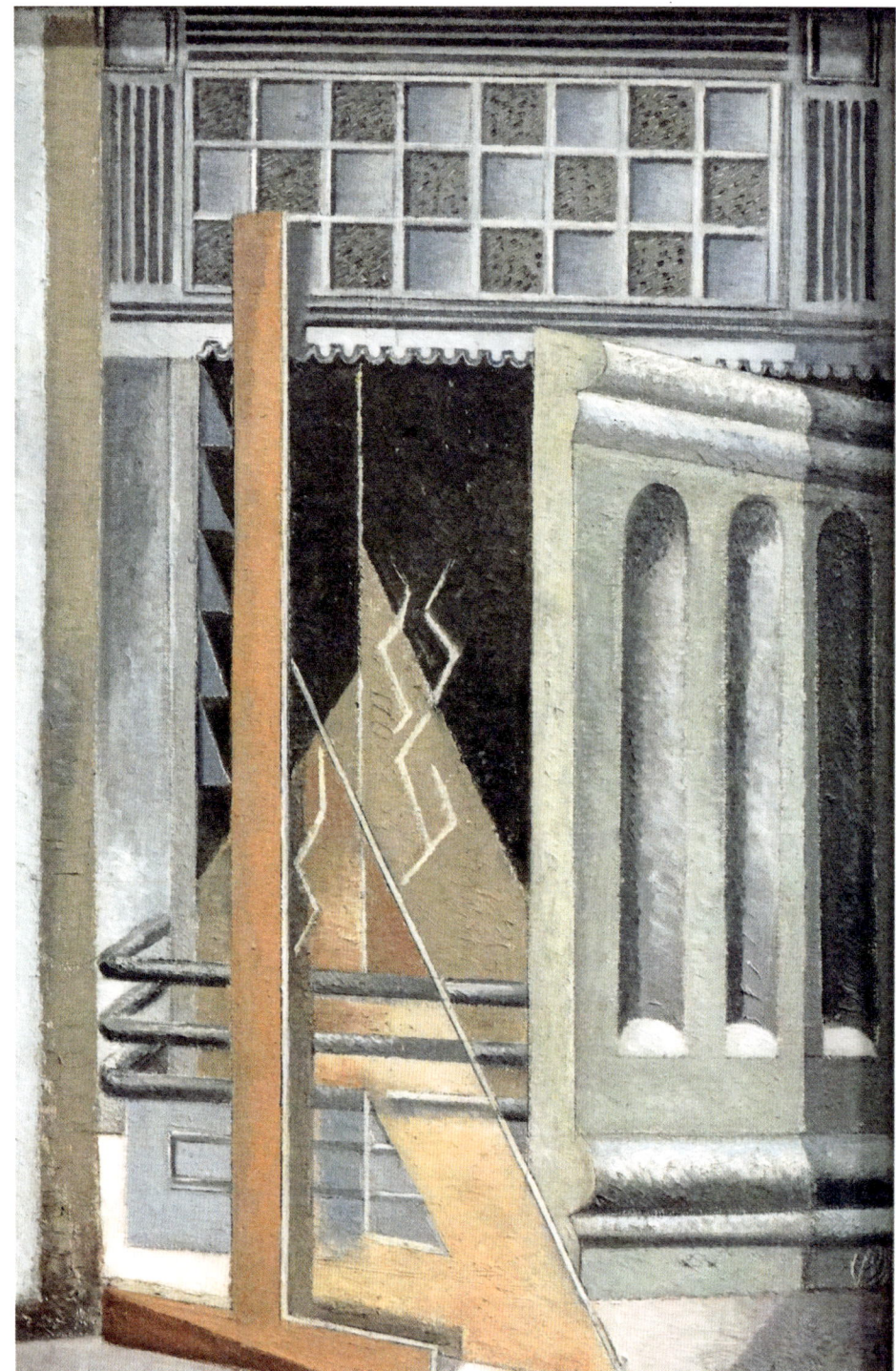

Lares, 1929
Oil on canvas, 31.5 x 47.6 cm (12½ x 18¾ in)
• Private Collection

Named after the protective spirits believed by the Romans to preside over the family home, *Lares* shows – rather than any really friendly warmth – a chilly De Chirico-esque concern with the geometry of dream.

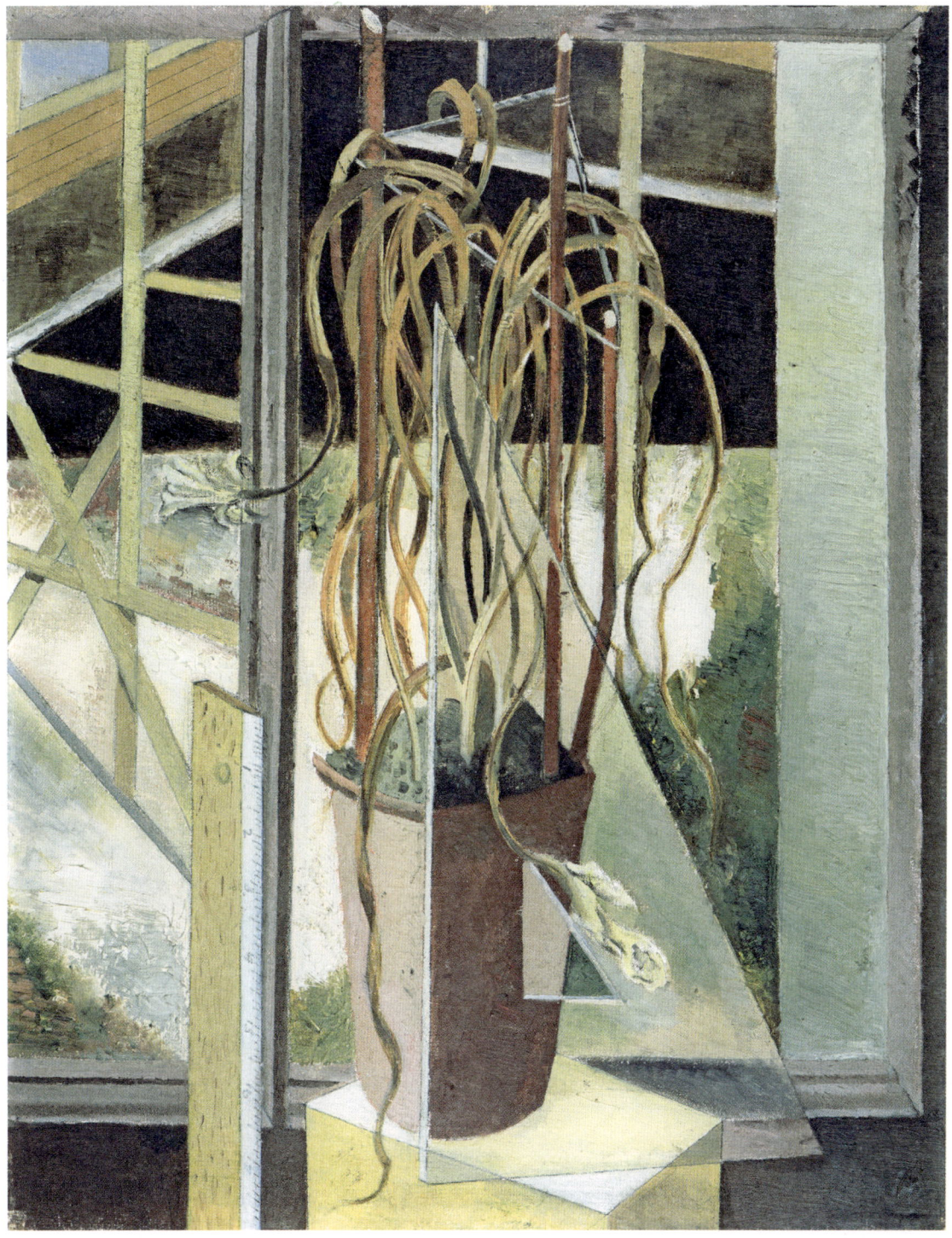

Dead Spring, 1929
Oil on canvas, 48.5 x 40 cm (19 x 15¾ in)
• Pallant House Gallery, Chichester

The oxymoron of the title is just one of several here: the flowing lines of the leaves contradict the regimented lines and angles we see through the window and the rule and set square we see inside.

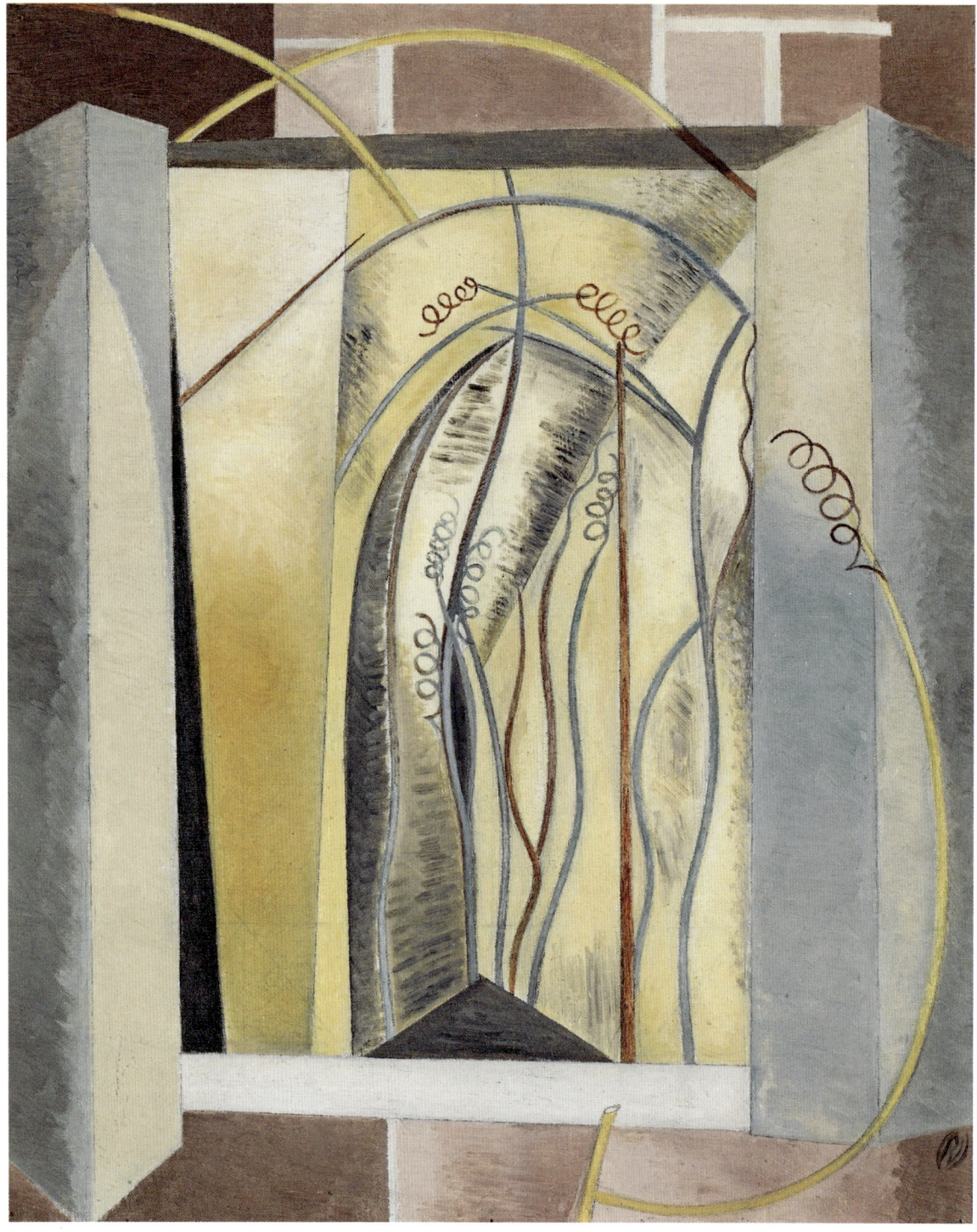

Coronilla Landscape, 1929
Oil on canvas, 61.2 x 50.8 cm (24 x 20 in)
• Fitzwilliam Museum, Cambridge

'O, what is that I think I see/ So pale beyond the yellow dusk,/ Beyond the trailing bitter flower/ And reek of marrowbone and musk?' In 'Coronilla', by Harold Monro (1879–1932), a mysterious *femme fatale* enthrals the poet.

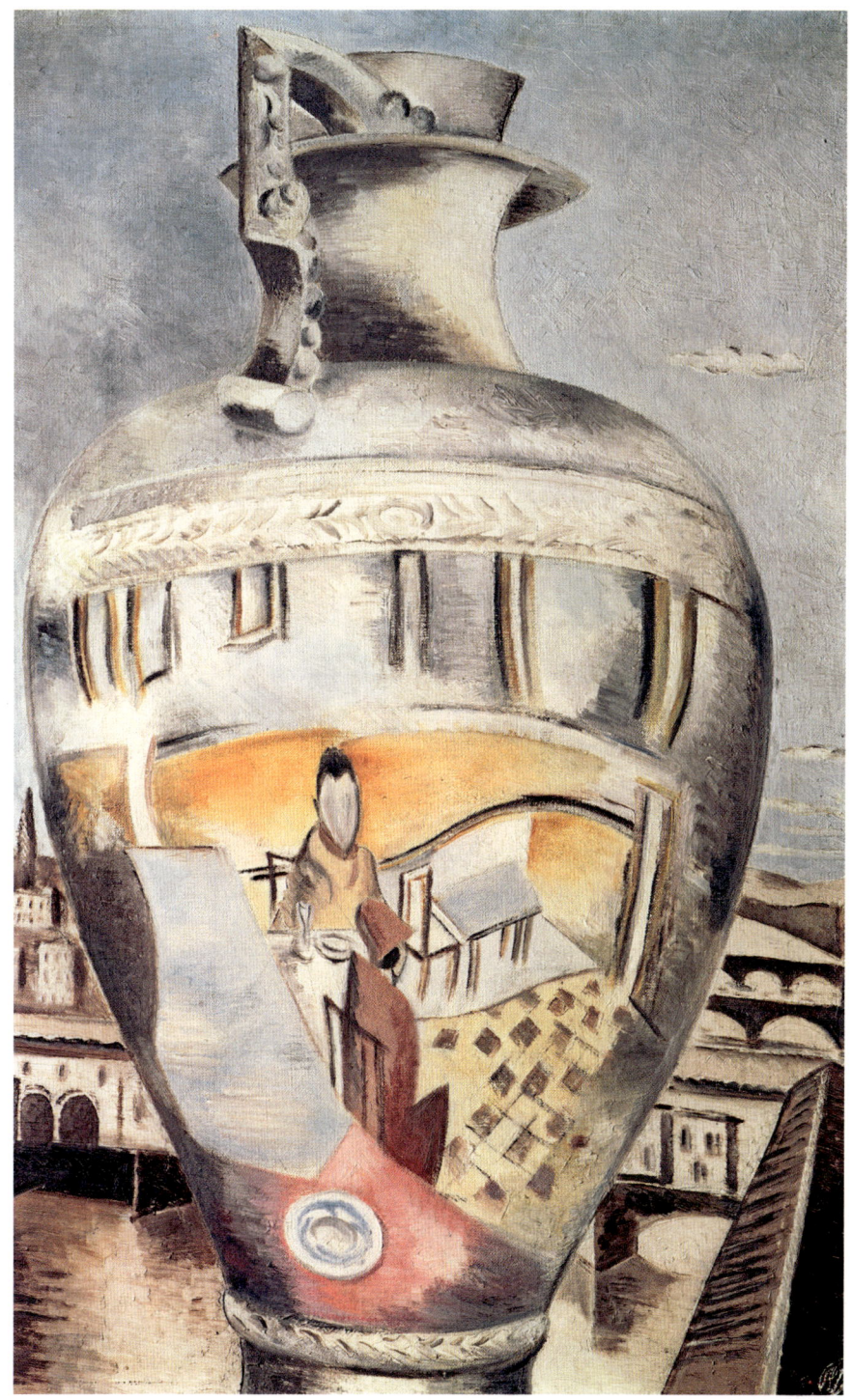

Souvenir of Florence, 1929
Oil on canvas, 68.6 x 43.8 cm (27 x 17¼ in)
• Yale Center for British Art, New Haven, Connecticut

Floating above the Arno and its bridges, this classical-looking amphora, suitable for oil or wine, reflects a restaurant interior, suggestive of good living. However, it would also easily double as an urn of death.

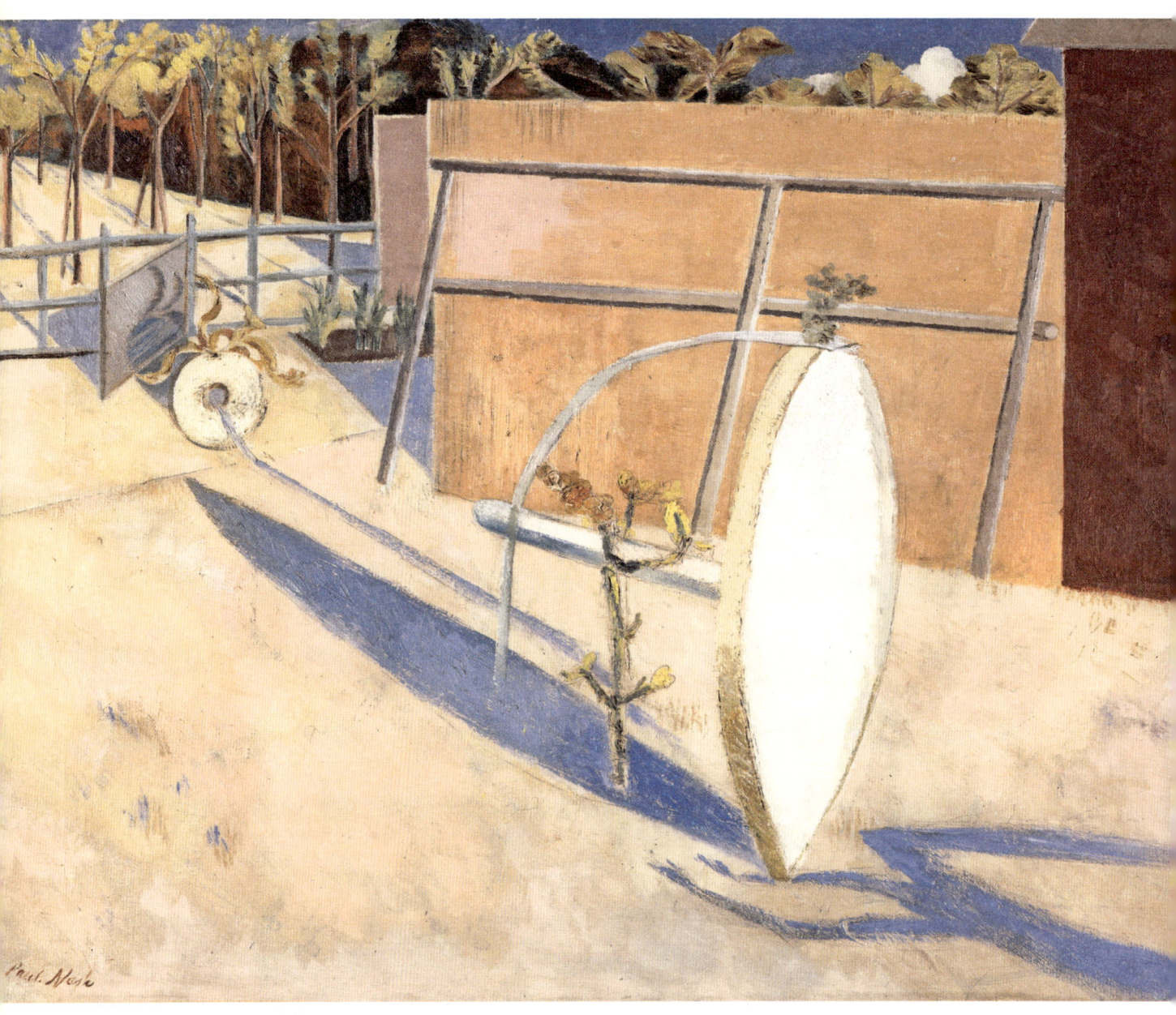

The Archer, 1930–42
Oil on canvas, 71 x 91.5 cm (28 x 36 in)
• Southampton City Art Gallery

The contraption is captured in meticulous detail, the logic behind it utterly obscure. The juxtaposition of plant and artificial forms is familiar (*Mirror and Window* (1924, *see* page 97) and *Dead Spring* (1929, *see* page 109). Again, though, the artistic purpose is unfathomable.

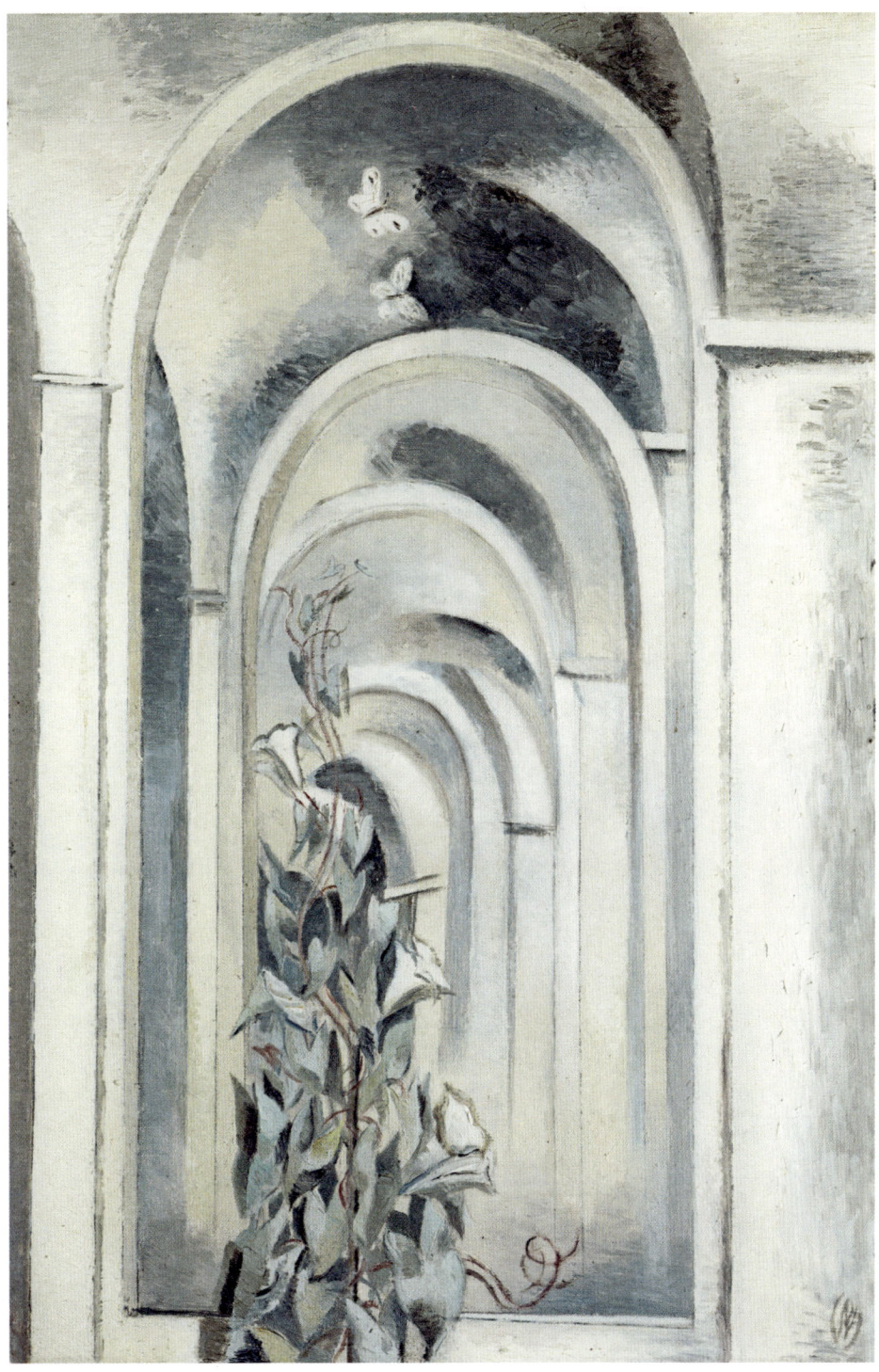

Convolvulus, 1930
Oil on canvas, 76 x 51 cm (30 x 20 in)
• Private Collection

Believed to be another response to Monro's 'Coronilla' (*see* page 110), the creeping convolvulus is emblematic of life's energy and love (like Blake's sunflower it follows the sun); the arches behind it the claustrophobic way to death.

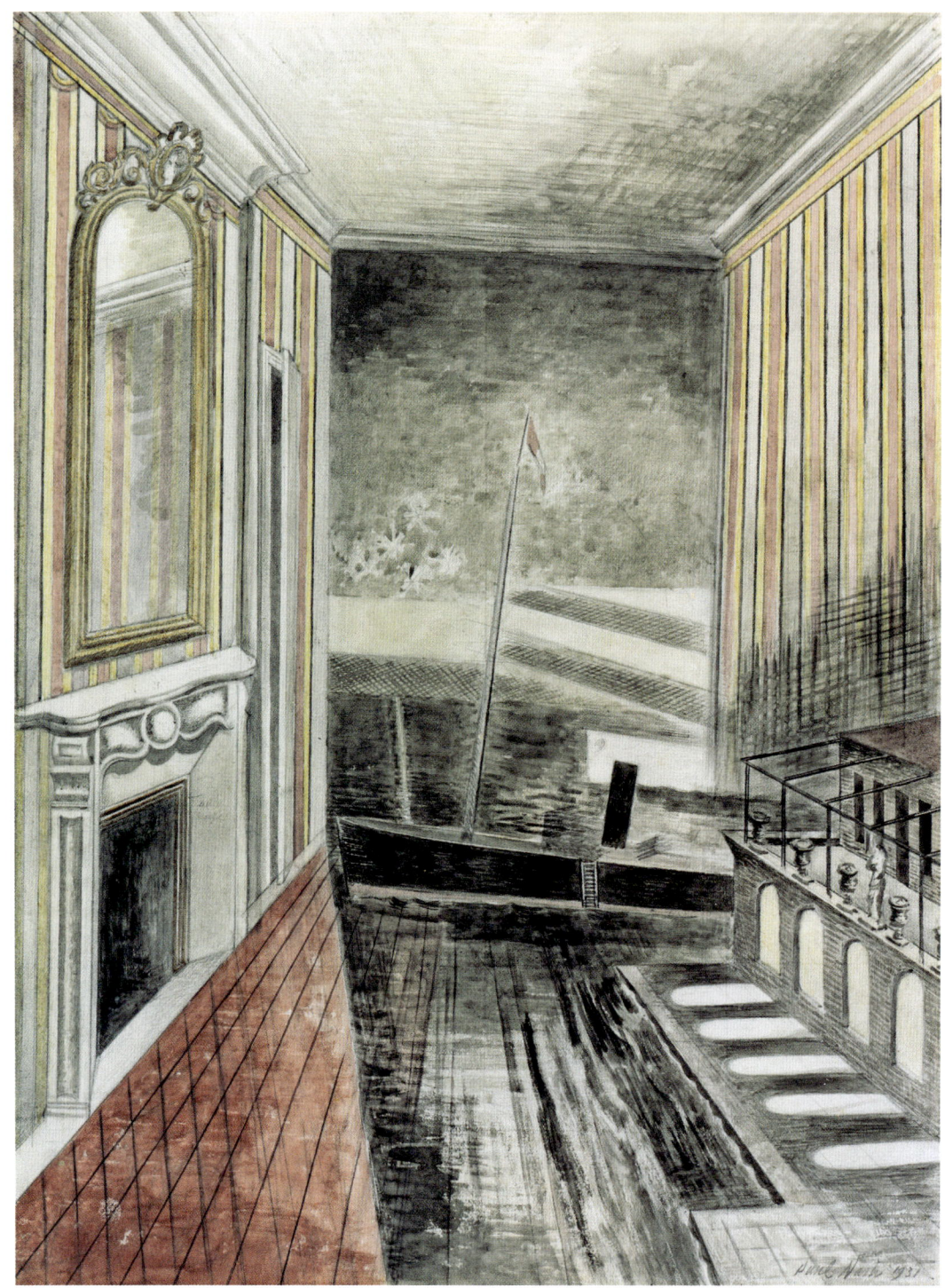

Harbour and Room, 1931
Watercolour and pencil on paper, 51.5 x 39 cm (20¼ x 15¼ in)
• Private Collection

An elegant interior coexists with a dark harbour reached by a Chirico-esque arcade. The play of outside versus inside (see, for example, *Mirror and Window* (1924, *see* page 97) and *Lupins and Cactus* (1927, *see* page 99), is here carried to surrealist lengths.

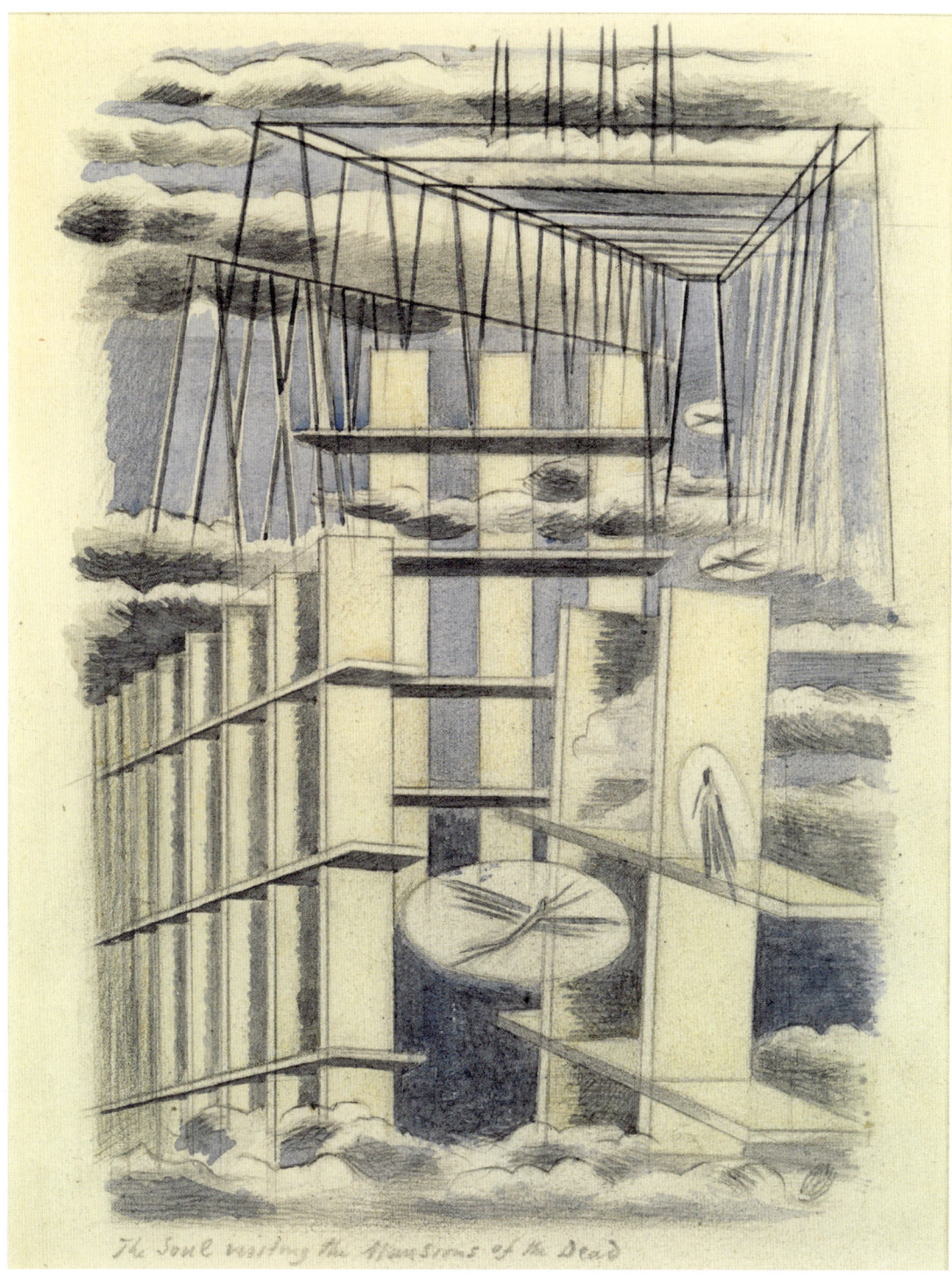

The Soul Visiting the Mansions of the Dead, 1932
Watercolour on paper, 21.5 x 16 cm (8½ x 6¼ in)
• British Council of Visual Arts, London

The title phrase came from Nash's reading of the meditation *Urne Buriall* (1658) by Thomas Browne (1605–82) for a new edition of which he was creating illustrations. Here, these 'mansions' are envisaged as airy and ethereal, geometric structures in the sky.

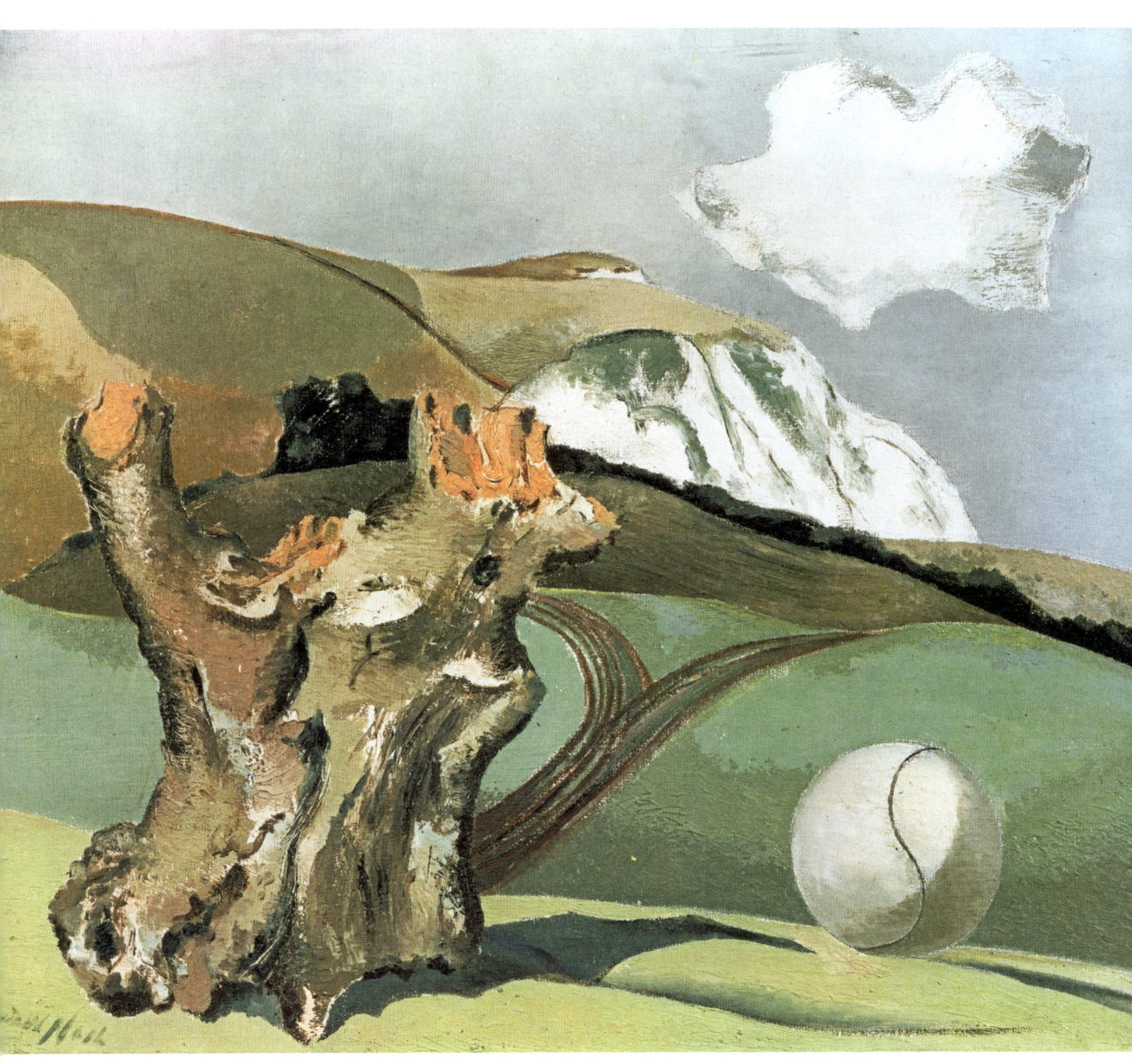

Event on the Downs, 1934
Oil on canvas, 51 x 61 cm (20 x 24 in)
• Government Art Collection, London

Whitecliff Farm on Ballard Down, just north of Swanage, was Nash's home while he worked on his *Dorset* Shell Guide – but it is clear he did not see the countryside in quite the same way as others.

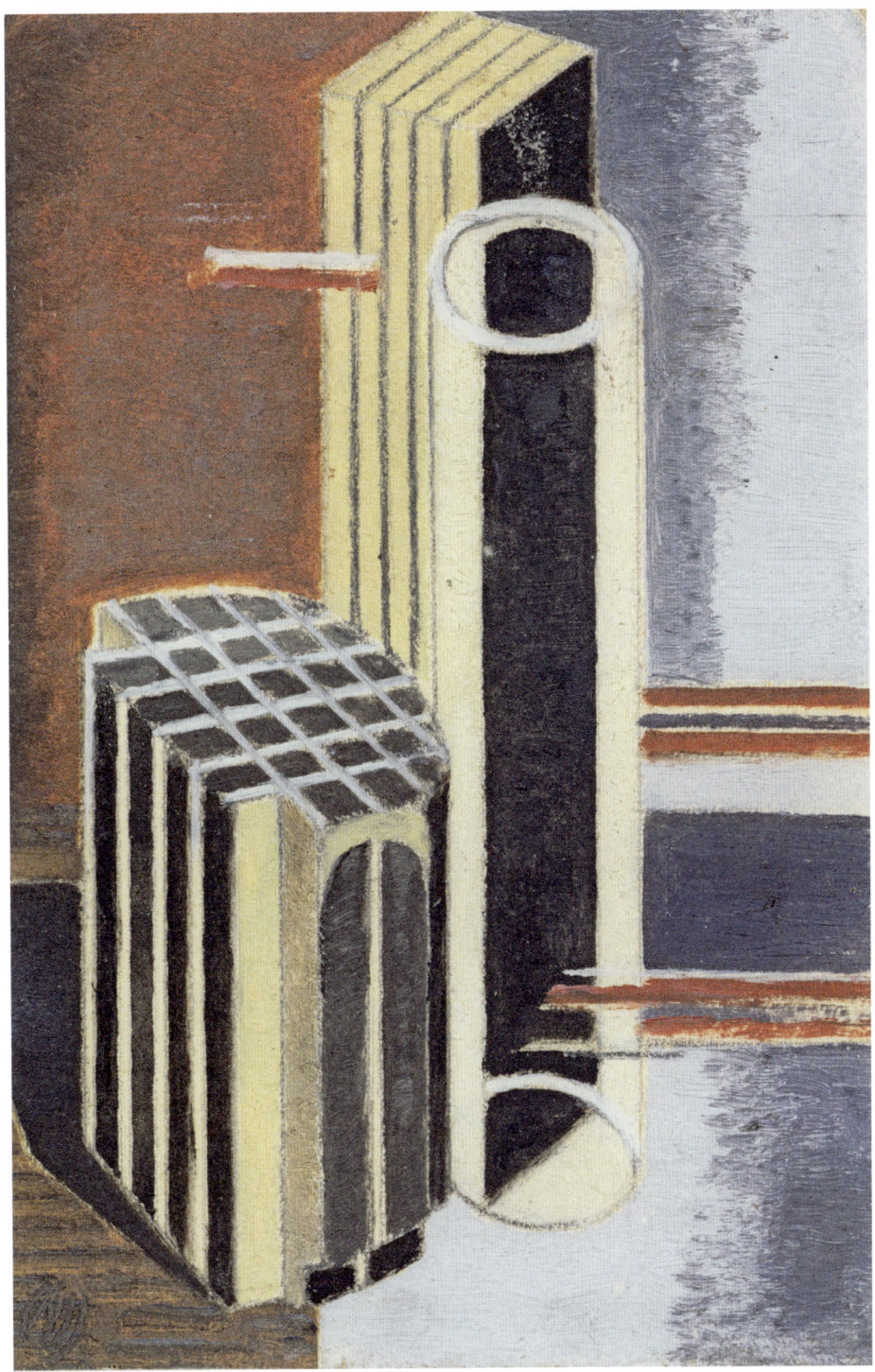

Composition (Design for Today), 1934
Tempera on hardboard, 12.8 x 8.9 cm (5 x 3½ in)
• Pallant House Gallery, Chichester

Nash, but not as we have known him: the earth tones are the nearest thing to landscape here. However, if the abstraction is surprising, certain things still seem familiar: the counterpointing of curves with angles, and of circles with straight lines.

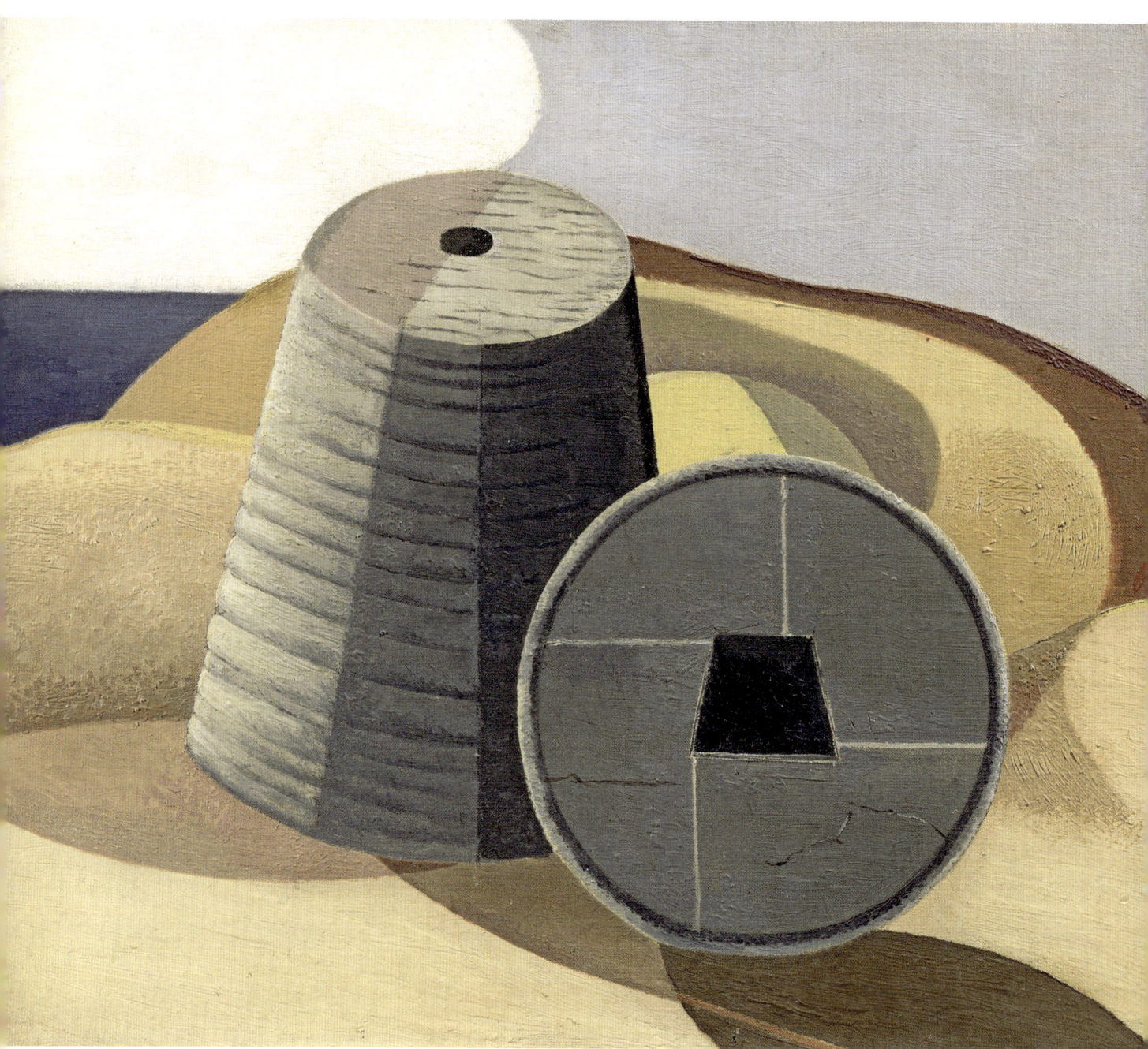

Mineral Objects, 1935
Oil on canvas, 50.2 x 60.3 cm (19¾ x 23¾ in)
• Yale Center for British Art, New Haven, Connecticut

This painting is not quite as abstract as it might appear, the shapes being based on bituminous discs cast aside by Dorset craftsmen making armlets from oil shale. Believed by antiquaries to be coins, they were consequently known as 'coal money'.

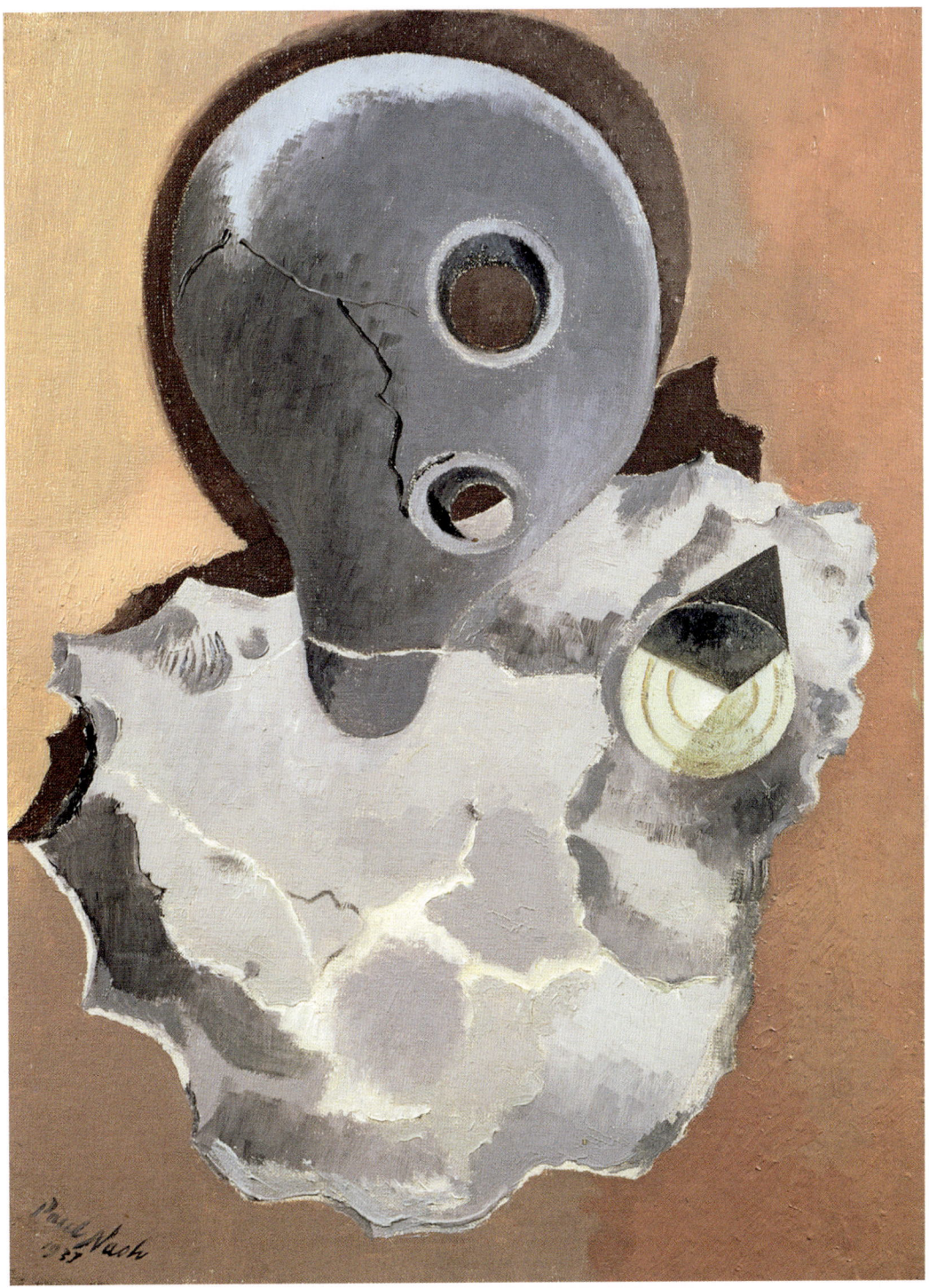

Encounter of Two Objects, 1937
Oil on canvas, 38 x 51 cm (15 x 20 in)
• Private Collection

The perforated pebble and the ragged grey flint were naturally occurring stones. A third 'object' on the right remains mysterious: it might be anything from a miniaturized aerial view of Silbury Hill to an item of Neolithic jewellery.

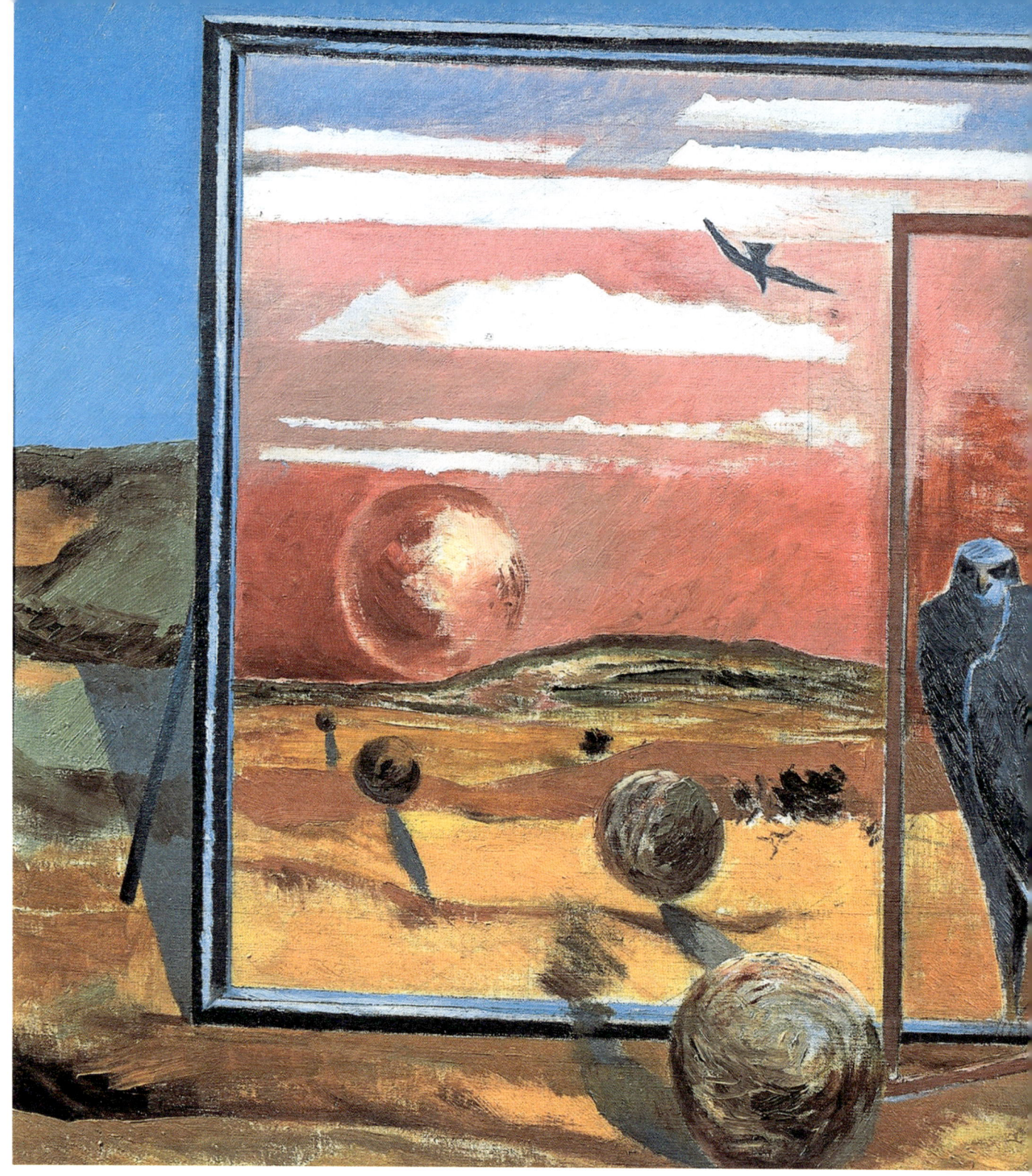

Landscape from a Dream, 1936–38
Watercolour on paper, 28.4 x 19.2 cm (11 x 7½ in)
• Tate Britain, London

This strikingly surrealistic painting still shows clear continuities with what went before. The mirror/window, the reflected spheres (the soul, said Nash), the narcissistic falcon (materialism) and, of course, the landscape of the Dorset coast.

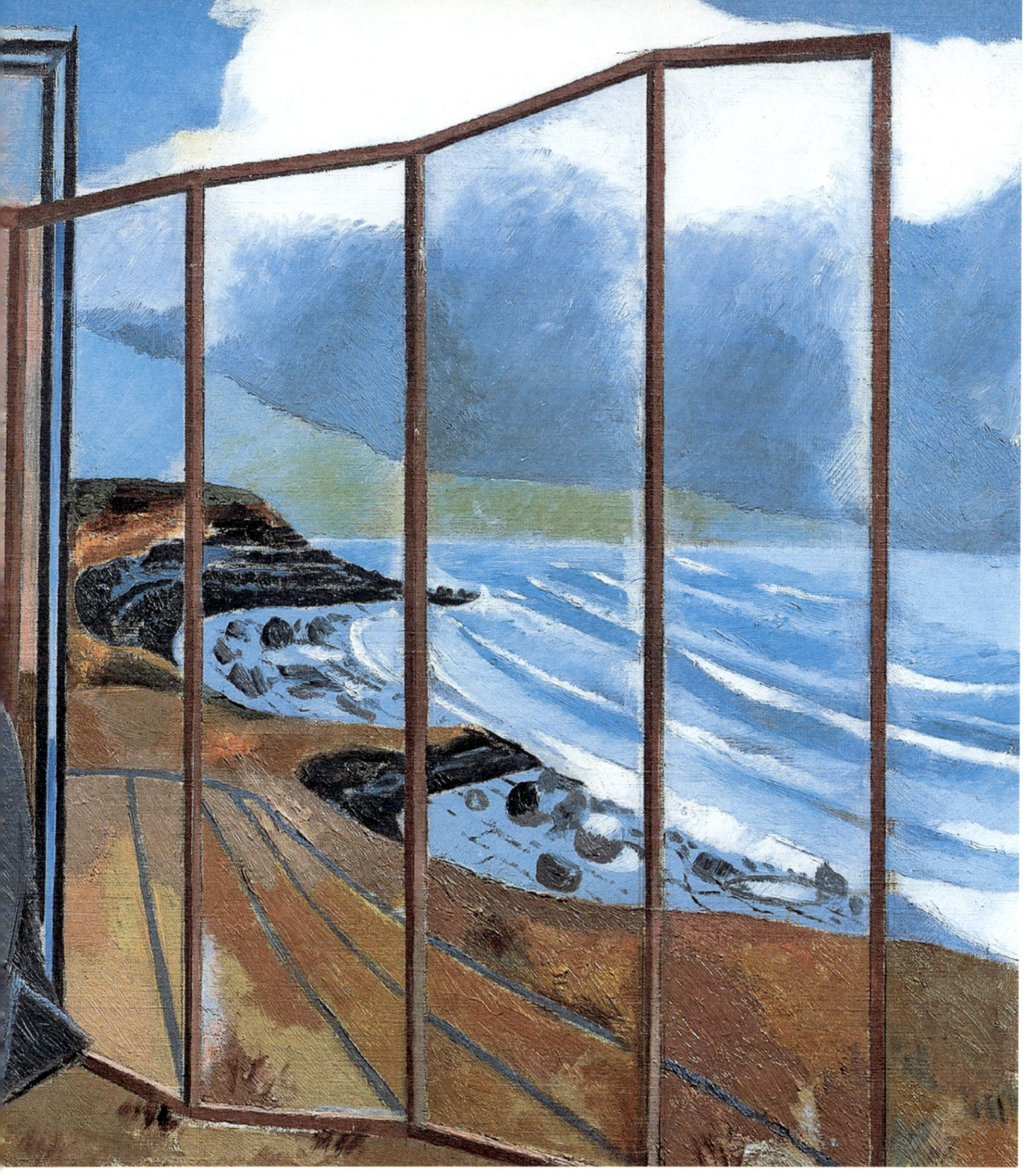

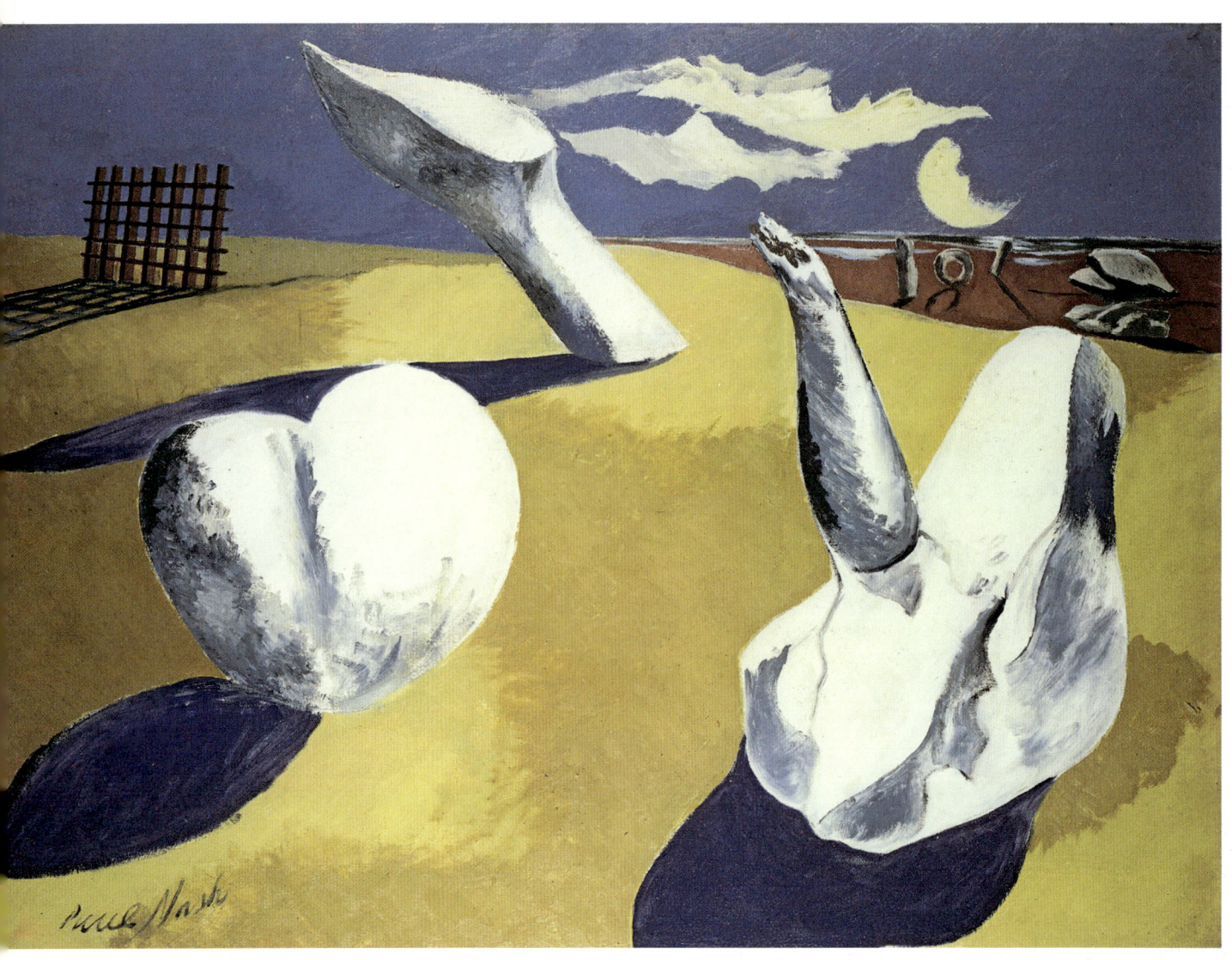

Nocturnal Landscape, 1938
Oil on canvas, 76.5 x 101.5 cm (30 x 40 in)
• Manchester Art Gallery

'Mock megaliths' crowd the foreground and the far-distance in this, the most Freudian phallic interpretation of Nash's works. Thought to have been 'found objects' – boulders, bits of antler, bone – they constitute a strange archaeology of the subconscious mind.

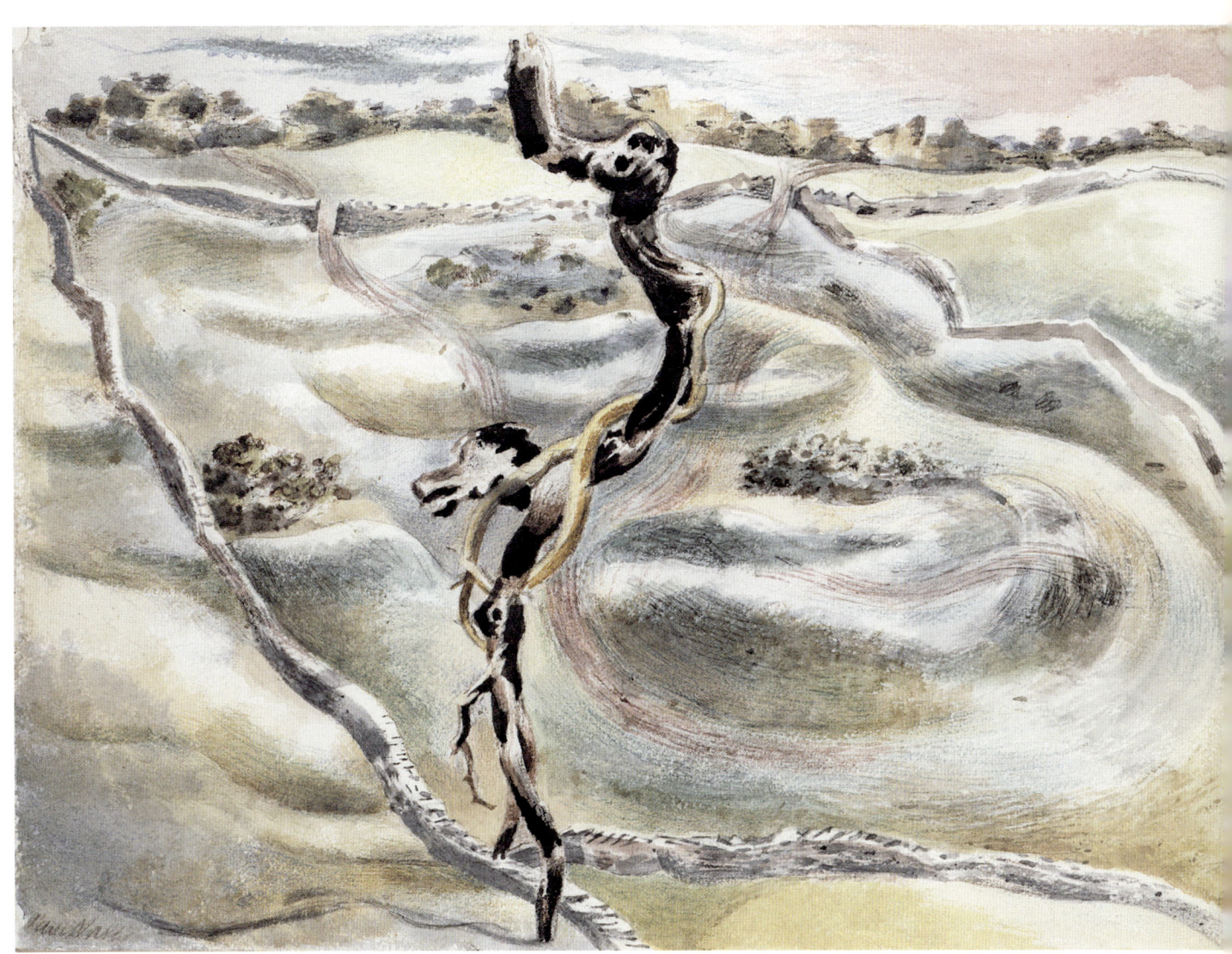

Object at Scarbank, 1939
Watercolour on paper, 28.5 x 39.5 cm (11¼ x 15½ in)
• Private Collection

The gnarled, knotty twists of a tree-branch 'rhyme' here with the snaking paths of dry-stone walls and dirt tracks, the nature of the landscape finding expression in a single object.

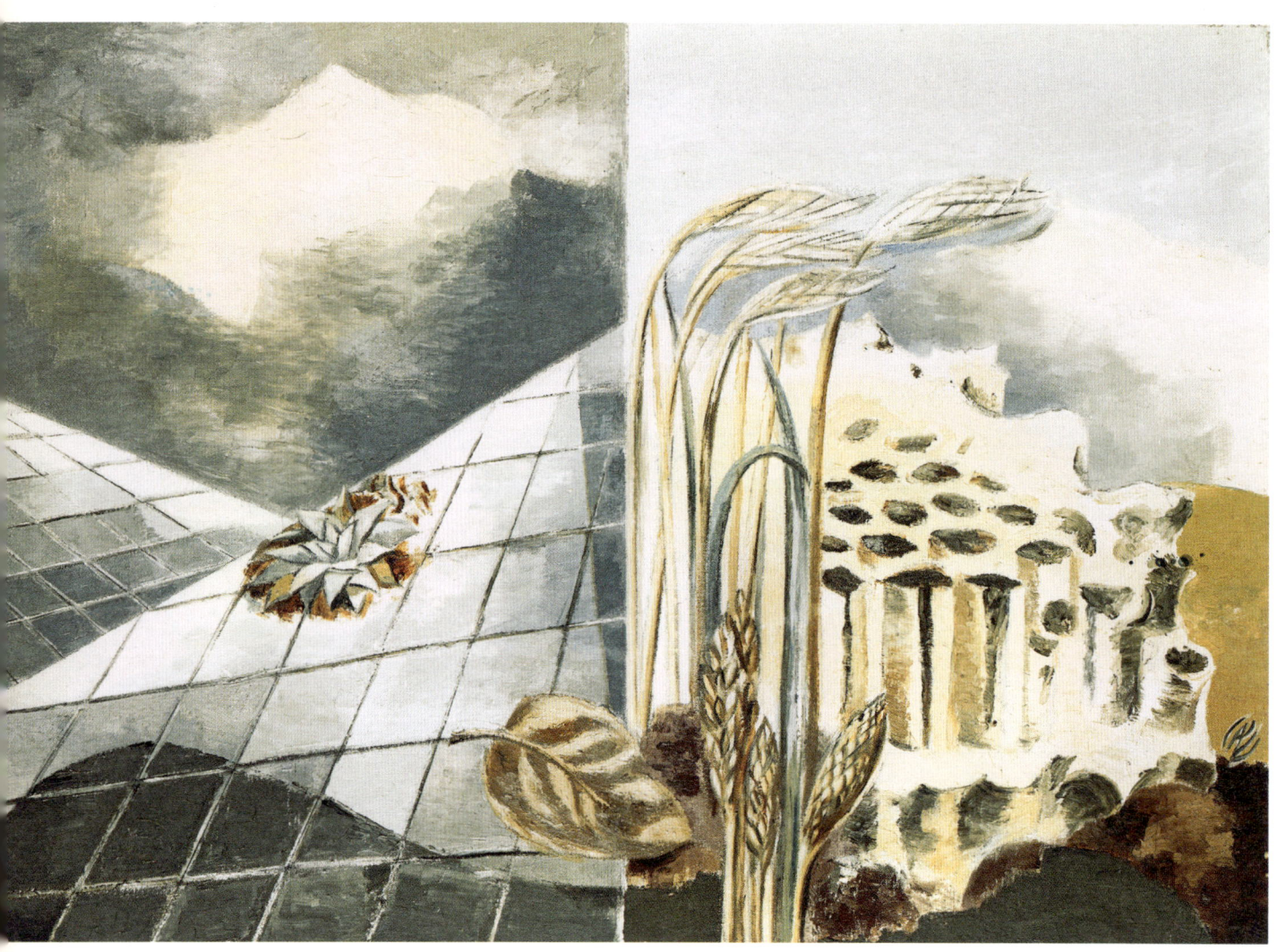

Summer, 1939
Oil on canvas, 55.8 x 80 cm (22 x 31½ in)
• Private Collection

This strange, surrealist 'summer' is divided into a diptych with a cloud that could be a snow-capped mountain, the square-scored slopes of an undulating landscape, and a lotus-blossom and stems of wheat, with a golden autumn leaf.

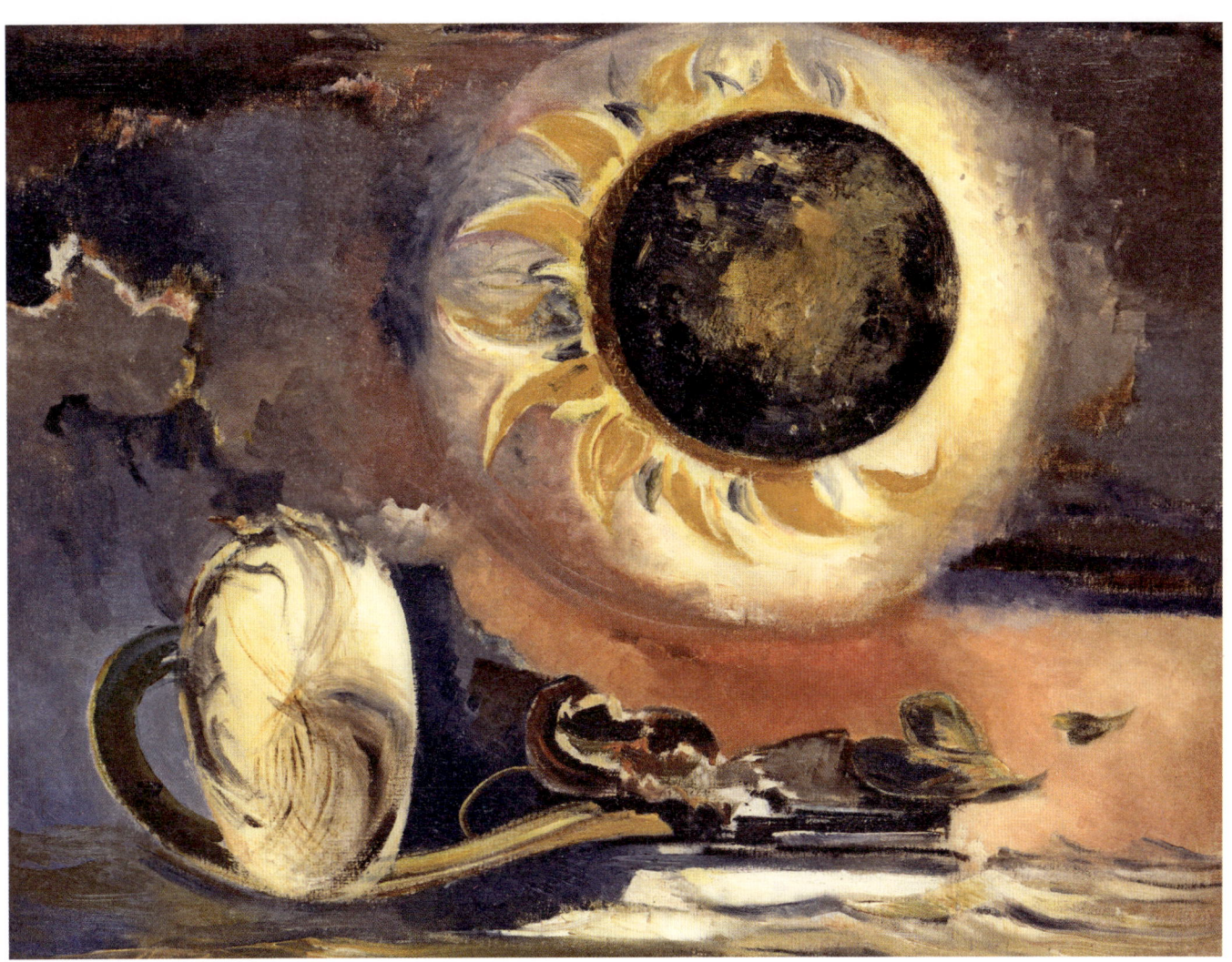

Eclipse of the Sunflower, 1945
Oil on canvas, 71.1 x 91.4 cm (28 x 36 in)
• British Council of Visual Arts, London

Did Nash foretell his own extinction in this glorious painting, created less than a year before he died? Or does the eclipse suggest the darkness the artist had to endure before he could find the light of inspiration?

Indexes

Index of Works

Page numbers in *italics* indicate illustration captions.

A

Archer, The (1930–42) 18, *112*
Au Bords du Bois (1921) 17, *94*

B

Battle of Britain, The (1941) 26, *50*
Battle of Germany (1944) *51*
Berkshire Downs (1922) *61*
Bomber in the Wood (1940) *46*
Book of Genesis (Heaven) (1924) 17, *95*

C

Channel and Breakwater (1923) *65*
Chaos Decoratif (1917) 15, *33*
Circle of the Monoliths (1937–38) *82*
Composition (Design for Today) (1934) *117*
Convolvulus (1930) *113*
Coronilla Landscape (1929) 17, *110*
Cumberland Landscape, A (1924) 17, *66*

D

Dawn, A (1912) *54*
Dead Spring (1929) 17, *109*
Different Skies, The (1939) *84*
Diving Stage, The (1928) *105*
Druid Landscape (c. 1938) *83*

E

Eclipse of the Sunflower (1945) 27, *125*
Edge of the Wood (1914–15) *57*
Encounter of Two Objects (1937) *119*
Event on the Downs (1934) 20, *116*

F

Farm, Wytschaete (1917) *30*
Field Path, The (1918) *58*
Forest, The (1930) *72*

G

German Double Pill Box, Gheluvelt (1918) *36*

H

Harbour and Room (1931) *114*
Howitzer Firing, A (1918) *39*

I

Interior Design (1920s–30s) *102*
Iver Heath, Buckinghamshire – Snow (1927–28) 13, *71*

L

Landscape at Fulmer, Buckinghamshire (1919) *59*
Landscape at Wood Lane, A (1913) 9, *56*
Landscape Composition (Objects in Relation) (1934) *78*
Landscape from a Dream (1936–38) *120*
Landscape of the Malvern Distance (1943) *89*
Landscape of the Megaliths (1934) 23, *79*
Landscape of the Moon's First Quarter (1943) *87*
Landscape of the Summer Solstice (1943) *88*
Landscape of the Vernal Equinox III (1944) 27, *90*
Lares (1929) *108*
Lupins and Cactus (1927) *99*

M

Mantel-Piece, The (1928) *106*
Menin Road, The (1919) 7, *44*
Messerschmidt in Windsor Great Park, The (1940) *47*
Mimosa Wood (1926) *69*
Mine Crate, Hill 60, Ypres Salient (1917) *35*
Mineral Objects (1935) *118*
Mirror and Window (1924) 17, *97*
Mule Track, The (1918) *37*

N

Nocturnal Landscape (1938) *122*
Northern Adventure (1929) *107*
Nostalgic Landscape (1923–38) 17, *96*
November Moon (1942) *86*

O

Object at Scarbank (1939) *123*
Oxenbridge Pond (1927–28) *70*

P

Pillar and Moon (1932–42) *76*
Places 16

Plage (1928) *104*
Pond at Souldem, The (1926) *68*

R

Raider on the Shore, The (1940) *48*
Ridge, Wytschaete (1917) *34*
Rye Marshes, The (1930) *74*

S

Sheepfold, Romney Marsh (1920) 17, *60*
Shellburst, Zillebeke (1917) 7, *31*
Shore, The (1923) *64*
Silbury Hill (1944) *91*
Soul Visiting the Mansions of the Dead, The (1932) *115*
Souvenir of Florence (1929) *111*
Spring in the Trenches, Ridge Wood (1917) *32*
St Pancras, London (1927) *100*
Stackyard, The (1925) 17, *67*
Still Life with Bog Cotton (1927) *103*
Study of a Wooded Landscape (1935) *81*
Summer (1939) *124*
Sunflower and Sun (1942) *85*

T

Totes Meer (1940–41) 26–27, *49*

V

View from a Window, Nice (1934) *77*
Void of War (1918) *38*

W

Wall Against the Sea (1922) *62*
We Are Making a New World (1918) *42*
Whiteleaf Cross (1931) *73*
Wire (1919) *43*
Wittenham (1935) *80*
Wood on the Hill, The (1912) 55
Wood, A – Illustration for King Lear, Act II, Scene iii (1926) 17, *98*
Wounded, Passchendaele (1918) *41*

Y

Ypres Salient at Night, The (1918) *40*

General Index

A
aeroplanes 25–27
Armstrong, John 24
Arp, Jean (Hans) 20
Artists' Rifles 14
Avebury, Wiltshire 23, 24

B
Betjeman, John 21
Bible *Genesis* 17
Blake, William 10, 12, 27
Breton, André 18–19, 20
    Surrealist Manifesto 19
Burra, Edward 24
Burt, George 21

C
Calvert, Edward 12
Carrington, Dora 11
Cézanne, Paul 11
Chelsea Polytechnic, London 10
Country Life 20

D
Dali, Salvador 20, 24
Davies, Hugh Sykes 19
De Chirico, Giorgio 18, 20
    Pittura Metafisica 17
De Creeft, Jose 20
Disney, Walt 26
Dorset 21–22
Duchamp, Marcel 20

E
Eliot, T.S. *The Waste Land* 8
Ernst, Max 20

F
Fascism 24
First World War 8, 14, 17, 18, 24
    Home Front 8
    Passchendaele 15, 16, 25
    Western Front 6–7, 8, 19
    Ypres 15, 27

Franco, Francisco 24
Freud, Sigmund 20
Fry, Roger 10, 11

G
Gertler, Mark 11
Giacometti, Alberto 20
Great Depression 24

H
Hepworth, Barbara 24

I
International Surrealist Exhibition, London 20

L
London County Council School of
    Photo-Engraving and Lithography 10

M
Magritte, René 20
Maiden Castle, Dorset 21–22
Miró, Joan 20, 24
Modernism 8, 11, 19
Moore, Henry 24

N
Nash, Barbara 9
Nash, Caroline 9, 12
Nash, John 9
Nash, Margaret 6, 7, 14, 15, 16, 21, 27
Nash, William 8, 9
Nazism 24
Nevinson, Christopher R.W. 11
New Verse 19
Nicholson, Ben 11, 24

O
Oakley, Mercia 13, 14
objets trouvés 20–21
Odeh, Margaret *see* Nash, Margaret
Owen, Wilfred 7

P
Palmer, Samuel 12
Picasso, Pablo 20, 24
Post-Impressionism 11
Pre-Raphaelites 10

R
Richmond, George 12
Richmond, Sir William Blake 11, 12
Roberts, William 11
Romanticism 10
Rosenberg, Isaac 7
Rossetti, Dante Gabriel 10
Royal Academy 11
Royal Air Force 25
Russian Revolution 8

S
Sassoon, Siegfried 6
Shakespeare, William *King Lear* 17
Second World War 24–25, 27
    Battle of Britain 25
Shell Guides *Dorset* 21
Silbury Hill, Wiltshire 22
Slade, University College London 10
Spanish Civil War 24
Spencer, Stanley 11
Stonehenge, Wiltshire 23
Surrealism 19–21, 24

T
Thorpe, Adam *On Silbury Hill* 23
Thurber, James 26
Tonks, Henry 10–11, 12
trees 13–14, 17

U
Unit One 24

V
Vogue 26
Von Clausewitz, Carl 25

W
Wadsworth, Edward 11, 24
West Kennet Long Barrow, Wiltshire 23
Wittenham Clumps, Oxfordshire 13–14, 22
Women's Tax Resistance League (WTRL) 14
Wood Lane House, Iver Heath 9, 13
Wordsworth, William 10, 12
World War *see* First World War; Second World War

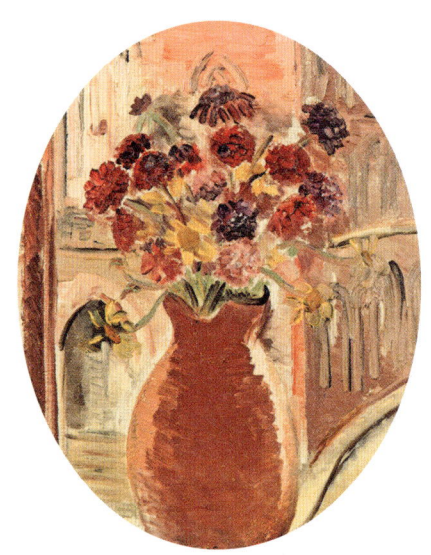

Masterpieces of Art
FLAME TREE PUBLISHING

A new series of carefully curated print and digital books covering the world's greatest art, artists and art movements.